Postmodernism and Islam

In this remarkable and accomplished book Professor Akbar Ahmed is a friendly and knowledgeable companion through the thickets of both Western and Islamic culture. As one of the world's leading Islamic scholars and an incisive Muslim commentator on the West, he is in a unique position to offer an indispensable guide to many complicated and vexed questions. He writes with a clear moral purpose: to reduce misunderstandings between East and West and to make what seems alien and strange to *each* culture intelligible.

Why do Muslims want to kill Salman Rushdie? How can the study of the Greek gods help to make sense of the current perceptions and misperceptions in East–West relations? Will Islam replace communism as the new enemy of the West? What is the relevance of postmodernism to Islam? Can West and East ever understand each other? In exploring these questions Professor Ahmed goes back into history and looks into the future. Emphasizing the role of the mass media in shaping our mental map of East–West relations, he analyses the ways the media turned the Rushdie affair and the Gulf war into a carnival of spectacle and entertainment. He makes use of the postmodern theme of the displaced, circulating image to show how images are used to tell stories – stories which are not always helpful or accurate.

Written with panache and an unswerving fidelity to truth, *Postmodernism and Islam* will help us to understand our times. Above all, it will be seen as a major enquiry into the study of Islamic and Christian relations.

Akbar Ahmed is the Allama Iqbal Fellow and Fellow of Selwyn College at the University of Cambridge. His previous books include *Pakistan Society, Discovering Islam* and *Resistance and Control in Pakistan*.

Postmodernism and Islam

Predicament and promise

Akbar S. Ahmed

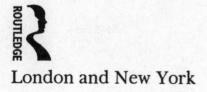

London and New York

First published in 1992
by Routledge
11 New Fetter Lane, London EC4P 4EE

Simultaneously published in the USA and Canada
by Routledge
a division of Routledge, Chapman and Hall, Inc.
29 West 35th Street, New York, NY 10001

Typeset from the author's wordprocessing disks by
NWL Editorial Services

Printed and bound in Great Britain by
Mackays of Chatham PLC, Chatham, Kent

British Library Cataloguing in Publication Data
Ahmed, Akbar S. (Akbar Salahudin), *1943–*
    Postmodernism and Islam: Predicament and promise.
    I. Title
    297

Library of Congress Cataloging in Publication Data
Ahmed, Akbar S. 1943–
    Postmodernism and Islam: Predicament and promise /
    Akbar S. Ahmed
    p. cm.
    Includes bibliographical references and index.
    1. Islam–20th century
    I. Title.
    BP163.A354 1992   91–39584
    297'.09'049 – dc20   CIP

ISBN 0–415–06292–6
        0–415–06293–4 (pbk)

Contents

For Nafees, with love

Preface

This book is an attempt to understand our times. And because it is about the age we live in some of the language and imagery may be disturbing and even offensive to those readers accustomed to the discussion of religion in traditional language and with customary reverence. While inserting the 'health warning' I also wish to point out that this is neither profanation nor gratuitousness; the eclecticism, syncreticism, irony and juxtaposition which cause – and will cause – cultural friction in our world are central to an understanding of postmodernism and will be examined; this is still little explored territory. A related theme I investigate is the ubiquitous presence of the media. The Western media are all around, stimulating, corrupting, influencing, shaping and challenging us. We cannot hope to understand Muslims without first understanding the nature of the Western media; this I will try to do.

I myself am ambivalent about the media. Although aware of its dangers – both in its destructive powers and seductive charms – I am also conscious of its great potential to assist in understanding and explaining the differences between disparate peoples. Its capacity to help bridge gaps is immeasurable. Future endeavour, whether academic, cultural or political, must take developments in the audio-visual media and recent communications technology into account; henceforth no one can be an island ever again.

Perhaps mine is a flawed picture; perhaps I am too influenced by my Asian background, perhaps by a Muslim perception of history and society. But without this exercise we cannot understand Muslims and their predicament in our age. I will, therefore, support my arguments with what I learned as a result of my forays into the Western media.

Take what for me were the highlights of the summer and autumn of 1991: I was on BBC TV's *Newsnight*, discussing Rajiv Gandhi's death with Jeremy Paxman; on *The World This Week* (Channel 4), presented by Sheena McDonald, I crossed swords with a US Congressman on nuclear proliferation (I am against nuclear weapons whoever has them); and I analyzed the Middle East with John Simpson again on *Newsnight*. On Radio I debated Christina Lamb's *Waiting for Allah* (1991) with her on BBC's *Outlook*, and spoke on the history of Pakistan for BBC's *Birth of a Nation* series; Melvyn Bragg was supportive of my new book, *Resistance and Control in Pakistan* (1991a), on *Start the Week*; and I was on BBC's *Any Questions?* with Ken Livingstone, MP, and Gillian Shephard, MP. (The trick question was about Nigel Kennedy's clothes on stage; I talked of Madonna's clothes – or lack of them.) For *The World Today* on the BBC I tried to explain the unsuccessful coup against Gorbachev in Moscow; for their *News Hour*, on the World Service, the kidnapping of a diplomat in Delhi by (it was believed) the Sikhs; and, again for the World Service, corruption in South Asia; for their *Analysis* I prepared a programme I was to present on the Middle East. Marina Salandy-Brown of BBC Radio 4 asked me to present a series of discussions with eminent British Asians, to be called *Only Connect*. I interviewed the Aga Khan for *The Guardian* and Diana Hinds interviewed me for *The Independent*. Finally, I plunged into Mark Tully's new book, *No Full Stops in India* (1991), to prepare for the *Third Ear* discussion with him on BBC Radio 3.

Enough, enough, I almost hear you cry. But this is not by way of impressing you, gentle reader, only to illustrate the extent of my involvement with the media. Chauffeur-driven cars to pick you up and drop you at your door; pretty, short-skirted young women with sultry voices to fuss over you; people in the street looking at you with a flicker of recognition in their eyes ('the telly don?'); members of your community flattering you ('thank God, we have a credible voice now') – all this is calculated to seduce; it is also illusion, as transitory as it is superficial.

More seductive and dangerous was the notion that appearing in the media confers a special wisdom and penetrating insights into human affairs. I was in danger of becoming the instant expert, the media guru, Mr Know-All. The alarm bells were sounding and I heard them loud and clear. My own discomfort was matched by that of my friends; they were becoming distrustful of the media exposure. Some Muslims, intrinsically suspicious of the West, asked: 'Why are you being invited so often?' 'Why are you talking to the "enemy"?' A few asked darkly: 'Have you sold out?' Those Muslim spokesmen, often self-appointed, who did not wish to share the media spotlight, were resentful of what they saw as an interloper (see Chapters 3 and 4).

However, all this was serving a serious purpose. It allowed me to participate in debates of importance and to present an alternative view. It was also giving me access to the Western media few Muslims would enjoy. This kind of participant observation, I knew as an anthropologist, was essential to a book dealing with the nature of the Western media. So, in spite of the dangers, in spite of the reservations of colleagues, in spite of the short-notice requests, changing schedules, unfriendly hours and long journeys that characterize dealings with the media, it was worth it.

Traditionally, social scientists neutralize the self in their academic work which reinforces their ivory tower image. I have deliberately used my experiences as sociological resource to make sense of what was going on around me. The consequences of the break-up of the cultural divides do not affect me alone but other lives also, as I will illustrate. Citing these experiences, therefore, becomes legitimate methodology (see also Ahmed 1991a).

The arguments in this book are impressionistic and thematic rather than sequential, exhaustive and chronological. The jumble of ideas and names, mingling and intermingling, the images piling upon images, the vast scope and dissolution of cultural boundaries suggest postmodernist methodology. In building my case there will be at times apparent contradictions and obvious circularity in the argument; there will be strange juxtaposition of people and places and even what seems deliberate provocation; this too reflects postmodernist method. The reader must bear with me. There will be, as I hope to show, an underlying structure to my argument.

The book itself grew out of a volume jointly planned with Ernest Gellner for Routledge; however, the publishers felt that both 'parts' would be better served as two separate, independent volumes. Although we were looking at the same problem we were covering two different areas and this was, perhaps, the most felicitous way of presenting our findings. After mutual agreement this is how we have proceeded. I would like to express my gratitude to him for his unfailing courtesy and support – and not only with regard to this project.

Also to be warmly acknowledged for their interest in this book are Syed Ali Ashraf, Christine Cottam, John Esposito, Anthony Giddens, Francis Robinson, Chris Rojek, Jane Steadman and Brian Street. In particular I owe my friend and publisher Chris Rojek double gratitude: for his help in an earlier book, *Discovering Islam: Making Sense of Muslim History and Society* (1988), and for his encouragement in the writing of this one. I would like to express the deepest gratitude to my wife for her support in the writing of this book. Although the book has benefited immensely from the responses of so many people I alone must shoulder the responsibility for the views expressed in it.

Some of the material in this book has appeared in different forms in *Asian Survey*, California, *History Today*, London, *Middle East Journal*, Washington, *New Statesman and Society*, London, *The Guardian*, London, *The Independent*, London, the *SOAS Bulletin*, London, and *The Sunday Correspondent*, London (1989–1991), and they are gratefully acknowledged.

I wish to dedicate this book to my daughter, Nafees, who was born in Cambridge in 1990. Nothing concentrates the mind of a middle-aged parent like the birth of a child. For me many questions about the future, intimating mortality, came tumbling out with Nafees. How long did I have with her? What sort of life would she lead? Would she be happy? Where would she lead her life? In what manner and for how long would she live? With only a few years left before the new millennium, with the planet and its inhabitants already showing signs of what looks like terminal exhaustion, these questions acquire a special edge.

Nafees will live, as a Muslim, in the postmodern world which is just beginning to shape our lives; therein lies the Muslim predicament: that of living by Islam in an age which is increasingly secular, cynical, irreverent, fragmented, materialistic and, therefore, for a Muslim, often hostile. However, postmodernism also promises hope, understanding and toleration – and this is where it connects with Islam. In an age of cynicism and disintegration Islam has much to offer. I, therefore, pray she finds inspiration in her faith and culture, to assist her in making sense of, and resolving, the predicament of living as a good, caring and decent human being in the postmodernist world.

Akbar S. Ahmed
Cambridge
November 1991

Chapter 1

Postmodernism and Islam

When Saddam Hussein invaded Kuwait in the summer of 1990 he abolished more than Kuwaiti independence. He also shattered the complacency of those who were dreaming of a stable and harmonious post-cold war New World Order for the 1990s which would set the stanchions in place for the political architecture of the twenty-first century. Within days George Bush and Mrs Thatcher were calling him Hitler; many Arabs, on the other hand, saw him as a champion and compared him to Nasser, even Saladin; Iraqis, hedging their bets, added the name of the pre-Islamic King of Babylon, Nebuchadnezzar.

Young soldiers, deep in America at one end of the world, and in rural Pakistan at the other, began to pack for duty on the Arabian peninsula; the Americans, who provide aid to Pakistan, had made an offer which the Pakistanis could not refuse and, therefore, they agreed to supply troops to fight alongside the Americans. Young Stuart Lockwood, one of the hostages in Baghdad, had his head patted by Saddam on television and instantly became part of history. Muslims everywhere protested at the presence of non-Muslim troops in the land of Makkah and Medinah. Arabs accused the Americans of being like Rambo. Palestinians, taking heart from Saddam's support, renewed the *intifada*, and their deaths in Jerusalem provoked talk of *jihad*, holy war, among Arabs; Israel, threatened by Saddam, once again evoked the spirit of Masada, the ancient garrison besieged by the Romans. The war that followed had about it the inevitability of Greek tragedy.

In the future, major international crises are likely to follow the same pattern, which was characterized by several features: first, the involvement of the media. The media were everywhere. Every gesture and every word of the main players like Saddam was news, to be discussed and analysed. Second, the interconnection of the world was made apparent, whether of people – our example of American and Pakistani soldiers – or of economies: not only oil supplies to the West but also the remittances of the South Asian workers were affected. Third, a feeling, a mood grew, fed by the media, that henceforth a crisis of this nature could escalate uncontrollably to bring about a world disaster. A global perception therefore formed which was not unanimous on cause and effect, but it reflected concern for the interdependence of life on earth and forced us to participate vicariously in the terrible decision-making processes.

Most of this was new and frightening, but there was an eerie element of *déjà vu* in the drama, as if, half-awake, we had seen some of it before. Over the previous two years another crisis had been simmering. In it we had heard the principles of freedom of expression being defended – Voltaire was often cited – against those Muslims who felt their religious beliefs were outraged by *The Satanic Verses* (see pages 169–77, for a discussion of the book). Muslims believed that the Prophet and his family were insulted and the authenticity of the Quran challenged. Ayatollah Khomeini elevated the Muslim response into an international affair by issuing a *fatwa*, a declaration, condemning the author, Salman Rushdie, to death; then, by dying, the Ayatollah left the issue suspended in mid-air to eternity; no Iranian could revoke or cancel it.

Shortly after the Gulf war it appeared to Muslims that yet another strand was woven into the rope being used to bind Islam: the story of the Pakistani and Arab bank, the Bank of Credit and Commerce International (BCCI), broke. Here was massive fraud, corruption, cooking of books, drugs, big names; these business-men could bring a blush of shame to the cheeks of J.R. Ewing. The media went wild with glee at what was one of the biggest banking scandals in history; the fact that most of the key players were Muslim added to the pleasure of the chase. The entire globe seemed to have been drawn into the BCCI story. Links were established with Abu Nidal on the one hand and Pakistan's nuclear programme on the other. It became the Bank of Cocaine and Crooks in the Western media. In 1991 the Western media were freely placing Muslims in the context of what they labelled a 'criminal' culture.

Ordinary, everyday, average Muslims may not agree with the *fatwa*, they may despise the military dictator in Iraq, they may loathe the fraud and corruption at the Bank, but they also resent the cavalier way in which they are treated by association in the media. They are still anxious to point out that the reality in each case is more complex than meets the eye; they will not have liked Rushdie's book, they will be vicariously thrilled that Saddam stood up to the West and spoke up for the Palestinians, even that the BCCI may be the target of Western wrath because it was the first major international Muslim bank.

There is no way an ordinary Muslim can make his views known in the media, which floods hostile words and images over and around him. He is portrayed as a fanatic over the book, politically unstable through the dictator and corrupt by the actions of the Bank. In the end, unable to convey his arguments, helpless and impotent, he is as cynical of Western motives as those of the military dictator and the corrupt bankers – they are all the same, he will say. But he is also as disgusted as he is confused with his own sense of impotence in shaping reality around him; he can no longer challenge what is real or unreal, no longer separate reality from the illusion of the media.

We note that Islam is the common factor intertwining most of the people mentioned above and ask: is Islam henceforth to be isolated and characterized as a force for anarchy and disorder? Islam, from the time of the Crusades, has been seen as barbarous, licentious, the enemy of Christianity; in our age, in addition, it is seen as anarchic and monolithic. The Islamic peril is now seen by many as the greatest threat to the West, beside which the Red and Yellow perils pale into insignificance.

But then we may consider other matters that have aroused controversy, for example, the antics of the popular singer, Madonna (and more of her later). Her songs, videos and stage performances have incurred the wrath of the Pope himself. So it is not only Islam which is the problem; something seems to have changed fundamentally in the way people are responding to the world.

QUESTIONS FOR OUR AGE

These contemporary crises were different yet in some ways similar: they forced us to ask questions; to challenge common assumptions; to look at the familiar in a different light. The kinetic energy which was created in turn sparked ideas and prejudices, controversy and argument. The crossing of cultural boundaries created the misinterpretation of foreign idiom causing great offence and agitation, great misunderstanding, on all sides. The crises brought together a bewildering collage of historical and popular images that, through communications technology, bonded the entire globe. The audio-visual media allowed, as never before in history, an instant access to news, an unsettling, dazzling juxtaposition of diverse pictures, a variety of discourses. High philosophy and comic-book ideas, historical facts and pop sociology jostled and mingled. All this was made possible by other recent developments, such as mass transport, the electronic and printing media and the development of the global economy.

It was the media that juxtaposed for us images of people like Hitler and Saddam, Bush and Lockwood, Rambo and the Pakistani soldier, Saladin and Nebuchadnezzar, Khomeini and Rushdie, Voltaire and the Iranians, the Pope and Madonna, and places like Masada and Makkah, Babylon and Jerusalem. The Rushdie affair, the Madonna controversy, the manner of the Gulf confrontation were harbingers of things to come – not subsidiary but central to our understanding. The exploration of this theme will be my concern. It is characteristic of the times we live in.

We are living in a period of dramatic change; structures that have held for generations are being pulled down. Changing, too, are notions of the self and of the other, of class, of ethnicity and of nation, although the nature and depth of these are still debatable. A perception is forming that we may be entering a distinct phase of human history, one following modernism and, therefore, tentatively called 'postmodernist'. However, the rupture with the previous period is not complete. For, if recent events in the disintegrating Soviet Union, Eastern Europe and South Africa represent postmodernist impulses, those in Tiananmen Square, those around events connected with the coup which almost ousted Gorbachev in August 1991, and those surrounding the Salman Rushdie affair suggest the strength of tradition and authority.

A host of questions, many of them of urgency for the immediate future, are thus thrown up for our consideration: Is there truth in the widely held assumption in the West that after the collapse of communism the next enemy is Islam? What does the New World Order we hear so much about mean for Muslims? Is the postmodernist age intrinsically hostile to Islam? Why do the media commentators, whether academics or journalists, so consistently and unanimously disparage Islam? And is the Muslim response, rejecting the Western media as biased, an effective one? If so, how long can they isolate themselves from the global civilization? Will the lampooning and vilification divert Muslims from the values of a religion that advocates compassion and balance? And where are these virtues, so much emphasized in the Quran, to be located in the present Islamic turbulence? Are the so-called moderates 'out' and the so-called extremists 'in' as a consequence of this turbulence?

What intellectual and cultural changes are taking place among Muslims? Why, for instance, do Muslims prefer baggy trousers to jeans? Is the mosque in danger of being replaced by the mall as the focus of Muslim social and community activity? What does the sermon in the mosque tell us? What does Islam have to say about the 'green' movement and ecology? How can Muslims retain their central Islamic features – family life, care for children, respect for elders, concepts of modesty and so on – in the face of the contrary philosophy of the postmodernist age? And how can they successfully convey the relevance of their beliefs and customs, their 'message', to the world community of which they are part?

We also go back to the past by asking: How does a religious civilization like Islam, which relies on a defined code of behaviour and traditions based on a holy book, cope in an age which self-consciously puts aside the past and exults in diversity? (The question is relevant to other religious cultures of Semitic origin.) How does it relate to the other major Semitic religions? What does it make of the influential civilization of Europe formed by the Greeks? How does European imperialism continue to affect Muslim culture and thinking?

These are important questions and need to be asked of our age. There are many theories in circulation, many processes afoot and many explanations at work. I will try to point to some. I cannot promise neat and tidy answers – nor are they always desirable. I will simply point to the pieces in the jigsaw puzzle that is our world.

Faith versus scepticism, tradition versus iconoclasm, purity versus eclecticism – it is difficult to relate Islamic postmodernism to Western postmodernism in any coherent or direct manner, or even to establish a causal relationship between the two. Although

Muslims may employ some of the conceptual tools of François Lyotard or Jean Baudrillard for analysis, there must be a parting of company on certain crucial points. While Muslims appreciate the spirit of tolerance, optimism and the drive for self-knowledge in postmodernism, they also recognize the threat it poses them with its cynicism and irony. This is a challenge to the faith and piety which lies at the core of their world-view.

In the end, Islamic and Western postmodernism may have little more in common than that they are coetaneous, running concurrently. What we can state is that they may be entering this particular phase of their respective histories through different gates, propelled by different causes, still unsure of certain features, like the nature of the media and formulation of their responses to it, and even with a different understanding of the very nature of the age.

GRAPPLING WITH POSTMODERNISM

As we intend to borrow the concept of postmodernism from one culture to apply to another, its definition becomes even more important. However, at its clearest it lacks clarity and its provenance is uncertain. Is it a historical period (postmodernity) or an up-to-date style (postmodernism)? Is it a literary conceit, a philosophic concept or an architectural notion? Is it an aesthetic variation, a response to the globalizing tendency, an arts style or social phenomenon? Is it an exclusively European phenomenon or can it be applied plausibly elsewhere? The tone of the questions is appropriate, for the term represents an age of ambiguity and irony; they warn us to remain circumspect in using it. But before attempting to define postmodernism we must consider modernism, that which precedes and which allows us to measure postmodernism.

Books containing ideas on modernism occupy a large space in any well-stocked library, but it is in the general sense of the *Oxford English Dictionary* definition that the term is used: 'modern view(s) or method(s), especially tendency in matters of religious belief to subordinate tradition to harmony with modern thought'. Modernism has come to mean the most recent phase of world history marked by belief in science, planning, secularism and progress. The desire for symmetry and order, balance and authority has also characterized it. The period is noted for its confidence in the future, a conviction that Utopia is attainable, that there is a natural world order which is possible. The machine, gigantic industrial projects, steel, iron and electricity – all were thought to be at the disposal of humanity to achieve this objective. The drive towards industrialization and reliance on the physical created an ideology which emphasized materialism as a way of life.

Nonetheless, doubts about modernism are expressed early by modernist writers like James Joyce and D.H. Lawrence. The critique of notions such as total 'progress' and those which generated them, like the Enlightenment, was already under way before the advent of postmodernist thinking (Adorno and Horkheimer 1979). Indeed, Chaplin's *Modern Times* is an indictment of the age of industrialization and the belittling of humanity, whether in Roosevelt's America or Stalin's Russia. 'Progressive', 'scientific', 'rational' – in all this there was no room for religion. At best it was relegated to Christmas and christening, at worst it was mumbo-jumbo to be stamped out with energy.

Anthony Giddens poses a central, though little raised, question in relation to modernism: 'Is modernity a Western project?' (1990: 174). His blunt answer is 'Yes' (ibid.: 175). It is the perception of modernity as Western which will help explain non-Western responses to it; for example, as we will see in Chapter 3, the rejection of the concept of the nation-state, one of the central features of modernity (ibid.). The fact that until the middle of the twentieth century Western imperialism was a vehicle for the project of modernism further underlines the point. It is in this context that we may see Charles Jencks's useful distinction between modern culture as élitist and inaccessible and postmodernism as popular and accessible (1984; 1990); non-Western people can more readily identify with the latter.

The contemporary formulation of postmodernism as a distinct phase succeeding modernism is rooted in and explained by the recent history of the West which is at the core of the dominant global civilization of our times (see pages 98–110). Our definition of this civilization is cultural/political and not geographical. At the core are the United States and Western Europe, but included are other nations, like Australia. There is a general consensus on how to order the world in economic and, increasingly, political terms, one which presupposes a cultural way of looking at the world. For this civilization much of the last half-century has been a period of prosperity and tranquillity unmatched in history. It includes large parts of the population and is characterized by a strong and widening economic base, unassailable democracy and an increasing sense of possibilities. Plague, starvation and large-scale war at home seem features of a distant, almost medieval, past. The present period has coincided with – indeed, is made possible by – the most sophisticated technological advances such as satellite dishes and fax machines which connect people everywhere.

However, this is still a Western view of history. The emphasis on the role of literary ideas in social and political life is a European phenomenon, part of its historical tradition. The belief that central planning and politics have failed, that new approaches are required, is now widespread. It is no coincidence that after the collapse of communism a playwright became the head of Czechoslovakia and a music professor lead 'free' Lithuania.

The term 'postmodernism' itself has been around for some time. Malcolm Bradbury traces its first literary use to thirty years ago. But he also points out that over the decades the term has come to mean different things to different people:

> The term twisted and turned as the years went by. The American novelist John Barth used it in two virtually opposite senses in two influential articles, 'The Literature of Exhaustion', written in 1967, at the height of Sixties experimentalism, and 'The Literature of Replenishment', written in the more sober year of 1979. In the first essay, he saw the dominant influences on fiction as Nabokov and Borges, and suggested that their fictionalist spirit revealed the 'used-upedness' of literary forms, leaving us in an age of quotation, pastiche and parody. In the second, he identified the central figures as Calvino and Márquez, and saw them as representatives of a new spirit in late twentieth-century writing, which had departed Modernist élitism and become the 'best next thing', drawing on magical realism and fantasy.
>
> If the term still eludes us, it does suggest we have lived through a time of notable artistic inquiry, an inquiry parallel to developments in science, cybernetics, computing, space-probe technology, genetic engineering and silicon age communications. It has been an era of global village eclecticism, when our typical writers often carry a double ethnicity, like Salman Rushdie, Kazuo Ishiguro, Timothy Mo.
>
> (Bradbury 1990)

Postmodernism in the end may just turn out to be a journalistic cliché, an undefined catch-phrase, and not really the herald of a new phase in human history. 'In becoming a household word, it has at the same time become something of a resounding cliché. Just about all the topical academic periodicals with any sort of connection to things cultural have published a special issue on postmodernism' (Lash 1990: 1). The trend continues, every discipline examining itself through postmodernist eyes. Griffin even brought God into his title: *God and Religion in the Postmodern World* (1989). Naturally enough, the most powerful office on earth, that of the President of the United States, has also been studied through postmodernist lenses (see Rose's *The Postmodern President*, 1988).

Titles such as *Heterology and the Postmodern* continue to be published, sending us scurrying for our dictionaries (Pefanis 1991; also see Douzinas and Warrington with McVeigh 1991; Roberts 1990). The over-kill in its use 'has come indeed to make a number of serious academics and intellectuals of a left political persuasion cringe. Periodical editors proclaim proudly that *we*'ve never had an issue on postmodernity' (Lash 1990: 1).

Scholars are already looking beyond postmodernism with titles like *Beyond the Post-Modern Mind* (H. Smith 1989). Indeed, Jencks has declared the term dead and proclaimed in its place a new phrase, 'The New Modernism' (Jencks 1990), although the new appears suspiciously like the old in this case. For others it is the Late Modern Age or High Modernity (the main features of which are radicalizing and globalizing – Giddens 1991: 243). However, 'despite the problems with the term itself – its relation to modernism, the meaning of "post", the periodization implied by the reference to modernism, and its co-opting of the modernism it apparently seeks to transgress – it has nevertheless entered the language, although what it designates is still very much at issue' (A. Lee 1990: x).

In this book we will range widely in order to understand postmodernism. I believe that while the sociologists and philosophers – like Gellner and Giddens in the United Kingdom, Lyotard and Baudrillard in Europe – attempt to explain the postmodernist age we live in, public media figures – like Madonna and Rushdie – personify it for the millions through their lives. We learn of the age through the theorizing of the former and the public personae of the latter (however averse they may be to being labelled 'postmodern' – as indeed Rushdie was in his interview; see

Ahmed 1991c). We learn of postmodernism through the ideas of the former, and the lives of the latter.

Characterizing postmodernism

Essentially concerned with ambiguity, the term 'postmodernism' is difficult to define unambiguously. 'We don't live in a world of clear images', Ian McEwan said on *The Late Show* (BBC2 TV, 7 February 1990). Lyotard, in *The Post-Modern Condition*, characterizes the postmodern as possessing an 'incredulity toward metanarratives' (1984: xxiv). It is 'an enigmatic and troubling postmodernity' (Foucault 1984: 39); 'a moment of gentle apocalypse' (Barthes 1989: xxii). For some it is more than merely 'troubling' and 'gentle' in its apocalyptic impact. It is panic culture: '*The Postmodern Scene* evokes, and then secretes, the *fin-de-millennium* mood of contemporary culture. It is a panic book: panic sex, panic art, panic ideology, panic bodies, panic noise, and panic theory' (Kroker and Cook 1988: i).

Let us attempt to identify some of the main features of postmodernism. Although we acknowledge the diverse sources – architectural, philosophical, literary – of the concept of postmodernism we will emphasize its sociological character. This is what our pragmatic analysis and discussion of contemporary events demand. The use of the term in the text will thus reflect some – or most – of the following features:

One: To approach an understanding of the postmodernist age is to presuppose a questioning of, a loss of faith in, the project of modernity; a spirit of pluralism; a heightened scepticism of traditional orthodoxies; and finally a rejection of a view of the world as a universal totality, of the expectation of final solutions and complete answers. In order to discover postmodernism one must look for richness of meaning rather than clarity of meaning; avoid choices between black and white, 'either–or' and accept 'both–and'; evoke many levels of meaning and combinations of focus; and attempt self-discovery through self-knowledge. The postmodernist condition corresponds to the collage of images and ideas that represents it – ironic, iconoclastic and free-floating. It declares its scope as universal, it embraces high- and low-brow, the serious and the frivolous with equal zeal.

For postmodernists, ideology, Marxist or Buddhist, is just one brand of many available in the shopping mall:

Post-Althusserian, postmodernist thinkers like Jean François Lyotard and Jean Baudrillard see Marxism as just one of a thousand brands on permanent sale in the supermarket of ideas. Assailed by hype, axe-grinding and missionary fanaticism on all sides people have begun to fashion their own designer ideology on the mix'n'match principle – perhaps a dash of Buddhism, streak of eco-fascism, spot of Althusserian cynicism, pinch of Adam Smith libertarianism and so on – all culled from a thousand half-digested sources.

(Horrie 1991: 5)

Something fundamental appears to have altered in the way a whole range of subjects – art, literature, science and even politics – is perceived: 'Jean-François Lyotard tells us in his influential book *La Condition postmoderne: Rapport sur le savoir* (1977) that "postmodernism" is "the state of our culture following the transformations which, since the end of the nineteenth century, have altered the game rules for science, literature and the arts"' (Kermode 1988: 134; also see Buxton 1990; J. Collins 1989; Connor 1989; Fiske 1991; Foster 1985; Glancey 1990; Harasym 1990; Harvey 1989a, 1989b; Jameson 1991; Jencks 1984; 1986a and 1986b, 1990; Kroker and Cook 1988; A. Lee 1990; Naisbitt and Aburdene 1990; Ross 1988; Schlesinger 1991; H. Smith 1989; *Theory, Culture and Society* 1988; Thompson 1990; the books of Alvin Toffler – especially his most recent, 1991 – lay the foundations for the apocalyptic vision of postmodernism).

The hero of a popular, serious novel, *The New Confessions*, captures the mood of the age in the concluding lines:

As I stand here on my modest beach, waiting for my future, watching the waves roll in, I feel a strange, light-headed elation. After all, this is the Age of Uncertainty and Incompleteness. John James Todd, I say to myself, at last you are in tune with the universe.

(Boyd 1988: 528)

Two: Postmodernism coexists and coincides with the age of the media; in many profound ways the media are the central dynamic, the Zeitgeist, the defining feature, of postmodernism (we will discuss the media in greater detail in the last chapter). The media entertain, instruct, educate, and pervert us, ceaselessly and with endless variety. The ubiquitous and powerful presence of the media as a primary element in any cultural definition was brought to our notice by Marshall McLuhan, in the first few lines of his then influential book *Understanding Media*: 'Today, after more than a century of electric technology, we have extended our central nervous system itself in a global embrace, abolishing both space and time as far as our planet is concerned' (McLuhan 1964: 3). Appropriately the sub-title of his book was *The extensions of man*. But McLuhan had also sounded the warning:

> The threat of Stalin or Hitler was external. The electric technology is within the gates, and we are numb, deaf, blind, and mute about its encounter with the Gutenberg technology, on and through which the American way of life was formed. It is, however, no time to suggest strategies when the threat has not even been acknowledged to exist.
>
> (ibid.: 17–18)

The nature and influence of the media as central to the understanding of power and domination are accepted widely today (see Chapter 6). Pictures on television can be as devastating to a country as a fleet of gunships blockading it or a shower of missiles falling on it. The killings in Tiananmen Square were seen by the international community on television, and the revulsion made the Chinese government outcasts. Dictators, like Ceausescu and Marcos, whose speeches were cut short on television, discovered that the failure was also symbolic of the collapse of their power.

The multi-media, multi-discourse, all-pervasive nature of postmodernism is repeatedly pointed out for us by analysts (J. Collins 1989: 112–113). The media – in particular, films – may thus be conceived in the most narrow Althusserian sense:

> 'Because every film is part of the economic system it is also part of the ideological system, for cinema and art are branches of ideology. None can escape; somewhere, like pieces in a jigsaw puzzle all have their allotted place', noted Jean-Luc Comolli and Jean Narboni in their seminal essay, 'Cinema, Ideology, Criticism'.
>
> (Nichols 1976: 24)

It is for this reason that a medium like cinema is a powerful instrument in projecting the dominant culture of the global civilization. Hollywood films have had for the last two to three decades the reputation of being the strongest advocates and exemplars of a centralized, homogeneous American culture (J. Collins 1989).

> According to film theory since the late 1960s, the enormous, widespread popularity of these films and their origins within an industry have made them the purest manifestations of how the American public has been led to think about itself by a highly sophisticated capitalist system. Popular film is allegedly the dominant or hegemonic ideology writ in celluloid.
>
> (J. Collins 1989: 90; for a similar argument with reference to television, see Buxton 1990)

Marshall McLuhan's global village metaphor is significant in dealing with the postmodernist media; in our age it is an actuality. No Western or Eastern, Muslim or non-Muslim divisions separate the pervasive presence of the media. Indeed some of the better known international postmodernist writers are from what McLuhan defines as 'backward or oral culture' (1964: 287); Rushdie is from India, Márquez from South America.

Three: The connection between postmodernism and ethno-religious revivalism – or fundamentalism – needs to be explored by social and political scientists. Postmodernists, it would appear, are better philosophers than they are anthropologists. While noting the fragmentation of social and political ideas and shifts in thought, postmodernists fail to link this process with the revival of ethnicity and religious fundamentalism. (How this revivalism is shaped by media images is discussed in the last two chapters.) Where nothing is sacred, every belief becomes revisable. Thus fundamentalism is the attempt to resolve how to live in a world of radical doubt. It is a dialogue with the times, a response to it. The unsettling contradictions and tensions we note in the major world religions are a result of the transnational moves towards unity; the question of the multiple interpretation of religion is thus also raised. In fact, an argument can be made that ethno-religious revivalism is both cause and effect of postmodernism.

Because the media allow both freedom of expression and broadcast of revivalist impulses, in a manner never before witnessed, the fire for self-assertion and self-identity is fuelled. (Even popular magazines like *Time* were addressing the question; a cover story asked: 'Who are they? Americans debate their identity', 8 July 1991). The revivalism expresses the importance of the nuclear family, the micro level, the personal, again in contradiction to modernism. The compulsive need for security in primeval and atavistic notions of lineage is a consequence of the fragmentation of the recent past; there is comfort in the womb. The quest for origins is therefore inevitable. The assertiveness, the elemental forces it unleashes, judders the modern state, however apparently secure, whether ethnic assertiveness in Canada and the USSR or religious assertiveness in India. In late 1991, after conceding independence to the Baltic states, Gorbachev warned of the ethnic fires that could consume the USSR and Eastern Europe (Croats and Serbs in Yugoslavia were already at each other's throats). The political map of many more recently formed states could be drastically altered in the coming decades; Bangladesh, breaking away from Pakistan, was thus a prelibation of things to come (also see Chapter 3).

The revivalist assertiveness challenges the modernist concept of large state structures, whether capitalist or communist (although some modernist writers like Yeats were using revivalism in this way early this century). Unfortunately, a loosening of the state structure and revivalism have not meant a more tolerant and pluralist society. On the contrary, they lead to sectarian violence. A kind of *Glaubenskrieg*, doctrinal war, a fight to the finish, appears to be the philosophy of the warring groups. (It is not too far removed from the vision of the future in the book *The Handmaid's Tale*.)

A personal witness to this brand of hatred, Anatoly Rybakov, the Soviet novelist, observes:

> I can state categorically that the manifestations of hate are not diminishing under the new pluralism, but growing in number and intensity. The escalation of hate has already begun, arising out of, and in the name of, nationalism. . . . Jewish cemeteries are being desecrated. Swastikas are proliferating, crawling on walls like malignant spiders.
>
> (Bunting 1990)

The momentous changes in the USSR are rife with danger because they are 'affecting millions of people . . . conditioned by that hate . . . pluralism may be throwing open the gates and unleashing a phenomenon that it may be unprepared and impotent to check' (ibid.).

Revivalist tensions spill across international borders, pushing countries into confrontation. If Hungarians are molested in

Romania there are processions and diplomatic protests in Hungary; if French Canadians complain in Canada they are heard in France; if Turks are persecuted in Bulgaria there are protests in Turkey; if Kashmiris are killed in India rallies in their support are held in Pakistan and the United Kingdom.

The word 'fundamentalism' has come to mean ugly, intolerant and violent religious fanaticism in the Western media; it is also a code, sometimes subliminal, sometimes explicit, for Islam. If a Muslim admits to being a Muslim he is in danger of being labelled a fundamentalist; such is the power of the media. But we must be cautious with the use of words like 'fundamentalism' with their specific association with Christian history.

Mesmerized as they are by Islam, the media often overlook the momentous surges of religious belief elsewhere in the world. Yet Christians in the United States, Hindus in India and Buddhists in Thailand present aspects of what the media define as 'fundamentalism'. The connection between Christian revivalism and the media is illustrated by examples such as the Global Satellite Network of the preacher Morris Cerullo of World Evangelism, who hopes that 1 billion people will submit to the teachings of Christ by the year 2000. Another Christian revivalist movement is noted among the Copts in Egypt, partly in reaction to the media coverage of Islam. It is typified by the public stance and life of the Coptic patriarch Shenuda.

One truth has emerged in our postmodernist world: that the concept of fundamentalism, as the media applies it, cannot be restricted to religion. Although Marxism-Leninism, fundamentalist communism, is disintegrating, for more than half a century it dominated large parts of the world. The works of Karl Marx and Vladimir Lenin were the fundamental holy scripture of Marxism-Leninism. These were among the best-selling and most translated books in the world. However, some, such as Marx's *Capital* and *The Communist Manifesto* and Lenin's *What is to be Done?*, have been more widely used than others (like the early work of Marx on human alienation) that raised embarrassing issues about autocratic government. The Marxists had pronounced God dead prematurely; judging from the full churches in the communist countries God has never been healthier.

Some commentators have introduced another group of fundamentalists: messianic capitalists (see the special issue on 'Fundamentalism' of the *New Internationalist*, August 1990). These are the leaders and captains of the dominant world civilization we have identified. They possess absolute faith in market forces as a solution to all human problems. Their doctrine is propagated by a network of influential private pressure groups such as the Heritage Foundation in the United States, the Adam Smith Institute in the United Kingdom, the Kiel Economics Institute in Germany and the Fraser Institute in Canada. Market fundamentalism has also influenced the World Bank and the International Monetary Fund in their prescriptions for poorer economies. As with the Christian fundamentalists, the values most prized by messianic capitalists are discipline, sobriety and hard work.

The intolerance generated by these movements is taking its toll even in societies traditionally considered immune, such as Western ones (also see below). The most sacrosanct of islands, the university, even in America, arguably the freest in the world, is susceptible:

> It is this sort of demand for intellectual conformity, enforced with harassment and intimidation, that has led some people to compare the atmosphere in universities today to that of Germany in the thirties. It reminds others of America in the fifties. 'This sort of atmosphere, where a few highly mobilized radical students can intimidate anyone else, is quite new,' Thernstrom says. 'This is a new McCarthyism. It's more frightening than the old McCarthyism, which had no support in the academy. Now the enemy is within. There are students and faculty who have no belief in freedom of speech.'
>
> (Taylor 1991: 5; also see Amiel 1991, Cockburn 1991
> and *Assignment: New War on Campus*, BBC2, shown on
> 7 May 1991 in the United Kingdom)

A hit song of 1989 by Billy Joel, 'We didn't start the fire', ends with the primal scream, 'I can't take it any more'. In vain he sings, 'But we tried to fight it'. The Americans, the words imply, are not responsible for the problems of the world. The title explains a feature of the postmodern age. Every group feels that 'We didn't start the fire'; the implication is that the other religious or ethnic group did. It is not a sentiment calculated to encourage dialogue or harmony.

Four: The continuity with the past, however apocalyptic the claims, remains a strong feature of postmodernism. The umbilical cord is not cut although it threatens sometimes to suffocate the baby.

Underneath the dross, the faddishness, the desire to be up-to-date are the positive features, like the philosophy of tolerance, the availability of choice, the accessibility of information, the democratization of public life, which would not have been possible without modernity and the past which forms it. So as we recognize Barthes in Flaubert, Foucault in Nietzsche, Derrida in Hegel we also glimpse in the magical realism of the postmodernists an even more ancient past going back to the Greek and Semitic myths (see the next chapter).

Perhaps the continuity with the past is strongest in postmodernist literature. Alison Lee, for one, is clear that the manner in which she uses postmodernism it is not a synonym for 'contemporary' (1990). 'Techniques that I discuss in relation to such novels as John Fowles' *The Magus* (1966, 1977b), Salman Rushdie's *Midnight's Children* (1981), or Peter Ackroyd's *Hawksmoor* (1985), are equally apparent in Miguel de Cervantes' *Don Quixote* (1604, 1614) or Laurence Sterne's *The Life and Opinions of Tristram Shandy* (1759–67)' (ibid.: x). (Salman Rushdie has emphasized the influence of the old tales, like those in *The Arabian Nights*, on his past work and the novel he is working on which reflects the culture of Arab Spain; Ahmed 1991c.)

Scholars conclude that there is much more continuity than difference between the broad history of modernism and the movement called postmodernism:

> It seems more sensible to me to see the latter as a particular kind of crisis within the former, one that emphasizes the fragmentary, the ephemeral, and the chaotic side of Baudelaire's formulation (that side which Marx so admirably dissects as integral to the capitalist mode of production) while expressing a deep scepticism as to any particular prescriptions as to how the eternal and immutable should be conceived of, represented, or expressed.
>
> (Harvey 1989a: 116; also see Giddens 1990)

Another expert cites Andreas Huyssen, that postmodernism 'represents a new type of crisis *of* that modernist culture itself' (J. Collins 1989: 113).

However, the continuities with the past involve irony and wit (Kermode 1988); 'And its response to reality is to treat it as unreal' (ibid.: 130; also see A. Lee 1990: 141). It is also a reassessment of the concept of 'realism', for 'Realism has not disappeared, but it is being challenged – and *that* is the function of postmodern fiction today' (A. Lee, ibid.). Another bond with the past is provided by the growth of the heritage industry (see Chapter 6):

> The growth of a museum culture (in Britain a museum opens every three weeks, and in Japan over 500 have opened up in the last fifteen years) and a burgeoning 'heritage industry' that took off in the early 1970s, add another populist (though this time very middle-class) twist to the commercialization of history and cultural forms.
>
> (Harvey 1989a: 62; also Ahmed 1991i; and Corner and Harvey 1991)

Five: Because large parts of the population live in urban areas and a larger part still are influenced by ideas originating from these areas, the metropolis becomes central to postmodernism (Eco 1986; Harvey 1989a and 1989b; Jencks 1984 and 1990; Raban 1974; Sennett 1991; Wilson 1991). The postmodernist condition is related to the growth of the city or, rather, the dramatic urbanization of populations in the last decades. But the city has moved beyond the vision of Le Corbusier and Max Weber as a planned abode for 'civilized' and 'rational' groups. Earlier studies of the city distinguished between the orthogenetic city – one which expresses traditional moral order like Buddhist Kyoto or Hindu Banaras – and the heterogenetic city (Mumford 1961). Energy, ambiguity, violence and disintegration characterize the latter; it is the direction towards which all cities are moving (for the city of the future, see Davis 1990).

Jonathan Raban calls the metropolis 'soft city', in his influential book of the same title:

> The city as we imagine it, the soft city of illusion, myth, aspiration, nightmare, is as real, maybe more real, than the hard city one can locate in maps and statistics, in monographs on urban sociology and demography and architecture.... Cities, unlike villages and small towns, are plastic by nature. We mould them in our images: they, in their turn, shape us by the resistance they offer when we try to impose our own personal form on them.
>
> (Raban 1974: 9–10)

The city is both an arena and metaphor for life, circumscribing as it defines. It is to the city that the challenge to modernism may be plausibly traced. City architecture oppresses at the same time as it creates a characteristic social environment. A dominating view of city life is provided by the general sense of anarchy that pervades it. It appears that traditional religious virtues, like kindness and compassion, associated with the great world religions have collapsed and been replaced by random and brutal violence:

> Today's manchild sees it as fashionable to kill a mugging victim. 'You take their stuff and you pop 'em', one kid told Brown. There are no more neighborhood Fagins who school their pupils in rational crime in which needless violence is avoided. Street fights are resolved not with fisticuffs but with semi-automatic weapons of high caliber; innocent by-standers are 'mushrooms' to be mowed down if they get in the way. The prospect of being sent to prison holds little terror; indeed, 'doing a bit' in the pen is regarded as a rite of passage.
>
> (Holt 1991: 27)

This milieu of violence was brought home to us dramatically by the widely reported New York jogger rape case. A white woman had been subjected to the most brutal sexual and physical violence by 'wilding' black youths in Central Park, and had been left for dead. Anyone, anytime, could be in her shoes. In another widely discussed case members of a gang called FTS, or Fuck The System, stabbed a young man to death for defending his mother in the New York subway. The FTS were stealing enough money to get to a discothèque. 'Because I have spent part of my professional life in places of combat', wrote Sydney Schanberg of *The Killing Fields*, 'I think it fair to say that New York is in effect in a state of war' (*The Guardian*, 12 September 1990). The latest Rolling Stones tour, perhaps acknowledging this state of affairs, is called *Urban Jungle*.

It was a nineteenth-century poet who captured the ugly face of city life in 'The City of Dreadful Night' (a phrase borrowed by Kipling to describe Lahore – although it is commonly held that he applied it to Calcutta; Kipling 1988: xii). His poem seems an apt description of urban life in the late twentieth century:

> The City is of Night, but not of Sleep;
> There sweet sleep is not for the weary brain;
> The pitiless hours like years and ages creep,
> A night seems termless hell.
>
> (James Thomson, in Gardner 1972: 739)

New York or, in Asia, Calcutta and Karachi, typify Carlos Fuentes' Makesicko city in his novel *Christopher Unborn* (1990):

'We killed the water.'
'We killed the air.'
'We killed the forests.'
'Die, damned city!'
'Come on and die: fucked-up city, what are you waiting for?'
(Fuentes 1990: 304)

The philosophy that propels its citizens is summed up in these lines: 'Don't hate yourself. There are better things to hate. Look at that house. Look at that store. Look at that car. Why don't they belong to you? It's up to you. Take them!' (ibid.: 439; for another literary view of the contemporary city, see Amis 1989).

The problem with the city is not that it dehumanizes man, but that it alters him. Women, egged on by post-feminist polemics and media hype about absolute equality, are hell-bent on the same path; so we heard about female serial killers, and in *Thelma and Louise* we saw a female buddy movie with the attendant murder and mayhem. However, thankfully, women still have some way to go before catching up with the levels of depravity achieved by the opposite sex.

In the city, man is tense, rushed, aggressive, harassed, neurotic, in short, de-humanized. Against this some will say, surely the human species has always been like this, starting from Cain and Abel. Perhaps there is some truth in this observation. But every society, throughout history and throughout the world, contains wonderful people: good-humoured parents, wise teachers, friendly neighbours, compassionate elders, hospitable strangers. In the city these are in short supply, a dying species, the freaks; here we discover a substantially mutated human society, one almost completely hostile and aggressive.

The urban violence and the random killings raise the spectre of life without justice, a species without compassion; and without these two there is anarchy and chaos – it is, as the French film title of Paris life proclaims, *A World Without Pity* (*Un monde sans pitié*). The city is in flames, as in the cult film *Streets of Fire*. We can no longer talk glibly of a return to the jungle. Even among the animals in the jungle order is maintained, and within the family group there is a greater protection and care than in many human societies. As a consequence the family unit is in the process of disintegration, with high divorce rates, alcoholism and drug abuse.

Paul Theroux's chilling description of travel in the subway in New York is as powerful a metaphor of urban life as we can hope for: 'It was a land impossible to glamourize and hard to describe. I had the feeling I was looking at the future' (Theroux 1991: 104). It is, of course, the simple Muslim, strong in faith, who refuses to allow even the dreaded New York subway to intimidate him: 'Then a Muslim unflapped his prayer mat – while we were at Flushing Avenue, talking about rules – and spread it on the platform and knelt on it, just like that, and was soon on all fours, beseeching Allah and praising the Prophet Mohammed' (ibid.: 93).

In *Black Rain* Ridley Scott extends the arguments he had rehearsed in *Blade Runner*. The nightmare is now universal. California or Japan, the entire world is terrifyingly similar. The hero is no longer a knight in shining armour but a corrupt cop. We are made aware of our ambivalence to the hero figure. The issue of racism is not hidden. The white hero responds like an average American or European to the stereotypes of the sadistic, chaotic and corrupt orientals. Once again Scott gives us a postmodernist feel and statement by juxtaposing images, values and attitudes. It is a vision the Japanese themselves depict in the futuristic animated film *Akira*.

The city is well on the way to becoming the satanic crèche, the urban nightmare of *Hardware*, the Los Angeles of *Blade Runner*, the Gotham City of *Batman*. And the time when life as we know it on the planet collapses is ominously near: 1997 in *Terminator 2 – Judgment Day*; 1999 in *Highlander 2 – The Quickening*. The year 1999 is also the one in which civilization as we know it ends in *Omega Cop*. The greenhouse effect and solar flares ensure that the ozone layer has collapsed; with it have collapsed law and order, and there is total anarchy on earth. Popular cinema appears to have written off the planet. Perhaps this is the customary spasm of the millenarians at the end of the cycle; but perhaps it is something more terminal, more apocalyptic.

Urban life in developing societies has traditionally revolted – as it has often fascinated – Europeans. Here is Lévi-Strauss, a distinguished European scholar, describing city life:

Filth, promiscuity, dis-order, physical contact; ruins, shacks, excrements, mud; body moisture, animal droppings, urine, purulence, secretions, suppuration – everything that [European] urban life is organized to defend us against, everything we loathe, everything we protect ourselves from at great cost – all these by-products of co-habitation never here [in the Third World] impose a limit on [urban life's] spread.

(in Geertz 1989: 40)

This was a generation ago. Today Western commentators would say that elements of disorder and decay in the passage apply to most Western cities. The Duke of Edinburgh, for one, in his usual forthright and succinct manner, observed that British cities were nasty, over-populated and smelly places to live in. His son, Prince Charles, sensitive to the pressures of contemporary urban life, would reject modern city architecture altogether.

In certain parts of some Muslim cities, like Karachi and Cairo, there is ample evidence to suggest that the urban terror has begun. Over-crowding, lack of civic amenities, collapse of law and order, endemic corruption and ethnic and sectarian violence create a general sense of despair and anarchy. So we conclude that the late twentieth-century city, whether developed – like New York and London – or developing – like Cairo and Calcutta – is a nightmare. Yet in spite of this – or perhaps because of it – a vigorous religious revivalism is also noted in most Muslim cities, as we will see below.

The city itself is not a bad idea. We recall imperial cities like Paris and London in the eighteenth and nineteenth centuries – their elegant avenues, grand houses, splendid parks. And a century or two earlier there are similar examples of Muslim cities – Delhi, Isfahan, Cairo. Yet we must not forget the misery of the working classes, tucked out of sight, and the ugly story of colonialism that helped nurture the European cities. For this we turn not to painters and poets with an eye to rich patrons but novelists like Dickens and Disraeli.

Even earlier, in Muslim Spain, we find model cities like Córdoba and Granada. Here we note a plural society, a multi-cultural richness, a tolerant synthesis of cultures, busy academics, public baths, open debates, flourishing arts, parks (for a romantic and idealized picture of Muslim Spain, see Irving 1990). A social symmetry was maintained; for instance, entire professions – artisans or goldsmiths – lived in one neighbourhood; or an entire ethnic group. Loneliness, the bane of the city, was thus kept at bay; the group reinforced, not subtracted from, a sense of identity.

The city was not a bad idea, and, above all, it generally worked.

After all, the notion of a city from early Greece – the metropolis – was that of a model society. It is in the late twentieth century that the city has almost broken down: in the muggings, breakdown of services, random violence, fear and isolation, life is becoming unbearable for many. We need to re-think, fundamentally, the notion of the city.

Six: There is a class element in postmodernism, and democracy is a pre-condition for it to flourish. The architects, dramatists, social scientists, writers, one is tempted to say the yuppies, those who provide the dynamics of a modern city, are at the core of postmodernism. Through the media their ideas are widely spread. The power of this class is based on knowledge and communication; it is, in Bourdieu's phrase, their 'cultural capital'. Postmodernism may thus be seen as essentially, though not exclusively, a middle-class phenomenon (see Lash 1990: 251).

Beneath the longueur of its language Marxism's enduring strength lies in the simplicity of its ideas and their broad appeal. It is easy to identify with the down-trodden, toiling masses against the exploiting, heartless capitalists. The formula goes to the heart, cutting across religious and ethnic boundaries. By contrast, postmodernism is vague and confusing, it appeals to the eye; the visual is an important element in postmodernism (Martin Jay, in the United States, has appropriately given his major work in progress the working title of *The Visual*).

Not unnaturally, Marxists are critical of postmodernism (Callinicos 1989; Eagleton 1991). They attack the postmodernists for the original ideologists' mistake of being non-historical and located in an eternal 'now' (Eagleton 1991). Lyotard's theories are thus rubbished as 'entirely vacuous', while Baudrillard is another 'cynic' and, for good measure, 'a nihilist' (ibid.). In practice, however, many postmodernist writers show the evidence of socialist ideas from the time before they apostatized.

While the middle class may provide an intellectual lead to postmodernism, it is the masses which help to define it. This is made possible through the process of democratization. Although it is undoubtedly the most desirable method of conducting human affairs, total democracy is still the closest thing to total anarchy. In reducing human thought and activity to the lowest common denominator it unleashes forces sometimes difficult to control; and the desire of the mob for blood and spectacle is close to the surface.

The Roman mob giving the thumbs-down sign loved nothing better than fellow humans brutally killed in front of it or news of its leaders, like Julius Caesar, being stabbed to death in the Senate. The pattern is visible throughout history; whether in the densely packed bazaars of Delhi in Mughal India when the populace waited to see the unsuccessful challenger to the throne blinded and in chains, paraded in humiliation on an elephant; in the French revolutionaries watching the aristocracy going to the guillotine in Paris in the late eighteenth century; or in the large crowds gathering in Lahore for the public whipping of petty criminals during the 1980s in General Zia's Pakistan.

With democratization, demotic impulses shape the age. And democracy took a long time coming. Starting in the last century it was a reluctant giving by the ruling classes of the vote, firstly to all white men, irrespective of birth, then, more reluctantly, to women and finally – and this is still an ongoing struggle – to the traditionally oppressed groups like blacks. It is the culmination of the process that explains the thirst for spectacle, for the blood of celebrities, for the vulgarization that is so apparent in the mass media. In this sense both the leader-writers of *The Guardian* and the *Sun* reflect the same democracy, though different aspects of it; one the high idealism of the literate élite, the other the gut vulgarity of the lager lout. The joining of sophisticated political satire and mob vulgarity demeaning the high and mighty are best seen in television shows like *Spitting Image* and magazines like *Private Eye* (more of which later). For Milan Kundera the fusing of cultures, the unbearable senselessness of being, the laying low of the mighty, is summed up in the poignant story of the death of Stalin's son (1985). The young man died complaining about faeces to an uncomprehending guard in a German prison camp.

From the actions of the President of the United States to the selection of the Top of the Pops and television ratings, to the rejection of communism in Eastern Europe and the USSR, it is the mob that helps to shape decisions today. Power, privilege, celebrity status are no longer the preserve of any one group. Even the most ordinary person – as Warhol, one of the exemplars of the age, enunciated for us – can become famous even if for a few minutes. (Appropriately, Warhol professed to be 'bored' with his prediction of the sixties that 'everyone will be famous for fifteen minutes'; his 'new line' was: 'In fifteen minutes everybody will be famous' – Augarde 1991: 222.)

Seven: Postmodernism allows, indeed encourages, the juxtaposition of discourses, an exuberant eclecticism, the mixing of diverse images. The postmodernist montage mixes the highbrow and the populist, the alienating and the accessible; the taste is eclectic, the outlook dégagé. Different styles and different historical periods are ours: we use French perfume and wear Marks and Spencer clothes, listen to rap and reggae, eat McDonald's food for lunch, watch an old John Wayne western in the afternoon and go for Indian tandoori to a Bangladeshi restaurant for dinner. Lyotard echoes the sentiment exactly by dismissing the eclecticism as 'the degree zero of contemporary general culture', 'kitsch' that 'panders' in the 'absence of aesthetic criteria' (Lyotard 1984: 76). The eclecticism feeds from the diverse and unexpected bringing together of widely different discourses:

> The radical eclecticism so prevalent in Post-Modernist texts like James Stirling's Stuttgart Museum (1984), Manuel Puig's *The Kiss of the Spiderwoman* (1978) or Ridley Scott's *Blade Runner* (1982) depends upon the juxtaposition of discourses (architectural, psychological, narrative, etc.) that are not only recognizable and discrete, but possessed of specific aesthetic/ideological values by which they assert their privileged status as representations of experience.
>
> (J. Collins 1989: 27)

It is this juxtaposition which allows postmodernism to subvert traditional images in the most startling and unexpected manner. Unconnected pictures link with one another to disturb or excite us. 'Postmodernist philosophers tell us not only to accept but even to revel in the fragmentations and the cacophony of voices through which the dilemmas of the modern world are understood' (Harvey 1989a: 116).

Theroux, in his recent black novel *Chicago Loop*, informs us that raisins have a mineral-oil glaze on them which causes 'anal seepage' (1990). Such is the postmodernist pursuit for information, however trivial, irrelevant or irreverent and the postmodern method of juxtaposition. The most unlikely ideas are thus triggered for us. Standing before a tranquil picture of rural life by Constable we are reminded of the threat to the ozone layer from the methane gases expelled from the rear ends of the cows; we marvel at the emerald-blue, translucent water at the beach into which a model in a television ad dives, and our mind turns to the

oil, garbage and filth it must contain; seeing a father with his child
we think of the disturbing incest stories in the media; eating fast
foods, like a hamburger, we worry about the poisonous preser-
vatives, the dangerous chemicals, we are ingesting; gazing at the
torso of a perfectly shaped model in tight-fitting jeans, the camera
focusing on the buttocks ostensibly to show the designer's label,
but also, not so subtly, suggesting a sexual message, we wonder
whether the model has been eating raisins.

The mixing of images, interlocking of cultures, juxtaposition of
different peoples, availability of information, are partly explained
because populations are mobile as never before. The mobility
continues in spite of increasingly rigid immigration controls.
Filipino maids in Dubai, Pakistani workers in Bradford, the
Japanese buying Hollywood studios, Hong Kong Chinese
entrepreneurs acquiring prime property in Vancouver testify to
this. This swirling and eddying of humanity mingles ideas,
cultures and values as never before in history. This aspect of
contemporary life was brought home to us when the Iraqi army
captured Kuwait in the summer of 1990 and netted peoples from
many lands, a veritable melting-pot.

The juxtapositions combine with the change, with the speed,
the variety of discourses, and the obsession with the new to
overwhelm and almost defy analysis. This is true even for the
experts. As a master of semiotics repined: 'All the professors of
theory of communications, trained by the texts of twenty years
ago (this includes me), should be pensioned off' (Eco 1986: 149).

*Eight: The idea of plain and simple language sometimes appears to
elude the postmodernist masters in spite of their claims to accessibility.* The
de-mystifiers and de-constructionists are themselves in need of
de-mystification and de-construction. They are often trapped in a
thicket of jargon, abstruse concepts and obscure terms. Both the
esoteric style and intellectual content reinforce the high-brow
impression of much of postmodernist thought. The parodist
becomes an easy target for parody.

Jean Baudrillard, the high priest of postmodernism, almost
asks for the following reaction to his recent book *Seduction* (1990).
The reviewer explains why postmodernists 'are not like you and
me' (J. Kemp 1990: 40). 'They do not use words as we use them,
or mean the thing that we mean by them. . . . Take obscenity, for
example. The field of obscenity is a vast and fascinating one, but
until now I never realised that it encompassed quadraphonics,

which along with the "Japanese vaginal cyclorama" stand condemned for "an orgy of realism". Meanwhile terrorist acts, by most people's lights the nadir of obscenity, simply "disappoint even as they exalt". (Sex, in case you were wondering, is merely the "economic residue" of seduction, about as obscene a description as one could wish for' (ibid.).)

In conclusion, we note that contradictory developments, disturbing paradoxes, puzzle the mind: a questioning of materialism, on the one hand, and an insatiable desire to join the consumerist order, on the other; individuals enjoy rights and privileges as never before in history, yet the state has never been as omnipotent as in our age. Another paradox of postmodernism is that 'Postmodern culture seems to proclaim itself as an avant-garde at the same time as announcing that avant-gardes no longer exist' (Lash 1990: 252). Another paradox is evident in the implosion of large political blocs, the most notable example of which is the communist one, and countries, like those in Western Europe, heading towards consolidation. A rejection of established religion alongside one of the most powerful revivalist waves in history in the major religions is also a paradox; so is the tacit admission of the need to view the people of the world as a common humanity and the unprecedented, widespread bigotry and intolerance costing lives.

With the anarchy of change, the plurality of discourses, we must also note the positive and exhilarating offering, what Barthes calls '*jouissance*', postmodernism brings to us: the importance of diversity, the need for tolerance, the necessity for understanding the other. The simple virtues, associated with the traditional Semitic religions – humility, piety, compassion, concern for the aged and the less privileged – seem to be fading from our memory. They already appear to belong to some fairy-tale, mythological past. It is time we retrieved them.

We need to interpret postmodernism in a positive manner; what tends to be emphasized in the flood of postmodernist literature is its sense of anarchy, rootlessness and despair. What is missed out are its positive sides, like diversity, the freedom to explore, the breakdown of establishment structures and the possibility to know and understand one another. Postmodernism need not be viewed as an intellectual conceit, an academic discussion remote from actual life in literary salons, but as an historic phase of human history offering possibilities not available before to such large numbers; a phase that holds the possibility of bringing diverse people and cultures closer together than ever before.

MUSLIM ENTRY INTO THE POSTMODERNIST PHASE OF HISTORY

In order to find an explanation of what is happening in Muslim society, it will be necessary to analyze postmodernism as a social science, taking account of its European origin. The current explanations are not so much wrong as inadequate to encompass the rapid changes overtaking Muslim society.

Let us first attempt to locate a postmodernist strand in contemporary Muslim thought. In spite of the flood of literature in the West – on art, architecture, literature – postmodernism has not made much of an impression on Muslims. Although some Muslim scholars identified the 'new situation' created by economic and political factors after Muslims had gained independence from the colonial powers, they failed to develop the arguments along postmodernist lines (Rahman 1984: 87; see Chapter 4 for a fuller discussion of Muslim scholarship).

Books such as *Debating Muslims: Cultural Dialogues in Postmodernity and Tradition* (Fischer and Abedi 1990) which raise the issue are rare. The few Muslim comments on postmodernism are tentative and sweeping; they dismiss it as a continuation of Western modernism, as destructive and doomed (Manzoor 1990), equated to 'Americanization', 'nihilism', 'anarchy' and 'devastation' (Abu-Rabi 1990). Indeed all the authors cited above equate postmodernism broadly with American civilization. This perhaps explains the Fischer and Abedi perspective which is based almost exclusively on Iranian data: from Iran in the 1980s the postmodernist world would be represented and dominated by the United States or, to use the name conferred on it by Ayatollah Khomeini, the Great Satan. Although this equation is also employed by some Western critics – for Kroker and Cook it was a 'panic' culture (1988) – it is, as we will see below, an incorrect simplification, a misleading reductionism.

There exists, therefore, an intellectual time-warp between Muslims and the West. So while postmodernism is already seen by some in the West as *passé*, yesterday's cliché, the Muslim intellectual continues to grapple with stale issues contained in modernism. Whether whining about European imperialism and Western decadence or beating the Marxist socialist drum, titles still use 'modern' (*Islam and Modernity*, Rahman 1984; *The Crisis of Modern Islam*, Tibi 1988; *A Faith for all Seasons: Islam and Western Modernity*, Akhtar 1990; and others). The response to post-modernism, to its wit and irony, to its scope and possibilities, is usually incomprehension or anger; it is as if two different peoples were speaking two different languages, representing two different time zones.

What then can postmodernism mean for Muslims? When does it become distinct from modernism or is it essentially modernism in another shape? Is it yet another concept borrowed from the West to be applied – or misapplied – to Muslim society like modernism itself, with its concomitant ideas of 'progress', 'rationality' and 'secularism'? Can the application of a term fostered in the European literary tradition be valid in Africa and Asia? How would Muslim leaders and intellectuals interpret the main features of postmodernism?

Muslim modernism

Before we consider these questions, let us clarify what we mean by modernism. We, too, rely on the meaning provided by the *Oxford English Dictionary* (see page 6). For Muslims, then, the definition applies to a wide range of activity from Islamic thought to political action, from architecture to modes of dress (see below). But there is a caveat to note: it is the subtle shift in the definition of the earlier modernists we discuss in this chapter to those we will mention later (in Chapters 3 and 4). The former were acutely aware of and underlined their religious culture and tradition; the latter tend to be dubious about the past.

The Muslim modernist phase was engendered by European colonialism. While more conservative Muslims would have no truck with Europeans – indeed many resisted them through armed struggle – the modernists wished to come to terms with and even incorporate elements of their civilization. Most sought synthesis and ideally looked for harmony between their own position and that of the Europeans.

One of the earliest and most influential modernist figures is Sir Sayyed Ahmed Khan, who lived in India in the last century. The college he established in 1875 in Aligarh, near Delhi, laid the foundations for what was to become a symbol of Muslim identity and lead to the Pakistan movement. The name of his institution, the Muhammadan Anglo-Oriental College; its conscious attempt to emulate Oxbridge in style and organization; the title of his book, *An Account of the Loyal Muhammadans of India* (1860) and his knighthood, in recognition of his services to the British, convey the essence of this modernist Muslim. The college – later university – was a rich source of recruitment for two other Indian modernist leaders, Muhammad Ali Jinnah and Muhammad Iqbal, who would go on to create Pakistan. Jinnah, too, consciously looked to London, where he was educated, for ideas on politics; Iqbal, who studied in Cambridge, frequently cites European writers in his work. Jinnah with his cigar, monocle, Savile Row suits and talk of Westminster style democracy – in a clipped English accent – is the modernist Muslim leader *par excellence*.

All this served a purpose. Modernism provided important weapons to Muslims like Sir Sayyed, Iqbal and Jinnah. Through their understanding of British ways and ideas they could engage successfully with the colonial power. These Muslims would turn the skills they had acquired from the British against them to best represent the interests of their community.

Muhammad Abduh, the father of Arab modernism and rector of Al-Azhar, and his disciple Rashid Rida, early this century, are the influential Arab modernists. Both were inspired by the late-nineteenth-century figure of Jamalaldin Afghani. Afghani's sympathetic interaction with European intellectuals on the one hand and advocacy of pan-Islamism on the other make him a central figure in Muslim modernism.

Across the Muslim world – Ataturk in Turkey, Amanullah in Afghanistan, the Shah in Iran (both father and son), Jinnah in Pakistan – leaders looked to the West for inspiration in moulding their societies and projecting modernity. Their actions expressed their position: Ataturk ordering the shaving of beards as symbolic of tradition; Amanullah encouraging the removal of the veils that women wore; the Shah suppressing the clergy and Jinnah rebuking admirers for calling him a 'Maulana', a religious leader.

In turn, the more orthodox would oppose these leaders. The pressure of the Muslim Brotherhood would be felt by Nasser; Sadat would lose his life to them. Jinnah, for many Muslims, was the 'Quaid-i-Azam' or the great leader, for others he was 'Kafir-i-Azam' or the great *kafir*, non-believer. The Shah of Iran became the symbol of a *kafir* for the Islamic revolution. The oscillation continues in Muslim society and explains an important dynamic of it.

Muslim leaders even after independence would continue to interact with, and borrow from, the legacy of modern ideas they acquired in the British institutions which had helped shape them: Lincoln's Inn (Jinnah), Sandhurst (Field Marshal Ayub Khan of Pakistan), Harrow (King Hussein of Jordan and agnates), Oxbridge (Zulfiqar Ali Bhutto and his daughter, Benazir Bhutto) or indigenous but British-style institutions (Nasser). There was the touch of a distinctly British code of political behaviour in their attitude to their main opponents: Jinnah admitting that Indian Muslims had lost their greatest friend on hearing the news that his arch-rival, Gandhi, had been shot dead; Nasser, after his military coup, allowing King Farouk to escape to the south of France in the royal yacht; Ayub, after his coup, permitting Iskander Mirza to proceed to London; Bhutto, after coming to power, leaving Ayub to spend his last years in his own home as a free citizen and not even bringing him to court on corruption charges as demanded by his party. This would change later. The Shah of Iran would be hounded to his death by the Ayatollahs and Bhutto himself hanged in jail like a common criminal because General Zia would not pardon him.

'Modern' was translated by Muslim leaders as a drive to acquire Western education, technology and industry. Ideas of democracy and representative government were also discussed, although with reservation on the part of the élite. For those who looked to the communist countries and Moscow for assistance, modernism also meant the imported ideas of secularism, socialism and state-controlled industrialization. In the 1960s economists and advisers from the two super-powers laid down the golden rules for modern progress, whether the Harvard economists in Pakistan or the Moscow planners in Cairo. Strong treaties or security pacts bound many Muslim countries to one or other of the super-powers: Ayub's Pakistan through CENTO and SEATO with the United States, Nasser's Egypt with the USSR. Prestigious central projects – Nasser's Aswan Dam, Ayub's capital, Islamabad – became symbols of national pride; the country's planners became the wise men behind the five-year economic plans which incorporated all aspects of life from health, to industry, to education; the government became the standard-bearer of modernity. The central issue was, as the *Oxford English Dictionary* informed us, to subordinate religious belief to harmony with modern thought.

There was thus a mimetic quality about Muslim modernism. Sometimes these leaders spoke out against the West, but tell-tale signs gave them away. Their Western suits, for example, suggested they remained in thrall. Scholars, like Hossein Nasr and Fazlur Rahman, would grapple with the Western concept of modernism in its relationship to Islam (for a fuller discussion, see Chapter 4).

If modern meant the pursuit of Western education, technology and industrialization in the first flush of the post-colonial period, postmodern would mean a reversion to traditional Muslim values and a rejection of modernism. This would generate an entire range of Muslim responses from politics to clothes to architecture.

For us the definition is literal: it is the period following that of modernism. With an important caveat or two we therefore accept the use of the term postmodern. We emphasize its European context and origin; and we point out that many of the features of modernism are continued, although in an altered form, in postmodernism. The application of the term thus assists us in better understanding the contemporaneous phase of Muslim history. In Muslim society postmodernism means, as we will see below, a shift to ethnic or Islamic identity (not necessarily the same thing and at times opposed to each other) as against an imported foreign or Western one; a rejection of modernity; the emergence of a young, faceless, discontented leadership; cultural schizophrenia; a sense of entering an apocalyptic moment in history; above all, a numbing awareness of the power and pervasive nature of the Western media which are perceived as hostile.

Discussions of postmodernism in the West relate it to an intellectual period with specific cultural characteristics and intellectual content. Writers are easily labelled: James Joyce is recognizably modern and Jean Baudrillard is postmodern. In the Muslim world there is a different emphasis, different markers, different understanding. Muslims would link the postmodernist phase to the political history of their nations. If postmodernism in the West was fostered by a milieu which encouraged the growing security and confidence after the Second World War, opposite forces were at work among Muslims. The catalyst may well have been provided by the political and military disasters after the first flush of independence from the colonial powers (although not all Muslim countries were formally colonized).

The defeat and humiliation of the Arabs in 1967 at the hands of Israel and the loss of territory – east Jerusalem, the West Bank,

Gaza and the Golan Heights – were followed shortly by the victory of India over Pakistan in 1971, which resulted in the loss of the majority province for Pakistan. Although in the Pakistan case the army was used to suppress the Bangladesh freedom movement and therefore drew widespread criticism, the spectacle of about 100,000 Muslim soldiers languishing in Indian prison camps was not an edifying one for most Pakistanis. These events did not have a recent precedent and were seen by Muslims to reflect the bankruptcy of their secular or modern rulers. Muslim humiliation was deep; morale was at its nadir.

The modern period had led Muslims into a cul-de-sac. Dictators, coups, corruption and nepotism in politics; low education standards; an intellectual paresis; the continuing oppression of women and the under-privileged and grossly unequal distribution of wealth were some of its characteristics. The multi-national companies and their visible efforts in supporting what was seen as a corrupt local élite, the large-scale migration from the rural to the urban areas and consequent social disruption in traditional life and the failure to build effective institutions of the modern state were other characteristics. Muslims were coming to the same conclusion as Giddens on the question of modernity (1990); they, too, saw it as 'a Western project'.

The reality of Muslim life was a far cry from the edifying and noble Islamic ideal (for a discussion of the ideal-type, which is based primarily in the Quran and life of the Prophet, see Ahmed 1988). Muslims, as most people who believe in God, asked if God had abandoned them. Other Muslims turned the question round: had they abandoned God? The answer pointed in the direction of Islam, and they turned to God (in troubled times this is a common theme in Muslim history: see 'Mahdism and millenarian movements', ibid.: chapter 3, section 6).

Islamic resurgence

For Muslims the 1970s began and were sustained with unparalleled Muslim activity: the Ramadan war in 1973; the Arab oil embargo in the same year, led by the vigorously dedicated King Faisal; General Zia's assumption of power in 1977 and his Islamization programme; the start of the Afghan *jihad*, to liberate Afghanistan in 1979; the bloody and violent attempt, also in the same year, by Juhaiman and his group, to seize the Kaaba in

Makkah – for Muslims the holiest of the holy, the action sent shock-waves wherever they lived; and, finally, the culmination of the decade with the coming to power of Ayatollah Khomeini at the head of the Islamic revolution in Iran, in 1979. Islamic activity was also noted in countries far from the Middle East like Nigeria and Indonesia. At all levels the Muslim leaders mentioned above consciously evoked tradition, whether in the rhetoric and idiom of politics, observing the fast during the month of Ramadan or wearing traditional dress, in particular avoiding the tie as a symbol of Western dress (see Chapter 5, 'Your jeans for you, my robes for me', for fuller discussion; also Ahmed 1990c).

Let us take the Ramadan war, which set the tone for the coming years. While the earlier wars with Israel were seen in terms of Arab nationalism and socialism, the Ramadan war was dense with Islamic symbols and rhetoric. The war was named 'Ramadan' after the sacred month of fasting during which it occurred; its code name was Badr, the first major victory for Islam led by the Prophet himself; those who died were not regarded as patriots but as *shaheed*, religious martyrs; and the battle-cry was *Allah-u-Akbar*, God is most great, the traditional call for prayer. (Almost twenty years later Saddam, the erstwhile socialist, would follow some of these steps during the Gulf crisis, including the stitching of *Allah-u-Akbar* onto the Iraqi flag.)

One of the key players in the Islamic revival was King Faisal. He first hastened the end of the Nasser era among Arabs by challenging Nasser's leadership. He then provided a vigorous Islamic direction to the Arabs and indeed the Muslim world. The first meeting of the Islamic heads of state in Rabat in 1969 was a personal triumph for him. The Organization of the Islamic Conference was formed with its headquarters in Jeddah. By helping to organize a similar meeting to the one in Rabat in Lahore, Pakistan, he was drawing non-Arab Muslims into the Middle East arena. Faisal's use of oil prices as a weapon in the 1970s also proved effective as it underlined the link with the region of those nations who needed oil. The millions of Muslims who were employed on the Arabian peninsula, especially those from South Asia, like the 3 million Pakistanis, provided further leverage.

But Muslim activity was not confined to battlefields and diplomatic conferences. A period of intellectual effervescence had begun. The first world conference on Muslim education was held in Makkah in 1977, and this generated a series of academic papers, books and conferences. Another equally autotrophic international attempt towards an 'Islamization of Knowledge' was made by scholars like Ismail al-Faruqi (1982), which challenged many existing modernist ideas. Muslim educationists like Ali Ashraf laboured to create an 'Islamic education' (1979, 1985); economists like Khurshid Ahmad worked on 'Islamic economics' (1981) and like Siddiqi on 'Islamic banking' (1983); sociologists, like Ba-Yunus explored an 'Islamic sociology' (1985); and anthropologists an 'Islamic anthropology' (Ahmed 1986a; for an overview see chapter 10, 'The reconstruction of Muslim thought', in Ahmed 1988). Books like Edward Said's *Orientalism* (1978), which forcefully argued that the West could know Islam only in an exploitative, hostile way, further provided ideas fuelling the challenge to Western scholarship. Muslim radical scholars carried this argument to its logical conclusion, rejecting everything from the West out of hand, and thereby set the pace, if not the agenda, for Muslim scholarship (see Chapter 4).

There was also an awareness that architectural designs imported from the West do not always meet local requirements. Architectural awards, like the Aga Khan's, helped relate the up-to-date to the traditional (as we note in Chapter 5). New, impressive, Islamic universities came into being at Al-Ain in the United Arab Emirates and in Islamabad in Pakistan.

Among Muslim nations these markers, events and dates, signifying fundamental changes, thus introduced an inceptive period, starting in the 1970s, which would be termed one of 'Islamic revivalism' or 'resurgence'. The tenebrific clouds hitherto obscuring Muslim endeavour began to shift and Muslims felt a sense of jubilation. Henceforth Islamic symbolism, signifying both form and content, would be increasingly visible in Muslim society. Although some of the personnel may have changed – Faisal, Zia, Khomeini and Faruqi are all gone – the Islamic tempo has not faltered.

Many of the elements we are witnessing are as old as the advent of Islam in the seventh century. The return to a golden past, the desire to live according to the Quran and the *sunnah*, the example of the Prophet, of his behaviour, clothes and personal rituals, have always been an ideal for Muslims. Educationists, reformers and visionaries have repeated this message over centuries. Nonetheless, the evidence suggests that Muslims are entering an even more self-consciously Islamic phase than in the recent past.

This is the bad news for those who dislike Islam. The good news is that Islam is not really about bombs and book-burning. This is a media image, one which has almost become a self-fulfilling prophecy, and the Islamic injunctions for balance, compassion and tolerance are blotted out by it. The holy Quran has emphasized 'Your religion for you and mine for me' (1989: Surah 109: 6) and 'There shall be no compulsion in religion' (Surah 2: 256). For Muslims, God's two most important and most cited titles are the Beneficent and the Merciful. This is not only forgotten by those who dislike Islam but, more importantly, it is forgotten by Muslims themselves. Chaining and blindfolding 'hostages' – however compelling the reasons – do not reflect compassion or mercy; nor does the murder of innocent Armenians in the USSR or Christians in the Sudan; nor does the brutality of despotic Muslim leaders, mercilessly killing their own citizens.

The public statues of the Great Leader striking up heroic poses, the terror and torture of an ubiquitous secret police, the megalomania and nepotism of the ruler, the mesmerized schoolchildren chanting his praise, were anathema to Islam. But Muslim leaders – as in Syria and Iraq – borrowed these from Uncle Joe; the Shah in Iran, although looking to the other uncle, Uncle Sam, for inspiration, also employed them. However, brutal despots are a feature of the modern age and not exclusive to Muslim countries. Pinochet . . . Ceausescu . . . Marcos; the list from different parts of the world is long. Securitate murderers, torture of dissidents and unparalleled corruption characterized the rule of all of them. And Western governments have honoured them, by honorary knighthoods in London and invitations to address the Joint Houses of Congress in Washington.

The general failure of the materialist model, whether Marxist at one end of the spectrum or capitalist at the other, also feeds Islamic revivalism. Both systems are widely seen in the Islamic world as based in materialism and are understood to have failed to provide social and political solutions: Marxism has usually meant a grey, brutal dictatorship, while capitalism is mostly characterized by alienation, greed and anarchy.

There is a danger of conveying the impression that there is a unity in Muslim perception and a totality in Muslim endeavour; this is manifestly not so. Bengalis, for instance, viewed the Pakistan army as a violent instrument of oppression; many Afghans accused the *jihad* of their compatriots of being funded and organized by the American CIA; many in Ayatollah Khomeini's Iran, including the Ayatollah himself, criticized General Zia's Islamization efforts in Pakistan as inadequate; in turn, many Muslims in the Middle East and South Asia condemned the Ayatollah's revolution in Iran as excessive. Critics were quick to point out the connection between military regimes and the use of Islam: to them Islam in Numeiri's Sudan and Zia's Pakistan was reduced to the chopping off of hands and whipping of petty criminals. Some scholars were cynical of colleagues who attempted to 'Islamize' knowledge, since merely appending the label 'Islamic' was no guarantee of academic quality. Sectarian champions, Shia or Sunni, denounced their rivals and proclaimed their exclusive ownership of the truth; smaller groups, like the Ismaili, Ahmadi and Baha'i, were dismissed as heretics and sometimes physically persecuted. Attempted suppression of multiple interpretations of the truth further exacerbated conflict within Islam, which emphasizes unity. The dynamics of the tensions in society are provided by people sometimes failing, sometimes succeeding in attempting to live according to the Islamic ideal-type (Ahmed 1988).

The exhilaration and promise of these processes thus raises questions as to the correct interpretation of faith, where society is heading, what order will emerge and who will lead Muslims? (The question of leadership among Muslims forms the main focus of Ahmed 1991a.) The discovery of the answers promises Muslims a period of volatility, excitement, disquietude and also frustration.

Perceptions of the Western threat

The West has studied Islam for centuries – through its scholars, libraries and now sophisticated technology – but in the main it has failed to understand both Muslims and their societies. Muslims, who rarely study the West, believe they understand through its words and deeds its hostility. The double misconception is refracted through the prism of philosophic and historical opposition; it is the canker lying at the heart of Muslim endeavour.

The implications of this argument are complex, even contradictory. Most recent opinion polls in the West confirm the impression that Islam is seen as the major 'next' enemy after communism (by 80 per cent of the British public, for example). There are few such surveys in Muslim countries but the general

Muslim response to the West confirms the impression that it is widely perceived as attempting to dominate and subvert Muslim societies through economic and cultural power. Muslims, therefore, fall back on and reinforce their own identity. Of course there is no such thing as a monolithic West; there are hostile, indifferent and even friendly individuals who people it. But, just as there has grown a media stereotype of Muslims in the West so there is a Western stereotype in Muslim minds. In particular, America, the powerful dynamo of the contemporary dominant world culture, repels as it fascinates Muslims. For some it is Utopia, which has attracted about 5 million Muslims; for others it is the embodiment of evil, indeed the Great Satan (we shall develop these arguments below).

Let us not fudge issues. There are differences of a philosophic and sociological nature dividing Islam from the West which are brought into sharp relief in postmodernism. In the next chapter, it will be seen that Muslims are further isolated because they rejected the ancient Greeks, whereas the other great monotheistic religions, Judaism and Christianity, interacted with them. This has led to significant consequences in the way different societies have organized themselves. Cultural differences – of clothes, for instance, which we discuss further in Chapter 5 – reflect deeper philosophic issues; so do those of time.

Patience, pace and equilibrium are emphasized in Islam. Haste is the devil's work, the Prophet warned. But the postmodern age is based on speed. In particular, the media thrive on and are intoxicated by speed. Silence, withdrawal, meditation – advocated by all the great religions – are simply not encouraged by the media. Unceasing noise, dazzling colour and restlessly shifting images characterize the media.

Even the Islamic ideas about domesticity, modesty and shame, which relate to both men and women, are misunderstood and mistranslated in the West. As Muslims point out, the secret to stable family life lies in the home. Western families, by contrast, appear to be heading in the opposite direction (see pages 242–53). Drugs, child abuse, domestic violence, divorce and alcoholism are the indicators of social breakdown. Scepticism, cynicism, ambiguity and irony contrast sharply with Islamic commitment and faith.

The derision of and antipathy towards Islam in the Western media cannot be blamed on the media alone. Many factors mingle, juxtapose and fuse. Some are rooted in history, others are contemporary: blame for the oil crisis, atavistic memory of the crusades, anti-Semitism (Muslims now take the place of Jews as alien, repugnant orientals: see the next two chapters), plain Western jingoism, the collapse of the communist states and the revival of the Christian heritage, the ire of those who dislike the holier-than-thou attitude of Muslims and the incapacity of Muslims to explain themselves effectively, have all helped to focus on Islam as the new enemy of the West.

The memory of the crusades fuses with contemporary responses to the availability of oil from the Middle East; the figures of Sultan Saladin from the time of the crusades and Sheikh Yamani of OPEC merge and fuse. Once again, the mosaic allows the juxtaposition of the most unlikely figures and events. Words originating in Muslim societies – *jihad*, *fatwa*, Ayatollah – become part of the universal journalistic vocabulary. In journalese, they are invested with new and specific meanings far removed from the original: thus fundamentalist becomes the code word for a violent Muslim fanatic.

Attacks on Muslim extremists – the fundamentalists of the popular press – easily convert into or carry over onto an attack on the entire body of Muslims. It is difficult to distinguish between the two types of Muslims created in the minds of the media. For non-Muslims, beneath the quiet façade of every ordinary Muslim there is a mad mullah struggling to emerge; the sooner and more effectively he is put down, the better.

Even non-Muslim writers who are sympathetic to Muslims are constantly vilified and under attack in the West. Edward Said, who is one such scholar, complained:

> You are seen either as a loyal American, or some kind of terrorist. . . . I've been working on a book called *Culture and Imperialism* which argues that the tactics of the great empires, which were dismantled after the first world war, are being replicated by the US, the main difference being that we are no longer dealing with an inert colonial world. Most of these countries are highly politicised and have recently acquired independence. But the American attitude has been that if there is a vital interest, invade. I am very hard put to describe the current conflict [in the Gulf] as anything but an imperialist issue. The American way of life is thought to be at stake.
>
> (Said 1990: 32)

Because the West's experts on Islam are home-grown, media images and stereotypes tend to be reinforced. 'Natives' of Afro-Asian birth – or those designated as Third World Scholars – who are asked to comment on Muslims are either not Muslim, or are 'nominal' Muslims (V.S. Naipaul, Fouad Ajami and Salman Rushdie, are three examples cited as Third World Scholars by Gordon 1989; see Chapters 3 and 4 below for a fuller discussion). Although of Asian origin, and capable of perceptive insights and high standards of writing, these scholars permanently live and work in the West; their marriages, their friendships, their interests and their futures are in the West. In various subtle ways they tend to voice what the West wishes to hear, see what it desires to see. More authentic voices, still more strongly attached to Asia, will rarely be heard. Muslims such as Khurshid Ahmad or Ali Ashraf are heard even more rarely, as rarely as Western scholars who are sympathetic to Islam (Edward Said perhaps being an exception).

This partly explains Muslim criticism – which can border on the obsessive – of the West and what it represents. It is this unfortunate relationship which provides the dynamics, the *frisson*, of the present encounter between Islam and the West. At best, the Western media marginalize Muslims (*The Jewel in the Crown*) or sentimentalize them (*The Far Pavilions*); often it deliberately and maliciously distorts their image (*Iranian Nights* – in this case with the aid of Tariq Ali, whom writers like Gordon would no doubt also term a Third World Scholar; also see Chapters 3 and 4).

Until today Europe has kept alive its memories of its Islamic encounters through culture, literature and folklore. The countries on the rim of the Mediterranean, once partly or fully ruled by Muslims, like Spain, Italy and Greece, celebrate their victory over the Muslims in annual festivals. In other European countries, like the United Kingdom, Germany and France, the large, visible Muslim immigrant underclass provokes religious and racist prejudice.

Here is a thoughtful English voice concerned with the Eurocentric perception of Islam:

All of these factors are pushing Europe to define itself in terms, not perhaps of Christian belief, but certainly of Christian heritage, and to emphasize as sharply as possible the distinction and the frontier between itself and the world of Islam. This may be unavoidable. It may in some respects even be desirable: if

Europe is to function successfully as a political entity its members will need some sense of a common heritage, and some criterion for deciding where Europe begins and ends. But the implications need to be considered very carefully. If the price to be paid is to make every Muslim resident in the Community feel that he or she is at best a tolerated alien, and every neighbouring Muslim state feel that it is looked on by Europe as an enemy, then that price is certainly too high. A more constructive and harmonious way to define Europe needs to be found.

(Mortimer 1990: 7)

A more constructive and harmonious way has not been found. On the contrary, the New World Order emerging in the 1990s is tending to focus on Islam with open hostility. At best there is an impatient testiness in its dealing with Islam. Too many forces have combined in this New World Order to counter this position. The Americans, in their role as the world's leading policemen, locate the bad guys in the Muslim world: Khomeini, Gaddafi, Saddam; the British, as enthusiastic followers of the Americans, vociferously support this position; the Russians are wary of their Central Asian Muslims; the Israelis, who influence America on Muslim matters, face the unresolved problem of their Arab population and neighbours. Predominantly Hindu, India is distinctly uneasy at the prospect of an Islamic resurgence which could lead to the secession of its province of Kashmir. Many countries thus have come to believe that they have a 'Muslim' problem.

There has grown, therefore, a tacit understanding, an instinctive sympathy, among those dealing with irate Muslims in different parts of the world. It is this conjunction that so effectively creates a general milieu of antipathy towards Islam. And it is in this context that the work of the chosen Third World Scholars on Muslims is viewed with undisguised suspicion by Muslims themselves (see the discussion of *The Satanic Verses* in Chapter 4). Their work forms the core of the pattern Muslims see as an international conspiracy. The mystery surrounding the untimely deaths of some of the key Islamic players on the world stage – Faisal, Faruqi, Zia – further reinforces the sense of a global conspiracy. It leads to Muslim paranoia.

In the face of this mutual hostility, especially the unsavoury and terrible onslaught of negative media images, the prognosis for the coming years is of culture clash and political tension. The pattern of the relationship between Muslims and non-Muslims appears to be forming. The more we are interlocked with each other, in our times, through technology, the more intolerant of and distant from each other we become. Instant, atavistic responses create instant misunderstandings.

MUSLIM DILEMMAS

'You keep on saying to Akbar . . . why don't you accept the human origin of your religion? Well, he can't', Ernest Gellner said sharply, coming to my rescue, in a television discussion on Islam. 'Islam has not', he further explained, 'been secularized. This is the great mystery about it. All the other world religions have softened, have permitted the ambiguity of meanings.' Gellner was right. For those who believe in Islam, the choice is between being Muslim and being nothing: there is no other choice.

Gellner had made this point on *The Late Show* (7 February 1990, BBC2), hosted by Michael Ignatieff, which included Ian McEwan, Frank Kermode (now Sir), Antonia Byatt (now Booker Prize winner), and myself as guests. We were discussing 'In good faith', Rushdie's first major public statement after months of invisible silence published in *The Independent*, 4 February 1990. No focal point emerged. The eminent literary figures talked airily of the notions of freedom of expression, principles of liberalism, the secular tradition and so on, while I tried to explain the social context of the Muslim response. Gellner, who, as a social scientist, must live and work in the villages and towns of the people he is studying, rather neatly put his finger on the problem, only to be shrugged off, uncomprehended.

Some problems of Muslim society

The question is: why is a religion advocating goodness, cleanliness, tolerance, learning and piety so misunderstood and reviled? Many of the currently accepted social positions in the West – on the undesirability of cigarettes, drugs and alcoholism, and the promotion of family life – have always been advocated by Islam. *Jihad* has become a dirty word in the media, representing the physical threat of a barbaric civilization. Yet the concept is noble and powerful. It is the desire to improve oneself, to attempt betterment and to struggle for the good cause. It is Tennysonian in its scope: to strive, to seek and not to yield.

I wish to avoid what I see as sterile sexist and religious polemics about Muslim women as I have already discussed the matter elsewhere (see chapter 9, section on 'Muslim women', in Ahmed 1988). But I feel it necessary to point out in passing the wholly incorrect, negative media stereotype of women as inanimate objects, submissively attending to the needs of their lord and master, locked away in darkened homes. I believe this is a stereotype partly reflected from the poor opinion, bordering on misogyny, that Western society, inspired by the ancient Greeks, holds of women (see below and in Chapter 6 of this book, 'Women as victims').

The potential of women in Islam is far superior to anything offered by Confucius in China or Aristotle in Greece, or to what Hindu or Christian civilizations offered. Muslim women are central to family affairs from domestic decision-making to rituals. Where their lot is miserable and they have virtually no rights, as in certain tribal areas, it is to be attributed to Muslim male tyranny, not Islamic advice and is in need of urgent redress.

We know that the modern political life of many Muslim nations has been enriched by the contributions of women. Miss Fatimah Jinnah, the sister of the founder of Pakistan, was one. She mounted the most severe political challenge to the military dictatorship of Ayub Khan in the 1960s. Two decades later Benazir Bhutto followed the same pattern, challenging General Zia and succeeding in becoming the first female Muslim Prime Minister, one of just a handful of women premiers in the world until that time. Begum Khalida Zia in 1991 continued the trend by becoming the first female Prime Minister of Bangladesh.

Muslims also face dilemmas in education. Away from the educated scholars, in the villages of Asia, Islamic scholarship faces serious problems (also see Chapters 4 and 5; in the latter, see 'The sermon in the mosque'). In lengthy and intimate discussions with orthodox religious scholars this was made plain to me. The outside world simply does not exist. The works of Marx or Weber are unknown. Faith and fervour are sufficient to carry all before them. This blocking-out provides Muslims with their supreme confidence but also poses the most formidable threat to them. And the threat is felt most sharply at the moment of realization that there are other, outside systems. It was first heard in the plaintive complaint of Aurangzeb, the Mughal emperor, to his tutor. The Emperor chided his tutor for filling his head with the most exaggerated notions of the Mughal Empire and dismissing the European kings as petty rajas. The same questioning is heard today among the more honest and intelligent *ulema*, the religious scholars.

These dilemmas provoke passionate responses. There is an interesting parallel in recent history which illustrates the principle prompting Muslim action against Rushdie. A century ago advancing European imperialism met Muslim resistance determined to defend the traditional way of life, from Sudan in Africa to Swat in Asia. The picture which symbolizes the clash is that of illiterate tribesmen, crying *Allah-u-Akbar*, God is most great, waving swords blessed by holy men, charging at the formations of European infantrymen, firing the latest, most deadly guns. The slaughter did little to dim Muslim commitment.

In our times the one picture which perhaps best symbolizes a similar clash between the West and Islam is that of the burning of Rushdie's book; it is the contemporary equivalent of the nineteenth-century charge. This time, Muslims, once again convinced that they were protesting against an attack on their beliefs, shouted *Allah-u-Akbar*, brandished matches endorsed by elders, and marched towards the waiting media. Once again the most advanced Western technology met Muslim faith; once again it was a massacre, this time of the Muslim image in the West. We witness again two mutually uncomprehending systems collide; monumental contempt and arrogance on one side, blind faith and fury on the other.

It is the nature of this complex historical encounter, exacerbated by each incident, which feeds into the Muslim incapacity to respond coolly and meaningfully. Muslims being killed on the West Bank or in Kashmir, their mosques being threatened with demolition in Jerusalem or in Ayodhya, India, are seen throughout the Muslim world on television and cause instant dismay and anger. The threat to the mosques has deep resonances in Muslim history. The one in Jerusalem is called after Umar, one of the greatest Muslims and rulers after the Prophet, the one in India after Babar, the founder of the Mughal dynasty. One is over a millennium in age, the other almost half a millennium. It is a milieu of distrust and violence within which Muslims see their lives enmeshed. The recent killings of Muslims by Muslims across the world – a Vice Chancellor in Kashmir, an Imam in Belgium, an aged writer in Turkey – is one response. It demonstrates the attempt to force greater commitment on the community, to push people off the fence, to obliterate the moderate and reasonable position; it also demonstrates desperation.

Muslims throughout the world cite examples of gross injustice, particularly where they live as a minority in non-Muslim countries. This group forms a large percentage of the total numbers of Muslims in the world today (see pages 141–53; for one of the most serious and academic journals on the subject, see *The Journal: Institute of Muslim Minority Affairs*, Jeddah/London). Their problems in non-Muslim countries stem as much from their powerlessness as the short-sightedness of those dealing with them. Repeated shootings and killings have led to desperation among Muslims. The state appears to have few answers besides the bullet and the baton (see Chapter 3, 'The tyranny of the nation-state'). Lord Acton would have sneered, repression tends to corrupt and absolute repression corrupts absolutely.

However, Muslims themselves are not blameless. Muslim leaders are failing in the need to feed and clothe the poor. The greatest emphasis in Islam is given to the less privileged. This, alas, remains a neglected area of attention as leaders prefer to fulminate against their opponents.

Muslim leaders are also failing in another crucial area. Those Muslims living in the West and complaining about racism would do well to turn their gaze on their own societies. Pakistanis have been killing Pakistanis, on the basis of race, in the most brutal manner possible for years in Sind province; political messages are carved into the buttocks of ethnic opponents. Kurds have been gassed and bombed in Iraq by fellow Muslims for decades. The sordid and all-but-forgotten matter of the future of almost half a million Biharis living in the most wretched camps in Dhaka remains unresolved. The Biharis, disrated to the status of alien creatures, maintain they are legitimate citizens of Pakistan. Their sin was the belief in an Islamic, united Pakistan. After 1971, in Bangladesh, they were seen as a fifth column. Islamic Pakistan is reluctant to allow residence to these Muslims – its legitimate citizens – and Islamic Bangladesh is equally reluctant to own them; so their lives remain suspended in the squalor and filth of the refugee camps. The concept of *ummah*, the Muslim brotherhood, is an excellent one; but it remains inchoate and needs to be pursued with more vigour than that presently exhibited by Muslims.

Also in need of pursuit is the notion of a just and stable state. Contemplating the 'prospects for the Twenty-first Century', a British Middle East expert concludes that the lack of 'a civil society' is the great bane of the Muslims (Mansfield 1991). Repression and stagnation – in spite of a certain record of durability in some states – mark their society. Lawyers and journalists are unable to work freely and businessmen operate in an economy which may be labelled 'socialist' or 'capitalist' but, in either case, is controlled by the state. Nevertheless, Mansfield is not entirely pessimistic, and ends with the example closest to him: 'Egypt has developed and maintained elements of a civil society and separation of powers within the state in spite of its long tradition of authoritarianism – from the Pharaohs, through Muhammad Ali and Cromer, to Nasser and Sadat' (ibid.: 348).

Muslim anguish

In recent decades Muslim cities have been captured (Jerusalem), Muslim states have been divided (Pakistan) and invaded by foreign forces (Afghanistan) and have disappeared altogether (Kuwait – in this case to reappear a few months later). Muslim struggle and sacrifice pass almost unnoticed in the world media (on the West Bank, in Kashmir and in Central Asia). But the villain in the drama is not necessarily a non-Muslim. In the case of Pakistan President Yahya was the main actor; in Kuwait it was Saddam Hussein. Here we have Muslim killing Muslim, not for any Islamic cause but for political and economic reasons.

In this period many Muslim leaders, heads of government, right across the Muslim world, have met a violent end by shooting (Sadat, Faisal, Mujib, and, starting with Daud, too many to name in Afghanistan). They have been hanged (Bhutto) or even blown up in the air (Zia). What Muslims have done to their leaders is more than matched by what the leaders did to their Muslim followers. Nightmare images are seared in the mind. State power – the army and police – has been responsible for the massacre of innocent country-folk and even entire towns in Syria, in East Pakistan (now Bangladesh), in Iraq and in Iran.

Furthermore, large proportions of the unprecedented wealth from oil revenues have been squandered on an unprecedented scale, in an unprecedented style. Call-girls in London and casinos in the south of France, ranches in the United States and chalets in Switzerland diverted money which could have gone into health-care provision, education and the closing of the vast gaps between the rich and poor. Oil money created an arrogance among some Muslims who have cherished a sense of special destiny around their family or clan. These antics provided legitimate ammunition for the Western satirists wishing to lampoon Muslims; they became the caricature of a civilization. Ordinary Muslims, therefore, have good cause to complain.

The main Muslim responses appear to be chauvinism and withdrawal; this is both dangerous and doomed. The self-imposed isolation, the deliberate retreat, is culturally determined. It is not Islamic in spirit or content. Muslims who are isolated and self-centred sense triumph in their aggressive assertion of faith. They imagine that passionate faith is exclusive to them. Yet we have pointed out a similar religious wave in Christianity, Hinduism and Buddhism. Preferring to ignore this, Muslims will point out that the Western world is intimidated by them, and fears their zeal. That Rushdie was driven underground is cited as one proof of this. It seems that Muslim spokesmen are in danger of being intoxicated by the exuberance of their own verbosity.

Because orthodox Muslims claim that Islam is an all-pervasive, all-embracing system, this affects the way in which Muslim writers and academics think. The increasing stridency in their tone is thus linked to the larger Muslim sense of anger and powerlessness. They advocate confrontation and violence, an eye for an eye, a tooth for a tooth; this attitude confirms the stereotypes of Muslims in the West. They argue that moderation has failed and that extremism will draw attention to their problems. Perhaps in the atmosphere of violence and blind hatred, of injustice and inequality, they have a certain logic in their position. At least they will be heard. They will force Muslim problems onto the agenda where more sober voices have failed and because we live in an interconnected world, no country can isolate itself from – or immunise itself against – Muslim wrath. Nevertheless, violence and cruelty are not in the spirit of the Quran, nor are they found in the life of the Prophet, nor in the lives of saintly Muslims.

Locating the essence of Islam

The Muslim voices of learning and balance – whether in politics or among academics – are being drowned by those advocating violence and hatred. Two vital questions arise with wide-ranging, short- and long-term implications: in the short term, has one of the world's greatest civilizations lost its ability to deal with problems except through violent force? In the long term, would Muslims replace the central Quranic concepts of *adl* and *ahsan*, balance and compassion, of *ilm*, knowledge, and *sabr*, patience, with the bullet and the bomb?

Balance is essential to Islam and never more so than in society; and the crucial balance is between *din* (religion), and *dunya* (world); it is a balance, not a separation, between the two. The Muslim lives in the now, in the real world, but within the frame of his religion, with a mind to the future after-life. So, whether he is a business man, an academic or a politician, he must not forget the moral laws of Islam. In the postmodern world *dunya* is upsetting the balance, invading and appropriating *din*.

Islam is essentially the religion of equilibrium and tolerance; suggesting and encouraging breadth of vision, global positions and the fulfilment of human destiny in the universe. Yet the non-Muslim media, by their consistently hammer-headed on-slaught, have succeeded in portraying a negative image of it. They may even succeed in changing Muslim character. Muslims, because of their gut response to the attack – both vehement and vitriolic – are failing to maintain the essential features of Islam.

Muslim leaders have pushed themselves into a hole dug by themselves in viewing the present upsurge simplistically as a confrontation with the West. They are in danger of rejecting features central to Islam – such as love of knowledge, egalitarianism, tolerance – because they are visibly associated with the West. In locating anti-Islamic animosity firmly in the West they also implicitly reject the universalism of human nature. But Allah is everywhere. The universal nature of humanity is the main topos in the Quran. God's purview and compassion take in everyone, 'all creatures'. The world is not divided into an East and a West: 'To Allah belong the East and the West: whithersoever Ye turn, there is Allah's countenance' (Surah 2: 115). Again and again God points to the wonders of creation, the diversity of races and languages in the world. Such a God cannot be parochial or xenophobic. Neither can a religion which acknowledges the wisdom and piety of over 124,000 'prophets' in its folklore be isolationist or intolerant. With its references to the 'heavens' above, the Quran encourages us to lift up our heads and look beyond our planet, to the stars.

The divine presence is all around; it can be glimpsed in the eyes of a mother beholding her infant, the rising of the sun, a bird in flight, the first flowers of spring. The wonders and mystery of creation cannot be the monopoly of any one people. The Sufis – like Iqbal – see God everywhere, even among the godless, not only in the mosque. In their desire for knowledge, compassion and cleanliness many non-Muslims possess ideal Muslim virtues. We note goodness and humanity in people like Mother Teresa, Mandela and Havel. Islam has always shown the capacity to emerge in unexpected places and in unexpected times. The true understanding of Islam will therefore be critical in the coming years – and not only for Muslims.

The structure of the argument

Beneath the diverse images and different pieces of the jigsaw puzzle I had promised a structure. Having outlined the frame and parameters of our discussion in this chapter, I will, in the next, go back to the beginning, back to the Greek gods and Semitic prophets. This is logical, for the Greeks and the Semites have moulded the civilizations of which we are part and which underline our common humanity and inheritance as have no other peoples. Islam will be located in the architecture of the Semitic religions, while looking for its interaction with the two other great religions, Judaism and Christianity. The influences on all three of the Greeks, who provide the matrix of European culture and thought, will then be investigated.

More than any other people the Greeks are the fountainhead, the base, of Western civilization; to revert to the Greeks is to seek purity, to establish roots. So, although the Hellenic path may appear like an unnecessary detour, I believe that we will be rewarded by the journey. For our purposes this exercise will allow us to trace how and where Islam became increasingly different from Western civilization. The intellectual tension between and the different temperaments of the two are thus the better grasped.

Chapter 3 touches upon the confrontation between Islam and

the West. Muslim scholarship in the context of postmodernism is examined in Chapter 4; after which Chapter 5 looks at the political understanding of culture and change. Finally, the nature of the Western media and their implications for Muslims are discussed. A comment on Western family life will also be made. For Muslims, history is not 'bunk'. It is alive, and its influences help explain Muslim behaviour and thought. This is also true, although in different ways, for non-Muslims. Even those who reject history and wish to live only in the present employ it in popular culture, albeit with irony and humour (as we see in the next chapter).

We will raise numerous questions, not all of which will be answered. What will become abundantly clear is that the most crucial battle of Islam, for its very spirit, has been joined in our age. I shall project an apocalyptic vision, juxtapose many divergent discourses, indicate cultural schizophrenia and ambiguity in the web of ideas that envelop us, and nonetheless give grounds for optimism, while raising more questions than can possibly be answered – and in doing all this I believe I shall suggest the spirit of postmodernism.

Chapter 2

Greek gods and Semitic prophets

At the end of the film *Blade Runner* Harrison Ford, the archetypal hero of the 1980s, asks, 'Where do I come from? Where am I going? How long have I got?' The very same questions – in almost the very same words – are asked by Stephen Hawking in *A Brief History of Time* (1988: 171). Futuristic Achilles or Cambridge professor, most of us, at one time or another, think of these questions. The ancient Greeks and the Semitic prophets help us with the answers.

In every area of life, from the names of the planets in the heavens to those of spaceships and rockets, in the designs of the latest architecture, in popular drama, in common ideas of politics and philosophy, not to mention the names of common diseases, the ancient Greeks continue to influence Western civilization. From vulgar kitsch to high philosophy their influences have never been more seductive and widespread than in contemporary culture. This is but natural in an age which revels in scepticism and wit, hedonism and eclecticism. Contemporary postmodernist writers like Foucault (1984; see especially chapter titled 'On the genealogy of ethics'), Derrida (Norris 1989; see chapter 3, 'Derrida on Plato') and Barthes (1989; see Part 1, 'On Gide and his journal') acknowledge the Greeks in their work.

However, Islam, unlike Christianity and Jewish civilizations which both absorbed and contributed to the Greeks, first accepted then rejected them from its system. Why this was so and what the consequences are for us today will be explored in this chapter. We will be able to understand better the Muslim lack of sympathy for Western postmodernism in the context of this historical rupture with the Greeks; conversely, the relative affinity of Christianity and Judaism to the Greeks helps explain their relationship to

postmodernism. The discussion will also illustrate the variation
and complexity of the diachronic relationship between these
different civilizations. It will thereby correct the simplistic vision
of those who reduce the relationship to formulas such as 'Islam
versus the West', 'Muslims versus Jews' and so on.

THE GREEKS AND THE SEMITES

The Greeks influence the dominant Western global civilization
more than we can imagine. The rhetoric, the posture, even the
crude philosophy of popular leaders like Ronald Reagan and Mrs
Thatcher are often labelled as Ramboesque. Yet Rambo violates
the primary Christian principle, 'Thou shalt not kill'. He is a direct
descendant, on the popular genealogical chart, to the original
mythological killing machine, Achilles. The link with the
primogenitor explains Rambo's phenomenal cult status; a legitimate atavistic nerve is touched. Even beneath mild-mannered
Bush – known to be a decent God-fearing, church-going Christian
– there is clearly a Rambo struggling to find expression. (Is it only
eerie coincidence that if you close your eyes when he is speaking
on TV you will hear the voice of that legendary cowboy Rambo,
John Wayne?) His sending of troops in 1990 to the Middle East,
the war that followed and his rhetoric about the crisis clearly
illustrate this. Both Achilles/Rambo and the Semitic prophets wish
to prevail; the key difference is in their method: the former use
brute force, the latter moral persuasion. Is Rambo, then, as
relevant as Christ in explaining these Christian leaders? And how
far did the Greeks infiltrate the other Semitic religions, Judaism
and Islam? How are we to understand the Greeks? To answer
these questions let us turn not to the Greek Shakespeare, Homer,
but to Shakespeare himself, the English Homer.

Shakespeare's *Troilus and Cressida* presents us with one of the
most penetrating insights into Greek society and politics. We see
champions who are treacherous (the slaying of Hector by
Achilles), lovers betraying each other (Cressida's betrayal of
Troilus), heroes objecting to generosity and nobility (Troilus to
Hector) and wives who are depicted as little more than
promiscuous sluts (Helen of Troy). But Shakespeare is never
simple. The gloom of this picture is balanced by people like
Ulysses, always wise, and Hector, always chivalric. However, apart
from these few sympathetic characters it is a world of cynicism and

disillusionment, of doom and despair, of lust and violence.

Shakespeare is, as usual, pointing out something for us we suspected all along but could not quite put our finger on. He is nearest the mark in depicting this side of the Greeks. Despite their positive contributions to civilization as we know it, theirs was an insecure society, marked by lust, violence, cynicism and anger, and their own writers reflected it with a high degree of accuracy. It is this aspect of the Greeks which strikes such a powerful chord in our day, Greek plays being widely produced even in non-Western societies like that of Japan.

While Achilles is the apotheosis of the warrior in a civilization intoxicated with war, Homer is its poet. The ferocious joy of battle is best captured by Homer. To attain immortality – to have people sing about you – heroic deeds had to be performed on the battle ground. Men thus fought for honour and to make a name. No ideological or moral argument was necessary. The Trojan war, we know, began with Paris eloping with a married woman. The Islamic approach to war is different.

A well-known story from the life of Ali, the great warrior and caliph of Islam, illustrates the Islamic position on war. As the champion of a Muslim army, Ali had to engage in hand-to-hand combat with the champion of the opposing non-Muslim army. Dropping his opponent to the ground, he leapt onto his chest and raised his sword to strike. At this point both armies were surprised to see Ali stand up and walk away; it seemed he had thrown away victory. 'Why', he was asked, 'did you do this?' 'Because', he replied, 'the man spat on me and I lost my temper. I would then have killed him because of my anger, not for the just cause of Islam.'

Although the Greeks did not invent murder and sex, they brought an unrivalled zest to them – a zest which would be imitated faithfully by the Romans who saw themselves as inheritors of the Greek legacy. Famous family moments in Greek tragedy include Oedipus killing his father so as to marry his mother; Electra killing her mother and Agamemnon, his daughter; and Atreus serving Thyestes' sons to him as a dish to avenge the seduction of his wife (here we see the prototype of Hannibal Lecter whom we will discuss in Chapter 6). Sex was riotous at all times. The zoomorphic nature of Greek divinity encouraged, not inhibited, coupling between gods and animals. Olympian gods coupled freely with mortals; the priapic top-god

Zeus was never one to miss an opportunity – even during his metamorphosis into a swan – of pushing his penis into any orifice; there was intercrural homosexuality; and the sexually explicit poses on vases and in the figures should not be forgotten. (Postcards of the satyrs with their enormous penises are the most popular items of demand by foreign tourists, much to the amusement of the present-day Greeks.)

In the gymnasium, where naked athletes worked out, the cult of male fitness was established. Physical and moral beauty were equated. The notion of homosexuality was thus made respectable (the island of Lesbos and Sappho also being part of Greek legend). Plato's *Symposium* is seen as supporting it.

The Greeks voted, in 416 BC, and after full democratic debate, to massacre the men and enslave the women of the island of Melos because it had remained neutral in one of their wars. Euripides' play *Trojan Women* (first performed in 415 BC) dramatizes the fates of Cassandra, Andromache and above all of Hecuba, when they are about to be shipped off to slavery. It is a grim two hours, an indictment of male violence and of the cult of victory.

Thucydides, one of the towering historians of all time, has written such a devastatingly frank analysis of the nature of war that he appears to glorify it. Some of his lines, like the following, are a forerunner of Orwell's 'Newspeak', of contemporary 'Nuke-speak' and cultural heroes like Rambo: 'moderation is the disguise of weakness; to know everything is to do nothing. Frantic energy is the true quality of a man; the lover of violence is always trusted and his opponent suspected' (Taplin 1989: 247).

Aristotle's 'women have no souls', indicated that they were marginal and ostracized in society (see Garland 1991 and Massey 1988); Socrates, the second most famous martyr after Jesus, dismissed his wife from the famous last group discussion before his death; the most celebrated Greek building, the Parthenon, on top of the Acropolis, was strictly a male preserve.

Anthropomorphic gods and divine mortals, it was difficult to differentiate the two. Gods and men reflected each other. Indeed, the malice and wrath of the gods visited upon mortals driven by human passions is a common theme in Greek literature. Consider the most renowned work of Greek literature, the *Iliad* by Homer. It is a paean to the glory of war and victory. Again and again, its characters find echoes in our world. Oliver Taplin refers to Achilles on more than one occasion as a Rambo, a killing machine, in his television series *Greek Fire* and the accompanying book (1989; also see Grant 1989, chapter 1, 'The wrath of Achilles').

The ideas of Plato, one of the key figures in Greek thought, continue to influence Western civilization. His notions of a natural hierarchy in society, of an ideal state ruled by a group of 'guardians' not unlike the upper-caste Brahmans of India in their unassailable high status, or the English ruling class; the assertion not only of male superiority but also of female inferiority, and his contempt for literati are still recognizable in certain phases of modern Western history. The young hero of Forster's *Maurice* reads Plato as a 'guide to life'. An attack on Plato is thus an attack on the basis of Western culture and philosophy.

However, Toynbee, Russell and Popper did attack Plato for suggesting the foundations of modern fascism. The German Führer wished to base his Third Reich on the Spartan model. The censoring of theatre, the down-grading of less privileged groups like the helots and the idea of mass gymnastics all came from Plato. During the rule of Hitler, architecture and other cultural models were derived from the Greeks. Albert Speer, in his architecture, consciously imitated the Greeks. The notions of purity of race, which led to that of the master race and the persecution of the Semites and blacks as 'impure', were inspired by the Greeks. Hitler's Olympics were more than the games; they represented a return to the fountainhead of civilization, an affirmation of original ideas, an understanding of history, a philosophic statement.

Greek influences also worked on the major artistic figures, from Goethe to Wagner. This may help to explain why Moses Finley's *The World of Odysseus* (1962) regarded Homer as an inhuman and pre-moral poet, and why the historian Arnaldo Momigliano described the *Iliad* as top of the list of the world's most dangerous books. Both were Jews with good reason to be wary of Germany's formative influences. Jews, as well as mentally and physically sick 'incurables', homosexuals, gypsies and members of the Slavonic races and all others regarded as dangerous to the health of the body politic, like trade-union leaders, intellectuals and churchmen, were objects of hate. Even the Scouts and Guides were banned.

Yet in a paradoxical and frightening twist, Plato has become the symbol of freedom and liberalism in America. There is, though, a growing awareness of the negative aspects of his

thought among younger radicals on campus who see him as a key
DWM, a Dead White Male, one 'who created Western civilization
from a phallocentric, gynophobic, racist and fascist viewpoint' (see
'Mind your language' in the *Weekend Guardian*, by Mike Bygrave,
11–12 May 1991).

But let us not be completely swept away by this persuasive
Shakespearean view of ancient Greek history. The humanity and
nobility of much of Greek thought are undisputed. In the ideal,
truth and beauty are inseparable; integrity is central to 'looking
good'. This is the lesson Keats learns from the Greeks:

> Beauty is truth, truth beauty, – that is all
> Ye know on earth, and all ye need to know.
> (John Keats, in Gardner 1972: 608)

The Greek legacy, which includes the theatre and debate,
sculpture and sport, continues to provide valued gifts for our
times. We will discuss them further at the end of this chapter (also
see Bernal 1987, Elias and Dunning 1986, and Taplin 1989).

Above all, the Greeks were concerned with ideas; with
establishing relationships between reality and illusion, form and
substance, fact and fiction. The heart of Plato's philosophy was
thus the realm of becoming; it was a world of shadows, always
all-changing, and because of its transient nature we could never
fully acquire knowledge and truth. Those who exploit half-truths
and shadows are the demagogues, the politicians. Plato loathed
them. He would have pointed out many examples of the
manipulation of the modern media from the lives of Ronald
Reagan and Mrs Thatcher. For him, far better was the
philosopher-king (Hitler's Germany was thus dense with Platonic
philosophy). Plato's preference was reinforced by his revulsion
against society for the manner in which his mentor Socrates had
been forced to commit suicide. Shadows, doubt, illusion, change,
transience, always questioning, always becoming, never com-
pleting: the foundations of Western postmodernism can be
legitimately traced to the Greeks.

Semitic societies

The Semites broke with the Greeks sharply in more ways than
one. Firstly, their fundamental concept of God was different. It
unequivocally distinguished between mortal man living on earth

and an immortal God up there in the heavens, all-knowing, all-seeing and all-powerful. The God on high spoke through chosen prophets and the divine words were embodied in holy books: the Jewish and Christian scriptures and the Quran.

The following story illustrates the central importance of the divinely inspired written word for the Semites:

> There is an old Jewish story about a gathering of rabbis who were debating a point of Holy Law. At the end of the meeting just one man stood out against the majority. But this rabbi knew that God was on his side and in exasperation called upon his divine ally to show his hand. 'If I am right,' said the rabbi, 'may the streams of Israel flow uphill.' And they did. But the majority was not impressed. 'If I am right,' said the rabbi again, 'may the trees bend to the ground.' And they did. Still the meeting was not impressed. 'If I am right,' he cried in frustration, 'may the voice of God sound in assent.' And a voice came from heaven in the rabbi's defence. But still the assembly was unmoved. 'We pay no attention to heavenly voices,' they said, 'because the correct determination of this point has long since been written down.' Moses in Sinai had revealed the sacred truth to their ancestors, and no voice in the universe could alter that. On the question of the sacred written word, even God might be in error.
>
> (Romer 1988: 107)

Secondly, total obedience was demanded by God and was expected to be given by the believers. Indeed, 'Islam' means submission or surrender to the will of God. Life, property and children were surrendered to God. Even death was not to be challenged. A Muslim accepts death as part of the divine pattern, as an inevitable conclusion to life on earth; there will be sorrow at the loss of a loved one, concern at imminent death, but rarely the primal scream to resist what, after all, is the 'appointed hour'; little of the passion of Dylan Thomas:

> Do not go gentle into that good night,
> Old age should burn and rave at close of day;
> Rage, rage against the dying of the light.
> (Dylan Thomas, in Gardner 1972: 942)

A pact, or covenant, was understood to be formed between God and the followers: obedience to divine rules in exchange for divine favours. No sacrifice was spared. Abraham agreed to sacrifice his son, like a man would a goat, as a gesture of total obedience. Thus the faithful were either the Chosen Ones, like the Jews, or the 'People of God', like the Christians, or the *ummah*, the Muslim community of believers. In each case, the orthodox drew lines around themselves to exclude the others.

Thirdly, a moral basis for society was introduced by the special messengers. Thus from Moses, who brought the Ten Commandments, to Jesus, whose divinity was theophanic and epiphanic for many of his followers, and Muhammad, who was *insan-i-kamil*, the perfect person, the Semitic prophets represented and propagated a moral order. Compassion, goodness and piety became important virtues in an understanding of Semitic soteriology. And this is at the centre of their crisis today: how to preserve timeless moral precepts in a rapidly changing world?

The patriarch hectored and advised but also provided patronage to his lineage, and even other tribes designated as belonging within the pale. The family and the community were emphasized. People were motivated to perform good deeds by the promise of rewards and punishments in the hereafter. Dos and don'ts in society were established. From high philosophy to the cut of the beard, a specific way of life was determined. In time, a rigidity far greater than perhaps intended by the prophets was established. Boundaries were thus laid down, defining the limits upon social behaviour, by the Semitic prophets.

Whatever their differences – and there are ancient splits which continue to colour politics in the Middle East, sometimes in the most violent forms – the three religions share many basic notions. The most important is that of God and the moral basis of life on earth. Furthermore, they also share the prophets who were lineally related through their eponymous common ancestors, Adam and Eve. (The 1990 Reith Lectures, titled 'The Persistence of Faith: Religion and Ethics in a Secular Society', given by Dr Jonathan Sacks, Chief Rabbi elect of the United Hebrew Congregations of the Commonwealth, could have been written by a Christian or a Muslim with their concern with virtue, faith and morality.)

Also shared are many of the holy places and holy myths. Jerusalem, for instance, is a holy city to all three religions – and hence the bitter dispute to possess it (there are numerous books on Jerusalem; Elon 1991 is just one of the most recent illustrating our theme; even Mark Twain wrote about his visit in *The Innocents*

Abroad and is temporarily solemn here). It is where Abraham prepared to sacrifice his son Isaac, where Solomon built his temple, where Jesus trod and from where the Prophet rose to heaven. Jerusalem thus became a symbol of a holy city. The metaphysical visionary William Blake wished to reconstruct England in its image:

> I will not cease from Mental Fight,
> Nor shall my Sword sleep in my hand,
> Till we have built Jerusalem
> In England's green and pleasant land.
> (William Blake, in Gardner 1972: 486)

There are other shared things. The succulent carp of Urfa in northern Mesopotamia is one. It has been a blessed fish – known as Abraham's carp – to all three religions for over a thousand years. It is never to be eaten, although there is no ban on fish in any of these religions. John Romer showed us many of these shared wonders in his television series and related book *Testament: The Bible and History* (1988).

However, an important difference between the three religions bears on political life. It is in their attitude to the state. For Islam religion and politics are fused. The Prophet – like the early caliphs who emulated him – led the prayers and the armies, ordered the collection of taxes, laid down the law and dispensed justice. In contrast, over the centuries, Christian church and state have become separate. Judaism falls somewhere between Islam and Christianity. Classical, rabbinical Judaism emerged only after the Judaic state had ceased to exist. For all three religions, however, the relationship between the church and the state has ranged between open hostility and an uneasy *modus vivendi* through the ages. The relationship remains volatile for Jews in Israel and Muslims in many countries.

Islam, unlike Judaism and Christianity, has no priesthood (for political complications arising out of religious functionaries assuming power, see Ahmed 1991a; for Iran, which is a special case, see Ahmed 1988). The mullah, found in some parts of the Muslim world, is not the equivalent of a rabbi or parish priest. He is a religious functionary specifically charged with tending the mosque and supervising rites of passage and no more. The Prophet had warned, 'There is no monkery in Islam.' This is a social fact of the utmost importance. Far-reaching consequences are observed. Islam allows a freedom of spirit and underlines the egalitarianism so pronounced in social life. The present attempt by some Muslim leaders to sound like high priests and organize a kind of theological police is against the spirit of Islam.

Other differences arise from cultural perceptions of one another. Jewish exclusiveness appears irritatingly tribal to Christians. The Christian anthropomorphic notion of the Trinity and the symbol of a dying, bleeding and tortured central figure on a cross baffles Muslims. It appears to underline a preoccupation with death and suffering. Islamic claims of being the final revelation of religion and social customs, such as the permission to marry up to four wives, are scorned by the others (though polygamy is reported in the Old Testament). Christians, imposing a Eurocentric historical frame on Islam, often enquire why it has not had a Reformation, an Enlightenment, a Renaissance – and when will it have them?

More bitter conflict centres on doctrinal matters: the Christians blame the Jews for Jesus' death – the eponymous Judas, in popular Christian culture, becomes the synonym for a treacherous friend, a betrayer; the mnemonic association, Judas and Jew, underscores the point. Christians also make scathing attacks on the Prophet and the Quran. Muslims, in turn, believe they possess the final revelation, question the very concept of the Trinity in Christianity and swear of the Oneness of God. Meanwhile, the Jews dismiss the other two religions as upstarts, declaring themselves the Chosen Ones, the exclusive favourites of God. This is what anthropologists call agnatic rivalry, the intense love–hate relationship between a father's brothers' sons.

Muslims self-consciously point out that they are chronologically the last in line of the revealed monotheistic religions. Offshoots like the Ahmadi in South Asia and Baha'i in Iran are considered heresies. In the fully developed nature of the Prophet, humanity is acknowledged to have reached the final development in human evolution as the Vicegerent of God on earth. Humanity has come of age. Henceforth, as far as Muslims are concerned, there will be no more prophets (though saintly figures, Imams and mahdis, are not precluded). The emphasis on the lack of a priesthood, and the rejection of merit based on wealth or lineage, underlines the egalitarian nature of Islam. Indeed, the earliest *muezzin* of Islam is the legendary Bilal, a black slave. Bilal's stature in Islamic history and mythology emphasizes the point for us.

The great historical clash between Christian Europe and Muslims for the holy lands, known as the crusades, is discussed in the next chapter as part of the larger encounter between the two. The long-lasting fear of the enemy created the myths and prejudices which colour the perception of each other into our times. However, officially, formally, perhaps the church has never been closer to Islam than in the present age. Here is the position of no less an authority than the Vatican:

> The Church also regards with esteem the Muslims who worship the one, subsistent, merciful and almighty God, the Creator of heaven and earth, who has spoken to man. Islam willingly traces its descent back to Abraham, and just as he submitted himself to God, the Muslims endeavour to submit themselves to his mysterious decrees. They venerate Jesus as a prophet, without, however recognizing him as God, and they pay honour to his virgin mother Mary and sometimes also invoke her with devotion. Further, they expect a day of judgement when God will raise all men from the dead and reward them. For this reason they attach importance to the moral life and worship God, mainly by prayer, alms-giving and fasting.
>
> (Watt 1991: 148–9)

There is clearly a desire to open a new chapter in Christian–Muslim relations:

> If in the course of the centuries there has arisen not infrequent dissension and hostility between Christian and Muslim, this sacred Council now urges everyone to forget the past, to make sincere efforts at mutual understanding and to work together in protecting and promoting for the benefit of all men, social justice, good morals as well as peace and freedom.
>
> (ibid.)

The above is from the section on Islam in the Declaration on the Relation of the Church to non-Christian Religions issued by the Second Vatican Council in 1965. Unfortunately this balanced and fair position is buried under the avalanche of Western negative media images. It is therefore lost on Muslims, who still associate the church with Western imperialism.

In spite of the general cultural antipathy, for most serious Muslim scholars the larger continuities and unity between the three religions outweigh the differences. The Islamic spiritual and social legacy derives from and acknowledges the Judaic–Christian traditions. The main figures are the same: Abraham, Moses, Jesus. The eponymous ancestor is Adam. Rituals, dietary laws and the vision of life and the hereafter are reflected in the earlier religious traditions. The notion of an all-powerful, all-knowing, eternal God is similar. In particular, several Islamic and Jewish traditions are alike: the prohibition of pork, the circumcision of boys, the prohibition of pictorial representations of God, the patriarchal family, the headgear for prayers, the religious rites for slaughter of animals and even the greeting, Jewish *shalom* or Muslim *salam*, which expresses the yearning for peace. Most important, the holy books of the earlier religions entitle their adherents to be placed in the category of *ahl-e-kitab*, those of the acknowledged Book. The Quran speaks favourably of the people of the Book. For example, Surah 3, verse 199, carries a universal message of goodwill and hope to all those who believe, the people of the Book irrespective of their religious label – Christian, Jew or Muslim.

Muslims can marry with the people of the Book, as the following account of the marriage of the Prophet to the Jew Safiyah informs us:

> Muhammad's tenth wife was Safiyah, who was taken as a prisoner of war in the Battle of Khyber. Her father and mother were Jews belonging to the two leading Jewish families. The father traced his ancestry to the Prophet Aaron, while the mother was a descendant of the famous Jewish tribe of Quraisa. Safiyah, whose original name was Zainab, was married to a well-known Jewish poet Salm bin Mishkam. But they could not get on, so the husband divorced her. Safiyah married again, this time to a Jewish warrior of great repute. She lost him, too, when he was killed in the Battle of Khyber, along with Safiyah's father and the other male members of her family. Safiyah was taken as a prisoner of war and became the maid of one of the Companions. Other Companions objected to this on the grounds that she was the daughter of one of the tribal chiefs and, therefore, she could only be assigned to the Prophet. Zainab also expressed her desire to become a Muslim and marry the chief of the Muslims. That alone, she said would help restore her dignity and status among her people. The Prophet then mounted her on his camel, covered her with his robe and accepted her as his wife. It was then that he gave her the name Safiyah.

(Zakaria 1991: 51–2)

Safiyah's interaction with other Muslims around the Prophet also illustrates normative attitudes in society:

> On her arrival in the Prophet's house in Medina, Muhammad asked Aisha if she liked her.
>
> 'But she is Jewish!' Aisha replied.
>
> The Prophet reprimanded her: 'So what? She is as good a Muslim as anyone else.'
>
> Once, Umar, during the Prophet's lifetime asked Safiyah whether she still maintained her Jewish links.
>
> 'I observe Friday and not Saturday', Safiyah told him bluntly, 'but I continue to have affection for my Jewish kith and kin. Islam does not prohibit that.' Umar was speechless. According to one account, she was very close to Fatimah, the Prophet's daughter and the wife of Ali, the fourth caliph. She bore the Prophet no children and died at the age of sixty. According to another account she had supported Ali's rival, Uthman, the third caliph, in their political wrangling. Safiyah had a mind of her own and maintained her dignity to the last.
>
> (ibid.: 52)

An account of Safiyah's marriage is an appropriate place to open a discussion of her religion, Judaism.

STAR

The historical significance of Judaism was that it was the first great monotheistic religion to base its belief and practice on sacred texts. John Romer relates history and theology in this passage:

> Why, of all the cultures living around the edges of the ancient Mediterranean, did the Jews alone produce such a set of sacred books? Obviously, there was a need to record the laws governing the covenant with Jehovah so that the people could adhere to the sacred contract from generation to generation. But there were also more immediate, more dramatic reasons: two disasters, two dislocations of national life, some five hundred years apart; first, the Exile to Babylon that followed the sacking of Jerusalem in 587 BC, and the second, the complete destruction of Jerusalem following the Roman wars of AD 70–135. Both these events threatened the annihilation of Israel. Through all of this, the sacred writings became the heart

of national identity, the ancient written law its shield. Sacred writings that were almost a swan song became the means of Israel's survival. The vice-like pressure of these two national disasters forced into being the Hebrew Bible, which is also the Christian Old Testament.

(Romer 1988: 107)

Nonetheless Judaism was influenced by the Greeks after the conquest of Palestine by Alexander. This influence lasted and was quickened even after the advent of Islam. In particular the *kalam*, philosophical or rational theology, and the school or sect of the Mutazila encouraged Greek thinking. Jewish Neoplatonism gave way to Aristotelianism, following the lead of al-Farabi, Avicenna and Averroes (for Greek influences on Jews and Muslims, and the resultant effervescence of a mutually rich culture, see Isaacs 1990). In particular, Averroes was a key figure, widely translated and read. Samuel ibn Tibbon, whose rendering into Hebrew of the famous *Guide for the Perplexed* (*Dalalat al-Hairin*; in Hebrew *Moreh Nebukhim*) by the Spaniard Moses Maimonides (1135–1204) had been approved by the author, translated Averroes. (Maimonides fascinates Muslims; see Calamus Foundation Lecture, London, 21 January 1991, of Prince Hassan of Jordan: 'Pluralism in Muslim culture: the example of Maimonides'.)

Though Maimonides, a many-sided scholar, was a contemporary of Averroes, he was unacquainted with his works when he wrote the *Guide*, the most important work of medieval Jewish philosophy. Subsequent philosophers would agree with his three essential dogmas: God's existence, revelation and retribution. In turn, the *Guide* influenced Christian scholasticism through Latin translations. The outstanding Jewish Averroist of the period is Gersonides (1288–*c*.1344). Like his mentor he was a man of many parts, philosopher, astronomer, mathematician and commentator on the Bible. Like his model he was reviled by the orthodox. His work was attacked by Crescas (1340–1410), whose critique resembles Ghazzali's refutation of Aristotelianism. Crescas also launched a devastating criticism of Maimonides. In Crescas medieval Jewish philosophy reaches its climax.

Between Jewish and Muslim culture a remarkable harmony and symbiosis are recorded. It is a fact which those locked in the terrible confrontation in the Middle East today would do well to recall. On the whole, Jewish culture and thought thrived under the

Muslims: 'The caliphs, once their original missionary zeal abated, showed themselves willing to accord an almost boundless toleration in return for a slender poll tax', notes the *Encyclopaedia Britannica* (1963, vol. 13: 55).

Thus the dignity of the exilarch, which existed from remote antiquity, was maintained with renewed magnificence. Intellectual leadership resided in the *gaon*, head of the academy, who developed the principles of the Talmud. The *gaon* Saadiah (882–942) exemplified the fruitful combination of Helleno-Arabic and Jewish culture. In particular the synthesis of cultures was to flourish in Muslim Spain: 'In Spain there came about a remarkable revival. The Jews knew no restriction upon their activities. . . . It was the Arab invasion that brought salvation' (ibid.).

The dark stain of European anti-Semitism

Symbiosis with Muslims in Spain is contrasted by Christian persecution of Jews in the rest of Europe. The antagonism relates to the birth of Christianity and is reflected in the Gospels. Christians widely believed that Jews were Christ-killers, that they had betrayed Christ and so must be punished. The myth of the Wandering Jew further added to distrust. It was common belief that they slaughtered Christians ritually during the Jewish Passover. The Christian crusades against the Muslims often commenced in Europe with a slaughter of the nearest Jews. Shylock's cry, 'Hath not a Jew eyes? Hath not a Jew hands, organs, dimensions, senses, affections, passions?', would echo through the centuries.

The theme of anti-Semitism is contained in the title, *Why did the Heavens not Darken? The 'Final Solution' in History*, of Arno J. Mayer's book (1990). There is a wealth of literature on the subject but I will point to a few recent books only – Dafni and Kleiman 1991; Dwork 1991; Edwards 1991; Hass 1991; Langmuir 1991; Read and Fisher 1989; Wistrich 1991; also see the 1991 ITV three-part documentary, *The Longest Hatred*. Mayer's title refers back to 1096, when a crusading army entered Mainz under the fanatically Christian Count Emicho, 'the oppressor of all Jews'. In his contemporary chronicle of this first church-sanctioned mass homicide of European Jews, Solomon bar Simson bitterly asks: 'Why did the heavens not darken and the stars not withhold their radiance, why did not the sun and moon turn dark?'

A century after the Mainz massacre, the English herded Jews

into York in 1190 and burnt them alive. This triggered similar incidents elsewhere in England and Europe (graphically shown in the BBC2 TV documentary *All the King's Jews*). In the thirteenth century, Edward I, an ardent crusader, reduced the Jewish community to outcasts, forcing them to wear yellow badges. He further weakened them by abolishing usury. His lead united royalty and peasantry, feudal lords and town merchants. By the end of the century Jews were declared a criminal community and expelled from England; they would not return in significant numbers for another four centuries.

The European medieval illustrations and woodcuts with the *Judensau* motif drive home the point of anti-Semitism with crude brutality:

> These sixteenth-century engravings are all based on the Wittenberg *Judensau*, a sculpture in Martin Luther's church at Wittenberg which Luther himself made famous. In his *Von den Juden*, Luther condemned all Jews as greedy and maggoty: 'You are unworthy to look at the outside of the Bible, let alone read inside it. You should read only the Bible which is under the sow's tail and gobble and guzzle the epistles which fall from there.' Subsequently Luther identified the sow with the Talmud.
>
> (Webster 1990: 76)

At the end of the fifteenth century in Spain, Jews, along with Muslims, were expelled from their homes, lock, stock and barrel. The movement against the Jews may be seen as a *Glaubenskrieg*. It would be repeated down to our times, finding its fullest expression in Hitler's Germany. The yellow star of David in Nazi Germany, reminiscent of earlier badges, would become the symbol of a cruelly persecuted people. Anti-Semitic propaganda films, like *Jud Süss*, were expensively produced with top actors and directors ('highly recommended', was Goebbels' response). But the groundwork for the German gas chambers, as we note, was prepared over the centuries.

Searching for answers, some Jews linked their misfortunes to loss of faith: 'Somehow I knew that Bolshevism, Hitlerism and all the misfortunes of humanity stem from this contempt for the Ten Commandments' (Singer 1986: 17). The brutality against them, therefore, ensured a renewed tenacity of faith, the need to cling to tradition:

It's no accident that Hitler and his theoreticians waged such a savage war against the *Talmud Jude*. These villains rightfully sensed that the Talmud and the Talmud Jew were their greatest enemy. A Jew without God can easily be persuaded that Lenin, Trotsky or Stalin will bring deliverance. Jews without God can believe that Karl Marx was the Messiah.

(ibid.: 37)

Norman Cohn spent a lifetime exploring one of the most enduring of the irrational impulses which lie behind European history – 'the urge to purify the world through the annihilation of some category of human beings imagined as agents of corruption and incarnations of evil' (Webster 1990: 15). Great fires like that of seventeenth-century London, for which a French apprentice baker was hastily hanged, are not necessarily started by anybody deliberately. They happen, but some sinister group of people has to be found to take the blame. Nero chose the Christians and they were put to death with original cruelty. Many were lighted up, when the day declined, to serve as torches during the night. Christian civilization, in turn, meted out similar cruelty to the Jews.

Anti-Semitism is far from dead in Europe today; indeed, there is ample evidence to indicate its vigorous existence in this random 'catalogue of hate' compiled by *The Guardian* for 1989–1990:

In a survey, 75 per cent of West Germans said there were too many foreigners in their country. Belgian police looked on passively as a group of skin-heads daubed swastikas on North African youths. Three Frenchmen murdered a North African 'just for kicks'. Near Avignon, France, 34 gravestones in a Jewish cemetery were desecrated. 70,000 racist attacks were recorded in Greater London.

(Njor 1990)

It is only in this century, in the United States, that Jewish culture has flourished to the highest level possible in a Christian country, in particular contributing to academic life and the arts. Indeed Judaism is widely recognized as a key factor contributing to modern Western life. As a leading Jewish intellectual provocatively pointed out: 'Judaism and homosexuality (most intensely where they overlap, as in a Proust or a Wittgenstein) can be seen to have been the two main generators of the entire fabric and savour of urban modernity in the West' (Steiner 1984: 194).

But we turn to a more conventional voice to sum up the modern plight of those who inherit the Semitic tradition; it speaks with equal authenticity for traditional Christians and Muslims:

> This Talmud Jew doesn't deal violently with any race, class or group. All he wants is to earn a living and raise his children and children's children to follow in the ways of the Torah and the Shulhan Arukh. He wants to raise chaste daughters instead of whores. He doesn't need modern literature, theatre, nude art. He doesn't change his outlook every Monday and Thursday.
>
> (Singer 1986: 38)

Jews and Arabs

This is what the ordinary traditional Jew wants. Indeed, this is what he hoped to find in Israel. The holy land – *Eretz Yisrael*, Hebrew for 'the land of Israel' – for the Jews has been a collective dream, a subconscious yearning, one carefully, lovingly nurtured for millennia. It has been an ideal, a Utopia, a land which promised milk and honey. It resonated in folk culture and literature. 'My heart is in the East, and I am in the uttermost West', sighed the eleventh century Jewish-Spanish poet Yehuda Halevi.

But there was the reality of dealing with another ancient people, the Palestinians, already living there. Their expulsion from their homes and their subsequent humiliation and further deprivation are at the core of the present tragedy between Jews and Arabs. Before we return to the discussion of Greek influences on the Semites we will look at the conflict between Jews and Arabs. It is of Homeric proportion, a veritable Greek drama.

Red and crimson sunsets on the peaceful beach, tanned healthy people relaxing in scanty swimsuits on the sand, bustling shopping centres, crowded discothèques, thriving farms – and always the fresh-faced, clean-limbed young soldiers patrolling discreetly to protect the citizen from terrorism – this is the Israel of the tourist brochure; this is its ideal self-perception (for pictures in this vein see the coffee-table book *The Israelis*, Elon 1985). But where are the Palestinians, the barbed wire, the weeping women, the dazed elders, the children with their stones, the filth of the streets after endless curfew? The Palestinians are invisible (as in Elon's book); they have been willed out of sight by the Israelis.

The last line of Grossman's novel, *See Under: Love*, would strike both Arab and non-Arab in the Middle East as ironic: 'We asked so little: for a man to live in this world from birth to death and know nothing of war' (1991a: 452). The Middle East has known nothing but strife and terror since the creation of Israel.

The cold-blooded killings of twenty-one Arabs in 1990 in Jerusalem which caused an international outrage had its origins outside that city. Auschwitz and Deir Yassin, the Six Day war and Black September, the Munich massacre, and the Ramadan war, Sabra and Shatilla are all links in the chain leading to the Jerusalem killings: signposts along the road of man's inhumanity to man. Europeans and Zionists, Nazis and Jews, Israelis and Arabs are all locked in the intense gridiron embrace of history – Hitler and Anne Frank, Golda Meir and Arafat, Rabbi Kahane and Edward Said, Bush and Saddam.

Julian Barnes, who gave us *A History of the World in 10^1/$_2$ Chapters*, describes the modern history of Israel, characteristically with a gun pointed at the speaker, in one whole paragraph:

> The Balfour Declaration. Jewish immigration from Europe. The Second World War. European guilt over the Holocaust being paid for by the Arabs. The Jews having learned from their persecution by the Nazis that the only way to survive was to be like Nazis. Their militarism, expansion, racism. Their pre-emptive attack on the Egyptian air force at the start of the Six Day War being the exact moral equivalent of Pearl Harbour.... The refugee camps. The theft of land. The artificial support of the Israeli economy by the dollar. The atrocities committed against the dispossessed. The Jewish lobby in America. The Arabs only asking from the Western Powers for the same justice in the Middle East as had already been accorded to the Jews. The regrettable necessity of violence, a lesson taught the Arabs by the Jews, just as it had been taught the Jews by the Nazis.

> (Barnes 1990: 55–6)

The crisis for Judaism, which quickened at the moment of its greatest political triumph, the establishment of Israel, has reached breaking point. Israel is not the vision of the Old Testament prophet Micah: 'They shall beat their swords into plowshares, and their spears into pruninghooks; nation shall not lift up a sword against nation, neither shall they learn war any more. But they shall sit every man under his vine and under his figtree; and none shall make them afraid' (Micah 4: 3–4).

The horrific memories of Nazi Germany and the centuries of persecution in Europe, conditioned the Israeli perception of and response to the world. 'Never again'; the determination of Jews to avoid what happened to them in Germany became national philosophy and foreign policy while the bitterness and hatred transferred in all sorts of complex ways to the Palestinians. 'We are Israel's Jews!', say the Palestinians, echoing Jewish history in Europe (Ascherson 1991).

It is this which perhaps best helps explain the extraordinarily harsh treatment of the Palestinian *intifada*; it is a *Glaubenskrieg*, with the Jews in a reversed role. As many writers point out, the miscegenation laws demanded by groups like Kach, their yellow shirts emblazoned with a black clenched fist, their public abuse of Arabs as 'dogs' and the demand for their total expulsion reflect their own persecution in Europe (see, for instance, Ian Black in *The Guardian*, summer, 1990).

The Palestinians have been pushed down to the lowest possible economic and social position in their own land. A Palestinian writer contemplates the wreck of his people's lives: 'As for those who are living under the Israeli occupation, they have had no chance of any economic development while their land and water were taken away. They have been permitted to serve the Israeli economy as virtual slave labour' (Shiblak 1991: 131–2; for another sensitive Palestinian writer on the plight of his people, see Aburiche 1991).

There is little but despair to contemplate:

How can one also describe the behaviour of the Americans' client in the Middle East – Israel's harsh occupation, its savage treatment and daily killings of the Palestinians, its refusal to honour the Security Council resolutions on the Palestinian question, or Israeli co-operation with the apartheid regime in South Africa and its arms supplies to the most ruthless dictatorships in Latin America?

(Shiblak 1991: 126)

Here the arguments always lead to Washington: 'The Palestinians, in the end, are the victims of the Americans' unequivocal support to Israel and the US/Israeli responsibility for the numerous foiled peace efforts' (ibid.: 126–7).

Tony Stark's television series, *Terror*, for Channel 4, provokes thought and sorrow as it traces the bitterness of the Arab–Israeli conflict first to the Holocaust, then to the activities of the terrorist Stern Gang and Irgun Zevai Leumi at the end of British rule in Palestine (also see book of the same title written by Conor Geary, 1990; other corroborative and equally powerful statements in 1990–91 came from *Malika's Hotel* set in Gaza, *40 Minutes*, BBC2; *The Promised Land, Assignment*, BBC2; *Under the Sun: Do They Feel my Shadow?* BBC2 and *Time Watch: Palestine – The First Intifada*, BBC2. The media interest may well have been partly responsible for the current spate of books on the subject: see, for instance, the 1991 catalogue of I.B. Tauris, London).

Somewhere, in the documentaries there is a scene of stunning brutality, taken from a distance and shown in slow motion, that stays in the mind. Heavily armed Israeli soldiers surround an unarmed Palestinian boy, a look of numb terror contorting his face, and pin him down to the ground. Then, methodically, with calculated force, they pound the boy's limbs, smashing them to pulp. It is a scene not calculated to inspire morale in professional Israeli soldiers, nor to quell the rebelliousness and hatred among Palestinians.

Suspension of civil rights, midnight knocks on the door, sadistic guards, terrified civilians, young prisoners urinating and crying with fear, torture rooms, cruel medics, prison towers, racial hatred and contempt for the prisoners and state policy which draws lines around an entire ethnic minority forcing them into one vast, prison-like existence. Are we talking of Nazis and Jews? No, these are Jews and Palestinians in Israel today. This is the picture as depicted by an Israeli prison guard profoundly disturbed by what he sees:

> For this is what the Palestinians have brought upon us by means of the *intifada*: they have deprived us, in the most unambiguous way, of the possibility of an 'enlightened occupation'. . . . It is not, at this hour, a matter of territories in exchange for peace. It is a matter of territories in exchange for our humanity.
>
> (Shavit 1991)

It is a doubly disturbing piece both for what it tells us of the condition of the Arabs and because, to the author, it conjures up Nazi images – towers, torture, guards, racism, cold-blooded brutality. No doubt as I write these lines there is an Arab Anne Frank locked in her room due to the curfew and scribbling in her notebook. No doubt, some day, we will read her diary with sorrow at her suffering and admiration for her courage.

Meanwhile, the killing of children continues with impunity:

Claxton quotes a UN report that puts the number of children shot dead in the past three and a half years at 56. Almost all died as a result of direct fire, *not* of random shots or ricochet. Not a single Israeli soldier has been imprisoned for the killing of a Palestinian child.

(Pilger 1991a)

The Arab neighbours remain an unknown entity. 'We don't really know anything about the Arabs,' admits Uri, an Israeli character in *The Smile of the Lamb*, 'we've buried them beneath our contempt' (Grossman 1991b). For the Israeli the Arab has become the stereotype of the enemy: 'Far ahead, in the mountains that rimmed the sky to the east, a weak light flickered. A Jordanian outpost? A Bedouin encampment? There lay the Land of Edom. The Kingdom of Transjordan. The city half as old as time. The enemy's home' (Oz 1986: 336–7).

Religious leaders and teachers, the wise people of a community, from whom we may expect talk of kindness and compassion, calmly support violence on camera. Civilians are not exempt from the terror. One religious leader admitted, without a touch of remorse, that he was responsible for the explosion that blew off an Arab mayor's legs. It was to teach him a lesson. Muslims, their faces covered, agree that Islam does not sanction violence but say they have no other choice. In a Jewish home, remote from ordinary contact with Arabs, the religious equations form with easy logic thus: Palestinians are terrorists; Palestinians are Arabs and Muslims; therefore Muslims are terrorists. This reductionism is made possible in the postmodernist age of the media and their instantly simplified images.

Although Rabbi Kahane's public position on Palestinians was one of the most extreme it touched a raw nerve in Israeli society. His assassination in New York in November 1990 further strengthened his following. Shortly after, Rehavam Zeevi, perhaps even more extreme, was appointed a minister in the Cabinet. However, this position is also widely criticized by Israelis fearful of extremism and what it is doing to their society (see 'Israeli censor's thick blue line', Ian Black in *The Guardian*, 5 November 1990).

A leading Israeli intellectual spells it out with courage, challenging the extreme views of the right-wing: 'And yet, if we are to hold any historical perspective, the only viable future for Israel, in coming generations, is to evolve a shared civility among its Jewish and Arab citizens' (Hareven 1991: 8). 'A shared civility', he explains, 'in a Jewish state will mean that Arabs will serve side by side with Jews as ministers in the government, as director generals in ministries and in economic enterprises, as heads of hospitals, as university professors. It will mean that after peace with our neighbours Arabs will serve in the army, and even before that they may serve in a civic service dedicated to community welfare. It will mean that Arabs will pilot El Al aircraft side by side with Jewish pilots' (ibid.: 9; there is some evidence of 'a shared civility' outside the Middle East vortex: Louvish, an Israeli living in London, dedicated his novel, *The Silencer*, 1991, to the Palestinian writer Abbas Shiblak, also living in London).

The alternative to a shared civility [the Israeli intellectual warns us] is a growing incivility, leading to alienation, polarization, and eventual strife in which Israeli Arabs will claim, as a few of them already do: if the Jews do not wish to integrate us in the structures of the state, then let us run our own affairs separately, autonomously, first functionally and eventually geographically. In the long term, not the external military threat but this internal risk is the greater danger to the security of Israel. It will not endanger the very survival of Israel; but it will deeply distort its life as a human society and will devoid its democracy of authentic content. . . . They will point out that we may be fast approaching the point of no return in the polarization between Arabs and Jews in Israel, and that once we have gone beyond that point the process will become irreversible.
(ibid.: 10; also see Domb 1982, Hareven 1983a and 1983b, and the work of writers like Amoz Oz and David Grossman)

The bitterness of the arguments, the razor's-edge divisions, have made redundant the need to apportion blame, to pronounce easy judgements on history, on political right and wrong. When we see reports from Israel on television showing a mother with tears streaming down her face, crying in grief for her dead child, do we really pause to enquire whose side it was on, Arab or Jew? A mother's grief is universal and we pray that the killing ceases; if we cannot, something is already dead in us.

The moral dilemmas, as the Jews are learning, are as terrible for the persecutor as the persecuted, the aggressor as the victim. 'The conqueror is also the conquered', Grossman tells us (1991b). Because of their hatred for the Palestinians, their quarrels with the Arabs and their anxious lives behind barbed wires and security guards, the Jewish citizens of Israel are farther than ever before from achieving the dream of living an ordinary life, 'in the ways of the Torah and the Shulhan Arukh'.

CROSS

Christ and Plato approach humanity from diametrically opposed positions. Christ spoke of meekness, kindness, love for the sick, the poor, the outcast and the crippled; Plato rejected these sentiments. The contradictions between the two create the tensions so apparent in European history, and are more than ever noticeable today in Western society. Nonetheless, Greek thought played an important role in Christianity from the earliest times and its traces are evident in the writings of St Paul and St John.

In the person of St Augustine, Platonic philosophy and the New Testament fused. Augustine followed this line of thinking in his treatise *De Trinitate* (On the Trinity). His mystical experience, his sexual nature and his Neoplatonic fascination make him one of the most extraordinary figures in Christianity. His mind was the crucible which fused Christian and Greek philosophy and transmitted it to medieval Christianity.

As a young student in Carthage, Augustine was profoundly moved by a treatise of Cicero which resulted in his enthusiasm for Greek philosophy. It convinced him of the superiority of the life devoted to the pursuit of thought, the *vita contemplativa*, over any secular ambition. When he wrote his treatise *De Vera Religione* (On the True Religion), around the age of 40, he was still thinking of Christianity in Neoplatonic terms. The Divine Word (*Logos*) in Christ is the spirit or mind illuminating reason through whom the human soul has access to the transcendent Godhead. It was only after his induction into office, which would lead him to a high position in the church, that he reluctantly gave up the dream of the *vita contemplativa*.

Even if he had not embarked on this intellectual exercise he would have been remembered for his famous autobiography, *Confessions*, in which, at the age of about 45, he told the story of his own restless youth and the discovery of peace, some twelve years earlier, in the Catholic church. (For a recent magisterial translation, see Augustine of Hippo 1991.) In fact, Neoplatonism had reinforced the Manichaean principle, that the path to God is by rejecting the body. For Augustine, this meant breaking the ties of sexuality. The story is told for all time in the *Confessions* and has continued to fascinate readers down the ages (the 1991 edition has headings which provide the flavour: 'Three lusts', 'Obscene literature', 'Alone I would not have done it'.).

In *De Civitate Dei* (The City of God), his *magnum opus*, he drew a picture of the two societies of the elect and the damned. His two cities are symbolic embodiments of the two spiritual powers which have contended since the Creation: 'The love of God proceeding to disregard of self, and the love of self proceeding to disregard of God' (*De Civitate*: xiv, 28). Augustine has left us the best portrait of himself and the justification for his eminence in his church in the following words: 'The true philosopher is the lover of God' (ibid.: viii, 1).

Links with the Greeks are thus clearly visible early in Christianity. Also visible is the relationship in the mosaic of ideas between the three religions: for instance, Augustine has a great influence on Aquinas, as does Averroes, whose contemporaneity with Maimonides we have noted. In the simplicity of their way of life, in their thought and in their dealings with ordinary people many Christian figures would resemble Muslim ones.

Christian mystics

Many of the saintly Christian figures would appeal to Muslims because of their mystical and gentle nature. There would be remarkable Sufistic resonances in them. In turn, Christians would find Sufism attractive:

> Whether we are Muslims or not, we are all surely children of One Father; and it is therefore no impertinence, no irrelevancy for the Christian scholar to aim at rediscovering those vital truths which made the Sufi movement so powerful an influence for good.

> (Arberry 1990: 134)

St Francis of Assisi could be a Sufi figure. The founder of the order of the Franciscans and principal patron of Italy, he came from a noble lineage. He was a happy-go-lucky young man. His confrontation with his angry father before the local bishop is as dramatic as any young man challenging parental authority. Taking off his clothes he handed them back to his father and, covered only by a hair shirt, said: 'Until now I have called you my father on earth. But henceforth I can truly say: Our Father Who art in heaven'. Like the Buddha he abandoned his comfortable home to search for truth and salvation in poverty.

Francis' mystical experiences, love of poverty and nature – he referred to 'brother sun' and 'sister moon' – and long illnesses made him widely popular. Contact with Islam might have come with a journey to the Moors in Spain in 1213–14, but sickness forced him to abandon it. Instead, it came through his trip to the holy places in Palestine in 1219, when the crusaders were besieging Damietta. The story is told that the Sultan was so impressed by him that, not surprisingly, he was given special permission to visit the holy places.

Church versus state

Greek influences, by the time of the Renaissance and Reformation, were pushing Europe towards more and more freedom of enquiry, something the church resisted. The general attitude, of following the logic of the argument wherever it leads, was the most important Greek contribution to Europe. The philosophical opposition of the church to, and silencing of, Galileo in 1633 point to important and far-reaching developments in the history of Europe.

Galileo became a crucial test case. He had published a book the year before, which his opponents claimed to be a defence of the Copernican theory, and for this he was condemned, though he avoided punishment by recanting. As early as 1543 Copernicus had made public his theory of the universe, according to which the Earth moved round the sun and not, as had hitherto been supposed, the sun round the Earth. But the ban on Copernican views by Rome had only a limited effect. The intellectual life of Western Europe was now as diverse as it was becoming fertile. Catholic theology no longer had a monopoly. In many European countries it was possible to have books published, even when they expressed views contrary to the established ideology of the country.

The struggle against the church was uphill. Religious bigotry had permeated society. Here is Calvin's Geneva:

Drunkards, dancers and adulterers were excommunicated, torture was used systematically, a child was beheaded for striking its parents and, in sixty years, one hundred and fifty men and women who had transgressed against Calvin's spiritual discipline were burnt at the stake.

(Webster 1990: 32)

Once again, the medieval illustrations, the woodcuts, speak of bigotry. Protestants farting in the face of the Pope was a popular one. Rome was named, like Babylon, the 'Scarlet Whore'. The three enemies of Luther's church were the Pope, the Devil and the Muslim.

In this sixteenth-century Lutheran woodcut Christ is shown trampling triumphantly upon a three-headed version of the apocalyptic beast. One of the heads is that of the Pope who spews out monks and demonic spirits. The second head is that of the Devil disguised as an angel. The third is that of a Muslim – specifically of the Turk who was seen at the time as a sign of the last days and as identical with Gog and Magog, the hosts of Satan who figure in Revelation 20.7.

(ibid.: 80)

The eighteenth and nineteenth centuries saw Christianity shedding some of its core features in the European drive to industrialization and later imperialism. Imperialism needed power and brutality to drive its engines, industrialization required the exploitation of labour and the greed of the industrialists to run its enterprises. While keeping the symbolism and rhetoric of Christianity, the spirit of Christianity – humility, austerity, piety – was replaced by an aggressive materialism. It was the face of Christianity, the triumphant imperial cross, which would be seen by the colonies of Christian Europe.

Memories of the Inquisition, the rigidity of the church, the ritual burning of those who had strayed, the pogroms against whoever was at hand – Jews, gypsies, women, the poor, the claims to absolute truth have left a revulsion against established religion in the West. It was Pombal, in Portugal, who, no longer able to bear the superstition and interference of the church, expelled the Jesuits, thus ending the Inquisition. Most of Catholic Europe followed. It became a rout for anti-clericalism. Even those inherently sympathetic to the church were gloomy. 'The Church', noted Thomas Arnold, 'as it now stands no human power can save.' For John Newman it was 'the veriest of nonentities'. In despair he wrote: 'Vanity of vanities, all is vanity!'

Western orientalists are quick to point out the hubris in their own civilization, as does Montgomery Watt citing another Islamic expert, Wilfred Cantwell Smith: 'It is my observation over more than twenty years of study of the Orient, and a little now of Africa, that the fundamental flaw of Western civilization in its role in world history is arrogance, and that this has also infected the Christian Church' (in Watt 1991: 109).

In our time the church is seen simply as a failed and out-dated system: the present Archbishop of Canterbury, George Carey, described it as 'a toothless elderly lady muttering ancient platitudes through toothless gums'. Secular society, is therefore a prize achieved after centuries, to be preserved at all costs. The slightest surrender to religion sends tremors through society. It is one reason why in the West there is an instinctive reaction against Islamic expressions of faith; it is a knee-jerk response to Europe's own unhappy experience with established religion.

Christianity is faulted on several counts in recent times by its critics: for its male bias ('The Bible story is profoundly patri-archal', is a typical lament by women writers; see Hampson 1990); for being too closely associated with European imperial colonization; for the role of the church during the two world wars (especially the first) where state-appointed priests urged the masses to their death; and for remaining silent at the treatment of the Jews, particularly in Nazi Germany. With rampant racism, materialism and arrogance, the Christian ideal is conspicuously absent in most societies of the West; there is Christian rhetoric perhaps, but not the spirit of Christ.

This is not to overlook the numerous brave and decent Christians – or lapsed Christians – who have adopted contrary positions. Perhaps in recent times Christian ideals have best been put into action when Polish priests fought for political and social justice against communists and those in South America against military dictators.

In the last half-century secularist forces, fired by materialism on the one hand and the communist imagination on the other, have culminated in a process begun centuries ago and put

Christianity on the defensive. The crisis for the modern church has taken interesting cultural forms. It began in the 1960s with rock music in church services. More recent developments include clergy who openly support homosexuality and free sex, and priests who, if not atheists, sound like atheists. For purists, the church has made far too many compromises; it has become all things to all men. The church no longer leads the flock but is led by it. The purists quote the Bible: 'What shall it profit a man, if he shall gain the whole world, and lose his own soul?' However, this flexibility has allowed Christianity a fresh vitality triggering a fundamentalist revival in many Western countries.

Christian fundamentalist groups range from Pentecostals, Baptists and other independent fundamentalist churches to 'charismatic' renewal movements in the mainstream churches, both Catholic ('Evangelization 2000') and Protestant. They have gained particular momentum in the 1980s and are strongest in the United States. Of the estimated 60 million born-again Christians in the United States, about half describe themselves as fundamentalists. From there they have spread the message to Latin America, the Philippines and parts of the Caribbean and Africa. Their vigorous missionary programme combines emotional religion with militant anti-communism.

However self-consciously secular the West has become, evidence of Christian culture remains pervasive in society although it may be the Christmas and christening-only variety (for the full impact of the media on the Western family, see pages 242–55). In the United Kingdom, on Good Friday, 13 April 1990, three of the four television channels ran films on Jesus, including *Jesus Christ Superstar*. This cultural expression reflects and maintains religious consciousness.

The poetic quality of the King James' version of the Bible explains its popularity among Christians. Because of their majesty the words recounting Creation rarely fail to move:

In the beginning God created the heaven and the earth. And the earth was without form and void; and darkness was upon the face of the deep. And the Spirit of God moved upon the face of the waters. And God said, Let there be light: and there was light. And God saw the light, that it was good: and God divided the light from the darkness. And God called the light Day, and

the darkness he called Night. And the evening and the morning
were the first day.

(Genesis 1: 1–5)

The very origin of the Gospels, which began as a series of
anecdotes, proverbs, reminiscences and stories – the 'sayings of
Jesus' which circulated among the earliest preachers of the faith
as they founded churches in Syria, Asia Minor, Egypt, Greece and
Italy – is romantic and simple in its appeal.

CRESCENT

For early Muslims Greek thought was seductive, and they
succumbed, indeed, 'certain Muslims' even considered Plato a
'prophet' (as Nasr pointed out in his Gifford Lectures, 1981).
Greek conceptions were used by them which led to the discipline
of *kalam*. Among the exponents of this view was the sect of the
Mutazila who became prominent during the Abbasids. The
Mutazila, 'those who stand aloof', were especially strong during
the reign of the Caliph Mamun (813–33). Mamun established a
library and centre for translating Greek books, and, eventually,
some eighty Greek authors became available in Arabic. One of the
most famous victims of the caliph was the jurist Imam Ahmed
Hanbal (780–855). He is one of the four venerated Imams of
Sunni Islam, whose school of jurisprudence dominates certain
parts of the Muslim world, particularly in Saudi Arabia. The Imam
was beaten and imprisoned. In the end, old and sick, he was
allowed to leave Samarra, the capital, and die in Baghdad. A
million people attended his funeral.

The Mutazila adopted Stoic teaching and were familiar with
Aristotle's *Categories*. They were influenced by Greek philosophic
and scientific thought with its emphasis on reason, logic and study
of the laws of nature. They believed in the freedom of the human
will over divine predestination. They relied on rational deduction,
in Quranic interpretation and theological interpretation. Reason
and revelation were regarded as complementary sources of
guidance from a just and reasonable God. The orthodox challenge
was not long in coming. Not unexpectedly, it came from the ranks
of the Mutazila. One of the pre-eminent Mutazila thinkers of his
time, Abu Hassan Ashari (d. 935) became the father of the Asharite

school of philosophy which came to dominate Sunni Islam in the central lands of the caliphate.

Ashari, like Imam Shafii in law and Ghazzali in theology, represented a synthesis between opposing positions. He stood midway between the extremes of Hanbal's literalism and the Mutazila's logical rationalism. He reasserted the doctrines and attributes of the omnipotence of God, the uncreatedness of the Quran and predestination. However, he drew on the language and categories of Greek thought that had now become an integral part of theological discourse.

Because of the movement to translate classical texts into Arabic, Muslim thinkers were able to appropriate Aristotle, Plato, Plotinus and the Stoics. They adapted these to their own context, producing an extraordinarily rich contribution to Islamic civilization. Men like al-Kindi and al-Farabi, Ibn-Sina (or Avicenna) and Ibn-Rushd (or Averroes) were among the intellectual giants of their times. Astrology, ethnology, science and medicine were included in their study. These were renaissance men, centuries before the word was used in Europe.

At the time when Greek philosophy and science were influencing the development of scholastic theology, philosophy (*falsafa*) was developing as a separate Muslim discipline. The Muslim *falsifa* (the plural of the Arabic *faylasuf* or Greek *philosophos*) – or Falasifa – went much further than the Mutazila in accepting the Greeks. One of the earliest was the Arab al-Kindi (d. 868). Another was the Persian ar-Razi (d. 923/32), whose book *The Spiritual Physick* has been described by the translator into English as expressing an attitude of 'intellectual hedonism'.

Even more notable was al-Farabi (*c.* 875–950). He defended his position in philosophy on a Neoplatonic basis. It was a position further refined by the Persian, Avicenna (d. 1037), considered to be one of the world's most renowned philosophers. Although these philosophers have an important place in any general history of philosophy, their work made little impression in the Islamic world.

The Arab intellectual crisis

The intellectual crisis for Muslim Arabs was reaching a head. Pressed between the contending positions of the orthodox and Sufi forms of Islam, and complicated by Hellenistic intellectual influences, Muslims searched for a way out of the impasse. This was the situation when Ghazzali (1058–1111) was appointed professor at the prestigious Nizamiyya college in Baghdad. He was only 33. His teacher, al-Juwayni (d. 1085), had alerted him to the threat to mainstream theology from the Falasifa. Having obtained copies of the works of Avicenna and others, he mastered these and produced an account of Avicenna's philosophy, *Maqasid al-falasifa, The Aims of the Philosophers*, which some argue is more lucid than anything by Avicenna himself. Ghazzali then refuted these teachings in his *Tahafut al-falasifa, The Inconsistency of the Philosophers*. Here he argues that they had ceased to be Muslims because they denied a bodily, as distinct from a spiritual, resurrection in holding that God knows only universals and not particulars, and in holding that the world had existed from all eternity. There were also seventeen other points on which he considered them heretical.

Nonetheless, it is important to point out that Ghazzali also demonstrated the extent to which some of the sciences of the Falasifa, such as mathematics, had nothing in them contrary to Islamic doctrine and were therefore acceptable. He even wrote introductory textbooks on Aristotelian logic with examples suited to the needs of Muslim theologians.

Ghazzali's *Ihya-ulum al-din,The Revival of the Religious Sciences*, was inspired by a vision of the Prophet, seen in Makkah. It is said of this work that 'if all the books of Islam were destroyed it would be but a slight loss if only the *Ihya* of Ghazzali were preserved' (Ghazzali 1980: 13). Al-Ghazzali has been called by scholars of Islam like Anne Marie Schimmel, 'the greatest Muslim after the Prophet Muhammad' (Schimmel 1975: 91). But Iqbal, contemplating the period, and himself the defender of faith against the Greeks, is not impressed. He is critical of Ghazzali: 'It was partly owing to this revolt and partly to his personal history that Ghazzali based religion on philosophical scepticism – a rather unsafe basis for religion and not wholly justified by the spirit of the Quran' (1986: 3).

As Ghazzali had written a refutation of Avicenna who had died in 1037, over twenty years before his birth, the Spanish Averroes (d. 1198) refuted Ghazzali in *The Inconsistency of the Inconsistency* (*Tahafut at-Tahafut*). Considered perhaps the greatest of the Arabic Falasifa, Averroes had a legal training and for most of his life served as a judge. He was well versed in the Greek sciences, studied Aristotle and wrote commentaries on some of his works, correcting many of the Neoplatonic misinterpretations current among the Falasifa. Despite his eminence he had no successors in the Islamic West and was hardly known in the East. Although he was a *qadi* (judge) he suffered a measure of repression from the orthodox. Perhaps his most significant achievement was the reintroduction of the genuine Aristotle to Western Europeans.

During the twelfth century the works of many philosophers, the central figure being Averroes, were translated from Arabic into Latin. This generated a surge of intellectual productivity in Western Europe, affecting science and philosophy as well as theology. The main influence of Averroes is to be seen in the Dominicans, Albertus Magnus (*c.* 1206–80) and Thomas Aquinas (1226–74). Siger of Brabant (*c.* 1235–82) and others came to be known as the Latin Averroists. They largely accepted Aristotelianism as expounded by Averroes. Aquinas, in particular, made it the basis of an all-embracing metaphysical and theological system, which is generally regarded as the high point of Western Christian thought in the Middle Ages. For many critics, both Christian and Muslim, there was little difference between *kalam* philosophy and that of Aquinas.

This was the sign of the times. The intellectual and cultural traffic was from Islam to Christianity. As Watt notes wryly: 'A much-quoted Christian writer of the ninth century complains that all the Christian young men are attracted by Arabic poetry, and are more interested in Arabic than in Latin' (Watt 1991: 76; also see my 'Spain's Islamic legacy', Ahmed 1991h).

This is how Umberto Eco describes the importance of Averroes in the development of European thought:

> The man responsible, a century earlier, had been Averroes, Moslem by culture, Berber by race, Spanish by nationality, and Arab by language. Averroes knew Aristotle better than anybody and had understood what Aristotelian science led to: God is not a manipulator who sticks his nose into everything at random; he established nature in its mechanical order and in its mathematical laws, regulated by the iron determination of the stars. And since God is eternal, the world in its order is eternal also. Philosophy studies this order: nature, in other words.
>
> (Eco 1986: 263–4)

In contrast to a Europe which, in the Middle Ages was beginning to enquire and probe, gather information and collect knowledge, the Islamic schools began to close the gates of *ijtihad* or innovation. It is no coincidence that the sack of Baghdad, the heart of the Islamic world, in the middle of the thirteenth century is the time when Thomas Aquinas, inspired by Muslim philosophers, was providing a Christian base for intellectual thought which would lead to European scholarship and, eventually, the Renaissance.

We do not know why philosophy began to decline in the Islamic east, after Avicenna, and the Islamic west, after Averroes. It was partly political decay and partly this new intellectual climate. A consequence was the atrophying of the sciences among Muslims. Perhaps the difficulties facing Islam in coming to terms with the thinking of modern Europe are not due to its rejection of Greek thought, but to its rejection of the Greek receptivity to new ideas. The Arab crescent was now on the wane.

There appeared to be an essential, irreconcilable contradiction in the study of philosophy for those who believed. Umberto Eco puts it thus:

> If the Koran says something different, the philosopher must philosophically believe what his science shows him and then, without creating too many problems for himself, believe the opposite, which is the command of faith. There are two truths and the one must not disturb the other.
>
> (ibid.: 264)

This is a simplification, a stereotype. Eco's argument is persuasively repudiated by Fazlur Rahman in this passage which reflects the spirit of questioning and intellectual effervescence which are the essence of the Quran: 'I can say without fear of contradiction that, for the Quran, knowledge – that is, the creation of ideas – is an activity of the highest possible value' (Rahman 1984: 158–9). Rahman then poses disturbing questions for those Muslims who would shut themselves from the world – those who, Eco would say, do not wish to be disturbed:

> Otherwise why did it ask the Prophet to continue to pray for 'increase in knowledge'? Why did it untiringly emphasize delving into the universe, into history, and into man's own inner life? Is the banning or discouragement of pure thought compatible with this kind of demand? What does Islam have to fear from human thought and why? These are questions that

must be answered by those 'friends of religion' who want to keep their religion in a hot-house, secluded from the open air.

(ibid.)

Rahman's arguments are amply supported by numerous sayings of the Prophet – 'the first thing created by God was the Intellect' – and those of Ali – 'God did not distribute to His servants anything more to be esteemed than Intelligence'.

Indeed Iqbal, himself a philosopher accused of being influenced by European ideas (see Raschid 1981), compared Greek thought to the Quran and found it wanting:

As we all know, Greek philosophy has been a great cultural force in the history of Islam. Yet a careful study of the Quran and the various schools of scholastic theology that arose under the inspiration of Greek thought disclose the remarkable fact that while Greek philosophy very much broadened the outlook of Muslim thinkers, it, on the whole, obscured their vision of the Quran. Socrates concentrated his attention on the human world alone. To him the proper study of man was man and not the world of plants, insects, and stars. How unlike the spirit of the Quran, which sees in the humble bee a recipient of Divine inspiration and constantly calls upon the reader to observe the perpetual change of the winds, the alternation of the day and night, the clouds, the starry heavens, and the planets swimming through infinite space.

(Iqbal 1986: 3)

Although it was not his primary intention, Ghazzali had effectively sealed the fate of Greek thought in Islam. Henceforth it would be seen as bordering on heresy. This reaction easily extended to other non-Islamic philosophy. In the realm of ideas it became second nature for Muslims to reject non-Islamic philosophies. Muslims would be encouraged to be inward-looking and self-sufficient. They would be quick to dismiss original or fresh thinking as *ijtihad* or innovation and to condemn it. 'The gates of innovation', the more orthodox would say, 'were closed centuries ago.' It was Iqbal who, provoking the wrath of the orthodox, pushed the gates of innovation ajar.

Where Aquinas had Christianized Aristotle, Iqbal Islamized modern European figures like Nietzsche, Marx and Lenin. With his Cambridge and Heidelberg education, he incorporated the major non-Muslim thinkers of the age into his work. In one of his most popular poems, Lenin is presented before God, sounding suspiciously like a Semitic prophet. But, like Avicenna and Averroes before him, his serious philosophic ideas are restricted to a limited circle, although his poetry is widely known and admired. For ordinary Muslims he is, above all, the poet who dreamt of a Muslim homeland in India: Pakistan.

The Greeks did not disappear entirely. They appear in unsuspected places. Ibn Battuta, the celebrated traveller, informs us that in fourteenth century India the orthodox Muslim king of Delhi, Muhammad bin Tughlak, studied Greek philosophical rationalism (Dunn 1989: 190). Wherever the rationalist system of scholarship remained dominant, the study of Plato and Aristotle is recorded even if only in small pockets. India up to the early nineteenth century and Iran to the present, not to mention other areas of the Islamic world, provide us with some examples. But what reduces the Muslim interest further, almost to the point of extinction, is the development of Islamic revival and reform in the context of Western colonialism from the nineteenth century onwards.

Although Greek philosophy may have withered among Muslims, memories of Greek culture remain in unexpected places and in unexpected forms. Sikander, the Muslim version of Alexander, although it is pre-Islamic, remains a popular name among Muslims (one of my younger brothers is so named); Aristotle is a symbol of knowledge among common folk; and there are towns named Alexandria, after the conqueror, across the Muslim world.

The last lines of Taplin's work on the Greeks echo the message of the Prophet (Taplin 1989: 264). Both point to the need to understand, to know, to read the signs around us; in the words of Clearchus of Aï Khanoum, KNOW THYSELF. The Greek saying matches an Islamic one. 'He who knows himself (his soul) knows his Lord,' said the Prophet. Self-discovery is indicated, self-knowledge presupposed. These are also the central notions of the postmodernist age.

Hellenic influences and Semitic traditions

Whatever the strength of the Semitic civilizations and the vagaries of fashion, the Greeks remain resilient. In Christian Europe, the juxtaposition between the 'pagan virtues' of the Greeks and the divinity of the Cross, the denial and the affirmation, is evident. Augustine and Aquinas and, nearer our times, Hume, Kant and Nietzsche, testify to this.

Consider three of the most important founding fathers of the modern Western mind, Marx, Nietzsche and Freud. Marx's doctoral dissertation (1841) was on the materialist and anti-metaphysical philosophers Democritus and Epicurus; Nietzsche became a professor of classics in 1869 before he was 30; and Freud was fascinated by many aspects of Greek culture – for example, Platonic love and catharsis – long before he coined the term 'Oedipus complex' in 1900. The influential *Dialectic of Enlightenment* cites the Greeks extensively (Adorno and Horkheimer 1979, see especially the chapter 'Odysseus or myth and enlightenment'). We have already pointed to the Greek influences on postmodernists like Foucault, Derrida and Barthes.

The Greek ethos helps explain in the West the marginalization of women, the aged and the poor; also the continuing importance of British public schools with their glorification of sport, masculinity, victory and élitism. The spirit, curricula and sports of the public school were designed to create leaders, those who would excel over others, be heroic like the Greeks, as they consciously claimed. The central position given to the classics at these schools was significant (the public schools traditionally provided the higher echelons of the Conservative party, which explains its symbol: the Greek torch). But Greek remained a slog at school, which prompted the famous remark of Churchill, who had struggled unsuccessfully with it at Harrow: 'So they told me how Mr Gladstone read Homer for fun, which I thought served him right.' It explains why the most aggressive and ardent of Christian bishops continue to be fascinated by, and look back to as the ideal, the 'Ancient Greeks' and their 'Ancient World' (Jenkins and Jenkins 1991).

In British India, the jewel in the crown, the distinctive buildings of the era of European classicism included Greek columns. The statues of the empire builders struck Greek poses, and the Indian Civil Service thought of itself as Plato's 'guardians' (the title of a volume by one of its members, Philip Mason, see Woodruff 1953–5, volume 1: *The Founders*, volume 2: *The Guardians*). Debates and amateur theatricals were vigorously encouraged. This tradition explains the participation of a British ambassador in amateur theatricals staged in Islamabad, Pakistan. The cultural event divides opinion among the diplomatic community, the English and north Europeans applauding it, the Muslims, long having rejected the Greeks, genuinely perplexed at the sight of a senior diplomat in make-up and costume and on stage. For them it is simply yet another example of the 'mad Englishman'.

'If you would seek his monument', says the epitaph to Sir Christopher Wren in St Paul's Cathedral, 'look around you'. A glance at the Rome of the Caesars, the London and Paris of European imperialism, the Berlin of the Nazis shows us how deeply rooted in Europe are notions of Greek architecture. The influence is also reflected in the other central buildings of the West (Summerson 1980). Washington has numerous examples with obvious Greek influences starting with Capitol Hill, the White House, the Washington, Jefferson and Lincoln monuments. Even Bokassa in Africa builds in this style, learning via Napoleon and via the French. Beneath every megalomaniac dreaming of empire there is an architect inspired by Greece struggling to find expression. Napoleon illustrates how quickly a republican idealist can slip into the posture and clothes of a Roman emperor with an eye to Greece. As Augustus Caesar said of Rome: 'I found it built of brick and left it in marble.' Albert Speer and Sir Edwin Lutyens have more in common than we imagine. During the First World War the British cast themselves as Athenians; their enemies, the Germans, as Spartans; they were echoing the Greek Peloponnesian war.

Many a modern nation casts itself as a new Greece. Recent literature continues to confirm Britain's attempts to play Greece to America's Rome, to use the image of Harold Macmillan (see, for instance, Hitchens 1990; also 'The Special Relationship', Wright 1991). The symmetry of the relationship – the United States as the mighty leader and the United Kingdom as loyal follower – is confirmed and mutually accepted. This is illustrated at all levels from major world events to cultural ones. Britain's unquestioning support for the Gulf war is an example of the former; for an example of the latter let us refer to the popular 1991 film *Robin Hood: Prince of Thieves*. Robin Hood is played by the American actor Kevin Costner, triumphant with the Oscars he won for his *Dances with Wolves*, and presently one of Hollywood's most bankable actors. A British actor plays the Sheriff of Nottingham. The responses were telling. It was not the absence of general comment at the incongruity of an American playing

Robin Hood without even attempting to disguise his accent but the sense of gratitude that a British actor was even allowed a role. Imperial memory of greatness and national pride seem simply to have faded. Britain is now almost a cultural extension of the United States, a willingly seduced acolyte.

The Greeks have even entered a heated controversy in America in the debate about race and colour. *Black Athena* (Channel 4 television, shown on 5 March 1991, based on Martin Bernal's book of the same title, 1987), using etymological, archaeological and literary arguments, puts forward the thesis that 'white' Europe consciously deleted the 'black', that is, African, origins of Greek civilization. Racism and anti-Semitism were at the root cause of this appropriation. This is not entirely convincing, but, for the blacks, the book provides further evidence of white perfidy and racism; it also illustrates the almost universal desire to appropriate the Greeks.

Perhaps the best-known and most widely accepted Greek contribution to the modern world is the event named the Olympics. The philosophy of a healthy mind in a healthy body is exemplified in the concept of the games. The athlete competes with honour and abides by the rules (at least, he ought to do so); he is, above all, a good sportsman. Logically the Olympics, which originated at ancient Olympia in 776 BC, are the ultimate media triumph for Greek philosophy. When they were revived in 1896, the moving force, Baron Pierre de Coubertin, recalling that the Greeks 'first conceived the idea of the development of body and mind through competition', judged Athens the appropriate setting for them.

The naked human body, glorified by the Greeks in art, was covered by the Semites. Its naked form not only represented a sort of physical arrogance but could also encourage prurience. Nudity was thus actively discouraged. The concepts of 'shame' and 'honour' were linked directly to ideas about the proper and improper sexuality of women. Statues were not encouraged – except among certain Christians – as they could divert worship from God. Judaism, Islam and most early Christians were emphatic about disallowing representation.

The connection between the ancient Greeks and the modern media is clearly discernible. On one level, present-day comic-book characters trace a link back to the Greeks: Superman to Icarus, Rambo to Achilles. On another level, the clean shaved face and the naked athletic torso and limbs, so beloved of the media, are inspired by the Greek athletes. They reflect so well the images the ad companies and sports firms wish to project. No more dramatic contrast can be provided than by the beards and baggy clothes of the Semitic elders vigorously arguing for their faith; it is an image conjuring passion and fury. Their position on popular contemporary issues, such as feminism and homosexuality, seem old-fashioned. To the young they appear as kill-joys, forbidding fun and laughter. In the media this translates as Jewish or Muslim fanaticism.

Pushing this line of argument further we encounter other interesting correlates: democracy, love for literature and music, drama, and the arts, on the one hand, and religious rituals, tradition and custom, on the other. The first leads to a state-of-the-art society, self-consciously the latest, up-to-date, fashionable and in vogue – indeed, these are the buzz words used to describe it by the media. In contrast, societies dominated by religion emphasize tradition, ancient custom and the past.

The results of all these drastic changes were far-reaching: as speed, strength and guile would be prized by the Greeks, piety, wisdom and sacrifice were honoured by the Semites. Where the Greeks sought the connection between cause and effect, the Semites depended on intuition and custom. Furthermore, there was the replacement of logic and reason by divine command, of open enquiry and scepticism by faith, of an amoral order by a moral one, of a flexible ideology prone to dissolving into anarchy, by one charged with a burning need to order and correct, and, most important of all, one set of ideas looking to the future, the other to the past. The consequences would be evident in the different attitudes to life, arts and science in society.

There is, consequently, a fundamental difference in the way the world is viewed from the two positions. One civilization views the world as a linear progression in which things generally get better. This is called 'progress'. People live and aim for tomorrow. The earlier Utopia is realized the better. Speed thus becomes an important factor in life. The legendary super-heroes – Alexander, Caesar, Napoleon – are *spericolato*, living their lives flat out. Evolution from primitive society to agricultural, industrial and post-industrial societies is seen as a logical movement. By contrast, in the Semitic tradition humanity began, literally, at the very top: the eponymous ancestors, Adam and Eve, started life in heaven. Their 'fall' also symbolizes mankind's fall from grace.

There is thus a tendency to hark back, one which encourages withdrawal and retreat from the world.

The Semitic prophets in ancient Athens would be seen as assumptive gnostics, dangerous visionaries and fanatics wishing to impose their own conceptions of divine will and order on society. Plato and Aristotle in a traditional Semitic society in the Middle East would be regarded as subversive heretics, misguiding people with their questioning talk and free reasoning. The first would provide a *frisson*, a promise of a better world, of happier times, for the believers; the cold logic and reason of the latter would be obnoxious to them.

CONCLUSION: 'NOUS SOMMES TOUS DES SÉMITES'

For a large part of humanity, the choice would appear to be between the Hellenistic gods and the Semitic prophets; in fact the divide is not so clear. The dynamic interaction of high technology, indigenous culture and Hellenism is one of the more interesting developments of the postmodernist era.

Modernism rejected the Victorian era and its values, reviving an ideal Greek model based on logic, progress and materialism, introducing the 'shock of the new'. Some, like Le Corbusier, went further by rejecting Greek influences altogether, including the Parthenon, long the base for Western architecture. Postmodernism, in turn, bears witness to the 'fragmentation of the old', and in the process re-discovers the Greeks. But this time the discovery is not innocent; it is laced with irony and self-consciousness. With recognition of Greek virtues and faults, it extols as it chides. We are a long way from the high Romanticism once accorded to the Greeks; Keats drooling over Greek vases and Byron over Greek women.

Besides, the societies of the three monotheistic religions have developed in ways which do not always correspond to the grand and noble vision of the Semitic prophets. Their unending and bitter disputes cause widespread misery and despair. Shaw, neither Greek nor Semite, perhaps best expressed this perspective: 'Christianity might be a good thing if anyone ever tried it.'

Nonetheless, the force of tradition inherited from the Semitic prophets remains a powerful one. It is in that sense we cite Massignon: '*Nous sommes tous des Sémites.*' The last lines of *The*

Penitent, which in many ways is representative of that tradition, express this belief:

> My morality would not prove that God is dead and that the universe is a physical or chemical accident. I see a conscious plan and purpose in all being, in man and in animals as well as in inanimate objects. God's mercy is often hidden, but His boundless wisdom is seen by everyone, even if they call Him nature, substance, absolute or by any other name. I believe in God, His Providence and in man's free will. I have accepted the Torah and its commentaries because I am sure that there is no better choice. This faith keeps growing in me all the time.
>
> (Singer 1986: 122)

Perhaps the most appropriate image with which to conclude the arguments in this chapter is that of the terrifying Semitic apocalypse. John Romer does so to conclude his *tour de force*, linking our world with the Bible:

> The blessings and faults of the Bible are still with us. Armageddon certainly is, with a new nuclear ring about it now. 'These spirits were devils with power to work miracles. They were sent out to muster all the kings of the world for the great day of battle of God the sovereign Lord. . . . So they assembled the kings at the place called in Hebrew Armageddon. Then the seventh angel poured his bowl on the air; and out of the sanctuary came a loud voice from the throne, which said, "It is over!" And there followed flashes of lightening and peals of thunder, and a violent earth-quake, like none before it in human history, so violent it was . . . the cities of the world fell in ruin' (Revelation 16: 14–19 NEB).
>
> (Romer 1988: 350)

The Quran has similar passages, evoking similar images of the 'Blazing Fire' (Surah 2: 119). These images speak to all of us – whether people of faith, people of the Book, or people who have no belief but are concerned about human life. They remind us of many things: to tread softly on earth; how closely interconnected our lives are; to care for the less privileged and the elderly; and to bear in mind that we are here for but a short time. In our times of ambiguity and cynicism, when people are so interlocked through modern communications technology and yet so divided through ethnic and religious hatred, it is a primary lesson worth remembering.

To sum up: the ancient Greeks provided a valid template for a world order and vision. The three great Semitic religions, though in some crucial senses at odds with the Greeks, nonetheless interacted with and absorbed their ideas in varying degrees. However, Islam, after an initial interaction, consciously rejected them. This rejection may help explain the deep-rooted cultural and intellectual opposition to Islam in the West where the ancient Greeks still matter. In spite of this there remain interesting resonances of a common humanity between Greek ideas and Islamic ones.

Had there been more Iqbals and Afghanis, or had Muslims continued to interact with the Greeks up to our times, would things have been very different for Muslim society? Would they have followed the European trajectory of societies which today have high economic growth, widespread education and stable politics? Or would European imperialism have nullified everything in any case? We have pointed to an important area of further investigation. In the next chapter we will look at some of the consequences of European colonialism on Muslims and its continuing impact.

By illustrating the diversity of Islamic history and the equally complex relationship of Islam with the major European cultural and religious systems we are better able to appreciate its responses to postmodernism. We have also set the stage for a comment on Islam in its dealings with the West and the dominant global civilization which it shapes. These have taken the form of long-lasting and deeply felt encounters which span more than a millennium.

Chapter 3

Confrontation and clash

Having introduced Muslims historically and in relation to their main protagonists, let us look at the major encounters between Islam and the West. By doing so we provide an overview which throws light on the present mutual antipathy that exists between the two. We will also examine the continuing colonial legacy, cultural and political, of Europe and its impact on Muslims. I will focus on South Asia, for it is here that one of the most remarkable and interesting encounters between Europe and Asia, Christianity and Islam, took place. This will also explain some of the existing contradictions in Muslim society which were created during the formation of modernism in these societies.

By better appreciating the processes of modernism that shaped these societies we are able to bring their postmodern features into bold relief. The juxtaposition and synthesis of diverse cultures, the irony and irreverence, are postmodernist; so too, are, the rejection of strong political centres and the clamorous demands of indigenous groups for recognition. We will explore both in this chapter. But first a comment on the historical encounter between Islam and the West. An appreciation of the encounter is not a parergon but central to our understanding of the relationship.

ISLAM AND THE WEST: A THIRD ENCOUNTER OF THE CLOSE KIND

Edward Gibbon recounts a chilling Muslim story in *The Decline and Fall of the Roman Empire*. When the first Muslims erupted from the Arabian peninsula in the seventh century and reached Alexandria, they sent a message to the caliph asking for instructions regarding the famous central library. 'If the books are in accordance with the

Quran, they are unnecessary and may be destroyed; if they contradict the Quran, they are dangerous and should certainly be destroyed', replied the caliph.

This is, of course, an apocryphal story and even Gibbon doubts its veracity. But it suggests the formation of negative images of Islam quite early in its history. It tells us how non-Muslims saw Muslims; also how Muslims are not able to see how the world sees them. The blind spot of Muslims, the incapacity to see how others see them, has historically created a false sense of self-sufficiency in Muslim society.

However, the pictures on television and in the newspapers of Muslims, death in their eyes, burning books in Bradford, were not a figment of the imagination. Others reinforce the Bradford ones: Libyans killing a policewoman in London; Palestinians hijacking passenger planes; Iranians seizing foreign embassies; and Indonesians blowing up the Borobudur temple in Java. It is, as pointed out elsewhere (Ahmed 1988), V.S. Naipaul's vision of Islam: 'Rage was what I saw . . . Muslims crazed by their confused faith' (*Among the Believers: An Islamic Journey* 1981; but this is the earlier Naipaul; ten years on he has softened both towards Islam and Hinduism in *India: A Million Mutinies Now* 1990).

These images stem partly from a lack of understanding of Islam among non-Muslims and partly from the failure of Muslims to explain themselves. Many of the negative images of Islam are not based on fact or reason. But as Johnson said: 'Prejudice not being founded on reason cannot be removed by argument.'

The present encounter between Islam and the West

The burning of books in Bradford brought into the open the present encounter between Islam and Western civilization, as it exposed the vast gaps in understanding between them, the violent passion on one side, the wall of incomprehension on the other. The encounter involves not only questions of religious belief and practice but also those of power and politics. An entire civilization is involved. On the surface, both civilizations appear vigorous and confident. Take Islam: about forty-four nations (around fifty with the Soviet Central Asian Republics) and about a billion people (Muslims tend to inflate the numbers). The present rash of political eruptions – whether in Kashmir, on the West Bank or Central Asia – points to the vitality in their societies. France has about a thousand mosques, Britain almost that number too (many of these converted flats and rooms). There are almost 6 million Muslims in Western Europe alone (over 1 million in the United Kingdom). However, these numbers exaggerate Islam's importance in Europe. Apart from small groups of local converts, most Muslims are immigrants or the descendants of immigrants. But the important point is that they are here to stay. In that sense they are Europeans.

The present encounter is coloured by the two earlier encounters, the first lasting centuries. It began with the rise of Islam, the arrival of its armies in Sicily and France, the duration of the crusades, and ended in the seventeenth century when the Ottomans were stopped at Vienna. Lasting centuries, the interaction between the two civilizations was deep at some points and marginal at others. It created in Europe an image of an aggressive and threatening Islam. Conversely, the encounters had little impact outside the Muslim areas of the Near and Middle East. From Mughal India or Indonesia, for instance, Western civilization was seen as distant and neutral, represented by traders and sailors. It was in the second encounter, in the last century, that the entire Muslim world was to be included in the colonial grip of European powers.

The brevity of the second encounter was matched by its ferocity. Lasting perhaps a century, the consequences of this encounter were devastating and in many ways are still with us. Social, cultural and intellectual life was affected and in parts damaged. Muslim responses varied. One came in the form of tribal uprisings. From the Sudan, where the Mahdi led the resistance, to Swat, where the Akhund symbolized it, the Muslim reaction appeared similar. These bold, passionate – if sometimes futile – responses created romantic images of the Muslim tribesman in the West as the 'noble savage': the Berber in north Africa, the Bedouin in the Middle East and the Pathan in north India.

At the end of the second encounter, after the Second World War, when Muslim nations began to emerge as independent powers, the difference between a triumphant Western civilization surging forward and a Muslim civilization racked with loss of intellectual confidence and direction was apparent. What the European imperialists did still matters in the Muslim world; it matters most in the creation by European fiat of the present political boundaries. Arabs in the Middle East, for instance, have good cause to blame outsiders for their political problems. Indeed, even the very term 'the Middle East' is Eurocentric; for Indians the region is 'the Middle West' or 'West Asia'.

Take the single most important key to contemporary politics in the Middle East: the Arab–Israeli conflict (also discussed in the previous chapter). It is widely seen as the source of all evils drawing in countries from across the world into the area. At the heart of this conflict are the origin and nature of the state of Israel. It is useful to be reminded that at the outset of the First World War, in spite of half a century of migration from Europe, there were still about 80,000 Jews in Palestine compared with about 650,000 Arabs. Today the demographic balance is quite reversed. The Arab plight in contemporary Israel – continued strikes, state oppression, unending curfew – illustrates how far down the road the two main protagonists have travelled. Arabs, who see Israel 'as a cancerous growth implanted in their body by the West' (Mansfield 1991: 346), ponder how different the shape of the Middle East would have been had the Zionist Congress accepted the British offer in 1903 of territory in Uganda. The West, therefore, is seen as a force in Muslim affairs.

Even a Muslim like the Aga Khan, who scrupulously avoids political controversy and is known to be sympathetic to the West, is concerned about the relationship between Islam and the West. He feels that Islam as a threat to order, as darkness, is never far from the Western mind:

> With Islam encompassing such a large area of the world with significant populations, western society can no longer survive in its own interest by being ill informed or misinformed about the Islamic world. They have to get away from the concept that every time that there is a bush fire or worse than that, it is representative of the Islamic world. So long as they make it representative of the Islamic world, they damage both themselves and their relations with the Islamic world itself because they are sending erroneous messages back. There is what I would call a 'knowledge vacuum'. It is hurting everyone.
>
> (Ahmed 1991g)

The present encounter, with its universal Western culture and pervasive technology, is perhaps the most forceful of onslaughts on Muslim civilization yet. Precisely because it is so amorphous and because it appears in the most unexpected forms in the most unexpected places, Islam appears so threatened and vulnerable. The VCR and TV need no passport or visa; they can invade the most isolated homes and challenge the most traditional values, and in their character and origin they are part and parcel of Western civilization (more of this later).

The global civilization: the triumph of the West

The West is at present the crucible of what is emerging as a universal culture, one united, quickened and even defined by what we are calling postmodernist developments. We call this 'Western' civilization in that the United States and Western Europe – predominantly white – are at its core, providing the ideas and technological discoveries that fire it. Within this civilization the United Kingdom, we pointed out, consciously plays Greece to the Rome of the United States, maintaining a 'special' relationship with it. English, therefore, plays an important role in this civilization, as the *de facto* lingua franca. Geographically, the civilization embraces non-Western nations like Australia and Israel, and even a non-Western people like Japan. After the emergence of Gorbachev, the USSR also looked for its place in this civilization. Other civilizations, even those distinct in their own traditions, like India or South-east Asia, are happily seduced.

If non-Western people have serious reservations about some components of the package – domination by American culture, for instance – they would still accept it for the other things it brings, such as democracy, human rights and literacy. So while middle-class 'superior' Asian intellectuals – Indians in Delhi or Japanese in Tokyo – will argue in the drawing room about the deleterious effects of Western culture on their society, their kids, wearing jeans, joggers and a baseball cap on their heads, with a Coke handy, will tell them not to make so much noise as they wish to follow the next episode of *Twin Peaks* on television.

An African or Asian in the favela or village would be forgiven if he thought the people in this civilization are almost interchangeable in their culture and media characters, their clothes, dialogue and style of living – that the white races all looked alike. The main characters are universal stars, globally recognized (see Chapter 6). The popular Australian television show *Neighbours* could be made in America – *Baywatch*, the American series, in Australia. The links between actors – or academics – across countries in this civilization are closer than ever before in history. What makes this instant exchange of ideas, images and values possible is the miracle of modern communications and the audio-visual media.

'The West', 'global civilization', 'the G-7 nations', 'the United States' and 'the United Kingdom' – we are using these terms loosely and interchangeably. Strictly speaking, each presents problems. We have pointed out that Australia is culturally and racially identified with the West yet is geographically not 'Western'; Germany, mighty Germany, has an under-developed eastern half hindering its growth. However, for our purposes the cultural borders of the nations that we have identified are flexible because they incorporate diverse peoples and embrace the entire globe; we may categorize them as forming the dominant world civilization. We also emphasize the central position created for themselves by the English-speaking nations – the United States, the United Kingdom, Canada and, indeed, Australia.

On the surface this civilization is defined by consumerism – junk food, clothes, leisure, rock music, television programmes, pop heroes, media celebrities. It also has a sacred pilgrimage place. Disneyland is like the Vatican for the Catholics, Makkah for the Muslims and Amritsar for the Sikhs. An entire civilization is here defined and many generations, in their millions, visit it. But unlike Rome, Makkah and Amritsar, Disneyland can be replicated. There are now two in the United States, one in Japan and another opening in France in 1992 (the one in Japan supports my point about some non-white societies aligning themselves with the West in the global civilization).

However, *Dallas* and *Dynasty*, Mickey Mouse and ET, Coke and jeans are only superficial symbols of this civilization. Central to it is the belief in capitalism, democracy and, related to it, the equality of women. At its best this civilization engenders a positive attitude to life, trust in science, a determined individualism, the urge always to find solutions, optimism and a respect for law. High standards of living, health and education are presupposed. The intellectual energy is exhilarating and unprecedented (over 60,000 books are published each year in Britain alone). 'The empires of the future', predicted that old imperial warrior, Churchill, 'are the empires of the mind'; a warning his Harvard audience, the élite of this civilization, no doubt took to heart.

As a commentator on American society observes, balancing its strengths and weaknesses:

> Nowhere has the debilitation of genuine literacy gone further (consider recent surveys of reading-comprehension and recognition in American high schools). But nowhere, also, have the conservation and learned scrutiny of the art or literature of the past been pursued with more generous authority. American libraries, universities, archives, museums, centres for advanced study, are now the indispensable record and treasure-house of civilization.
>
> (Steiner 1984: 429)

A time of crisis is a good time to judge a civilization. So, rather than looking at the Western technological achievements or successful democratic functioning of governments – which are in themselves impressive – let us look at the human response to political crises where human lives are involved. The return of the hostages – Brian Keenan, John McCarthy, Jackie Mann, Terry Waite and Terry Anderson – brought home several points to us.

The first was in the example it provided of the double misconception that defines dealings between Islam and the West. Muslims complained: why was the West so agitated about a few hostages, when thousands of Muslims had been killed or displaced due to the Western backing of Israel? They failed to realize the central importance of the individual, the single citizen, in Western society. The West condemned Muslims as barbaric for hostage-taking but did not connect cause and effect: they did not recognize the deep political injustices that drove the Muslims to these acts of desperation.

Nonetheless, it forced thinking Muslims to question: could Islam, the most important names of whose God were the Beneficent and the Merciful, ever support the kidnapping and torture of a sick man in his late seventies? Was this medieval Middle Eastern method really the most effective strategy with which to solve political problems today?

Then there was the personal dignity and humour of the hostages under the most harrowing circumstances and the warmth and support of their people – from government ministers and ambassadors attending them, to the media giving them top priority, to the person in the street refusing to forget them. Clearly, underneath the disintegration and dehumanization in the

West there were still wells of human feeling. Consider the youngest hostage and, therefore, the one with the most to be bitter about.

McCarthy's humour and charm, above all his lack of bile for his captors, were wholly commendable. In that moment of freedom from the night of captivity he symbolized a person any civilization could be proud of. For the demonstration of grace under pressure I salute John McCarthy. I also salute the Friends of John McCarthy, especially Jill Morrell and Chris Pearson, for not giving up hope and for unflinching loyalty.

The rapturous welcome of a nation moved to tears ('A very British Hero', wrote James Dalrymple in *The Sunday Times*, 11 August 1991; 'True Brits', declared Peter Millar in the same paper on 29 September 1991); the modest but self-possessed hero, quintessentially English; McCarthy was as the English like to see themselves. In writing of McCarthy the tabloids described him as the 'typical' English boy deriving his strength and poise from 'typical' rural England. They were right. The human drama provided us rare insights into the reservoirs of tradition and stability which still survive in rural society, which hold off the apocalyptic tidal wave of change coming from the cities.

Living in the English countryside I have observed that most villages still exhibit the social structure, values and organization of traditional society. My book *Out of Cambridgeshire* may never be written, but I can confirm this in the activities of those enjoying bowls and playing cricket on the village green, worshipping in the village church, gossiping in the village shop. And unlike dwellers in the cities they still smile and say 'Good morning'.

Western civilization is now the dominant, universal expression of humanity. Its most powerful weapon lies in the media, especially television (see Chapters 5 and 6). Dictators and nations have felt the impact of the media. Whoever controls the media is in control, McLuhan would have intoned, with Baudrillard assenting.

The ultimate proof of this argument, one confirming the cultural triumph of the West, came in August 1991 in Moscow: Boris Yeltsin hearing over and over again, for inspiration, Elvis Presley's 'Are you lonesome tonight?' during the critical days waiting for the military crackdown (see 'Elvis helped Yeltsin triumph' by Martin Walker in *The Guardian*, 26 August 1991). Cultural triumph in another direction came in Kuwait: George

Bush became one of the most popular names after the Gulf war for new-born Arab babies.

Within the context of this culture and its values instant celebrities, whether prostitute or princess, obsess the media and become universal figures overnight. The media allow the unthinkable, defying all racial stereotypes of a generation ago: in the late 1980s pop-star hysteria around a Russian leader – leading to a neologism, 'Gorbymania'; Japanese humour, *Kazuko's Karaoke Klub*, live before British television audiences and Japanese heavyweight wrestling shown as a regular, mainstream British weekly programme called *Sumo*; an Indian, Pamela Bordes, sells her sexual secrets to the British press and within weeks is a media star, Bombay planning feature films on her. (British MPs and newspaper editors in the late 1980s beat a path to her door clutching the rumoured sum of £500 in their sticky palms – although it is doubtful whether this is what Mrs Thatcher meant when she talked of the 'enterprise culture' for her Britain.)

A shouting and waving fan-following for a Russian political leader? Popular appreciation of Japanese humour? An Indian sex queen? These were unimaginable in the West a generation ago. They suggest the dissolving of racial and social stereotypes; it is the nature of the postmodernist age that makes this possible. The universal culture is thus not wholly defined by race or colour; it confirms the eclecticism and universalism that postmodernists profess.

The global civilization means dictators can escape to anywhere in the world from their countries when their people revolt against corruption and nepotism; it also means – as the cases of the Shah of Iran and President Marcos show – that they can be harried to an early death through relentless court notices and the media which are everywhere, ever-present, ever-judging. This is not good news for dictators; but it is hope for all oppressed people; also for those who enjoy the spectacle of the high and mighty suffering retribution.

A New World Order?

A political cartographer with a bold eye for simplification would reject the clumsy apparatus of global classification that has prevailed so far – First, Second, Third World, North–South, East–West and so on. He would divide the world map in the 1990s into two major categories: the civilizations that are *exploding* –

reaching out, expanding, bubbling with scientific ideas, economic plans, political ambitions, cultural expression – and those that are *imploding*, collapsing on themselves with economic, political and social crises which prevent any serious attempt at major initiatives. The former are, above all, exploding with optimism, with sights firmly fixed on the future; the latter are weighted down by their history, traditions, 'certainties', their ethnic and religious hatreds.

Whereas the Western or global civilization, in essence the G-7, is the example of the former, much of the rest of the world falls into the second category. South America, our cartographer would muse, has its corrupt dictators and chaotic inflation; Africa has its civil wars and starvation, and, at the heart of South Asia's problems lies the all-destroying communal violence which constantly pushes India and Pakistan to the brink of war – perhaps a nuclear one next time – and their per capita incomes below $400; China appears paralyzed with a geriatric leadership and economic stagnation, a situation from which the USSR emerged, to find itself staring at disintegration and civil war.

The imploding nations are in no position seriously to challenge or offer plausible alternatives to the exploding civilizations for world leadership. Only the Muslim world offers a global perspective with a potential for a role on the world stage. It does so in different ways: whether exporting a key element that drives the engines of the West or producing leaders (from Gaddafi to Khomeini to Saddam) whose actions challenge the West through regional or even global designs, or in the 10 million Muslims actually living in the West. Only the Muslim civilization appears poised both to implode and explode.

Western civilization – whenever historically exploding from Europe – has meant death and destruction: from the time of the crusades (usually launched with a wholesale massacre of Jews, setting the pattern for Europe's treatment of its minorities), to the sixteenth century when it wiped out the entire native population of the Caribbean; from the devastating consequences, in Africa, of slavery and transportation in the death-ships, to the decimation of the autochthonous tribes of Australia and the United States. And in the two world wars that shook this century Western civilization fought itself. Nothing on this scale had been seen before. Western civilization enveloped the entire globe in the madness of war; millions and millions of people were killed and entire nations obliterated.

The effects of the imperial explosion of eighteenth- and nineteenth-century Europe in the traditional societies of Africa and Asia haunt them still. Europe perverted what it could not destroy. They brought electricity, the telephone and the railway, Europeans announced imperiously. True, there was a beneficent contribution too. The colonies have also to thank the English, as we will see below, for bringing their language, their notions of politics and the game of cricket. But deportation, barbed or electric wire around villages and cultural mutants were another part of the colonial legacy. When they departed, Europeans drew ill-contrived boundaries to create nations, sometimes dividing tribes and villages in two. In one case, India and Pakistan shared a railway station: the platform was in one country, the ticket office in the other. Many of the problems of the Middle East and South Asia are traced directly to those hasty and ill-conceived exercises in nation-building.

The United States, it argues, has no imperial past; it is the greatest democracy in the world. This is correct. And individual Americans in private are often warm and caring people. But, in its role as the champion of the West from the middle of the twentieth century onwards, America has begun to acquire the historical, psychological and geo-political characteristics of an imperial power: an Imperial Rome in ancient history and an Imperial Europe in contemporary times. Visions of a New World Order, despatching troops all over the world to enforce it, and providing a lead to other nations in almost every human activity are imperial signs (or neo-imperial, if you like). The United States may be a reluctant Roman entrant to the imperial club, but is nevertheless there with the Romans and all the others.

The actions of America when dealing with native, non-white populations, therefore, have ominous historical resonances and do not inspire confidence; the treatment of the American Indians in the last century set the tone: Hiroshima and Nagasaki in 1945, napalm and carpet-bombing in Vietnam in the 1960s and the horrors of the Gulf war in 1991 were a logical sequence. The motto and promise of the typical American soldier to 'bomb them into the Stone Age' is as much a philosophical statement as a reflection on a historical and cultural tradition.

Each stage, each assault, is marked by a significant development – a quantum leap – in weaponry. The weapon comes to symbolize the epic nature of the triumph: the Colt 45 and

Winchester '73 – repeat-action revolver and gun – in the second half of the nineteenth century against the American Indians, the A-bomb against the Japanese in the middle of this century and the latest high-technology weapons deployed against the Iraqis at the end of it. The fact that the enemy did not possess the same weapon and was therefore disadvantaged had something to do with the outcome of the struggle. The imperial dictum about the Maxim gun best summed it up with smug honesty and clarity: the white man had it, the natives did not. But no quarter was given, no mercy shown by the victors; it did little to endear them to the vanquished.

It was precisely the revulsion against this philosophy which had helped to create the non-aligned movement in developing countries after independence. Those African and Asian leaders – like Nasser, Nehru and Sukarno – who hoped to avoid the trap of falling into one or other super-power camp nonetheless found themselves enmeshed in varying degrees in their global confrontation. Momentous action was often matched with symbolic gestures: Nasser nationalized the Suez Canal in 1956 while, at international social functions, he publicly refused to drink Coca-Cola as it represented American culture.

However, in the 1980s, change was taking place in both camps in opposite directions. While the United States surged ahead in political and military might, the USSR began to falter. *Perestroika* and *glasnost* had altered not only Soviet society but Soviet foreign policy as well. The Soviets were no longer prepared to back the Arabs merely to spite the Americans. Indeed, *glasnost* for Israel means more Jews to be settled on the West Bank and the replacement of Palestinian workers even from their menial jobs.

General Schwarzkopf, the Commander of the Allied forces in the Gulf war, publicly expressed his poor opinion of Saddam as a military leader. Saddam was not much better as a scholar of international affairs. He should have appreciated the changed international climate. Again and again the Soviets had come to the aid of the Arabs. After Nasser's defeat in 1967 they replaced his military losses and eventually had some 10,000 military advisers in Egypt. In 1973, when Arab armies proved they could take the initiative, the USSR again forced the United Nations Organization through the threat of unilateral action to declare a cease-fire in order to prevent Israeli victory.

It was Saddam's misfortune to be left facing the full might of the United States without the comfort of knowing that the USSR was waiting in the wings to pick up the pieces. It is this asymmetry which has upset the traditional balance in the Muslim world. All the old equations must now be thrown out of the window. The new reality is reflected in Israel's triumphant vindication as an ally of the United States (Sadat's declared view was that the United States held 99 per cent of the cards in the Middle East – a fact confirmed by the Madrid conference in 1991).

Previously, in the recent modern past, Afro-Asian countries had acquitted themselves honourably against aggressive Western powers; in the end they triumphed over the superior power, forcing it to quit. The French had to pack up and go home in Algeria, the Americans in Vietnam, the USSR in Afghanistan. It had been costly and bloody but victory was sweet; it was the triumph of David against Goliath. America in particular had its nose tweaked in the 1980s in the Middle East, when it tried to rescue its hostages in Iran and with the Shia suicide squad in Lebanon, but the Gulf war was different. Never before in history was a war so brutally, effectively and totally conducted with the aid of such sophisticated technology, and the results were as uneven as the power of the two sides. The Stealth bomber, the Cruise missile, the laser-guided 'smart' bomb, the Patriot missile, the TIALD and the MLRS, all supported by the latest satellite technology, made the Iraqis deaf, dumb and blind. After the war Muslims were asking who is next? Libya? Pakistan? There is no shortage of pretext: accusations of terrorism in one case, a nuclear programme in the other.

Afghanistan is another Muslim nation which finds itself precariously attempting to maintain a balance in the wake of the New World Order. It was the heroic Afghans who, without flinching, challenged the USSR when it was a super-power. The Victorian phobias that hung over the land like a pall – the Great Game, the fear of the Russian push to the warm waters, the mysterious stirrings of Central Asia that sent a flutter through the ranks of the political officials south of the Khyber Pass – have evaporated. Once favourites of the West, they now find themselves discarded like a pair of old boots. Hungry, divided and with no prospects in sight of a return to normality after a decade of civil war, they confront the costs: about 1 million dead, over 5 million displaced and the entire fabric of society in tatters. They may well ask: what was the struggle and sacrifice all about?

After the Gulf war the imperial triumphalism is unrestrained.

John Pilger, one of Britain's most perceptive journalists, bitterly ruminates on the aftermath of the war:

> The victory parades have been run again, in between the Alka Seltzer ads and the child abuse hot lines. 'We could have easily done it without the British and French', wrote the foreign editor of the *St Petersburg Times*. '. . . You can call this America assuming its God-given role as leader of the forces of light and night. You can even call it America as Head Honcho, Big Kahuna, Numero Uno . . .' The effortless, fluent inanities are now virtually unopposed. Power is unabashed, and celebrated with all the ignorant certainties that echo the totalitarianism over which the Now Generation claims to have triumphed.
>
> Forty million Americans have no medical care [he notes with disgust], yet power triumphant has been reason enough for the Congress to approve $2 billion for a weapon called a Superconducting Supercollider. And the Pentagon confidently expects much more: $500 billion for weapons for which an enemy is still pending, including $24 billion for Ronald Reagan's Star Wars fantasy.
>
> (Pilger 1991b)

There is a school of thought which holds that the United States as an economic and political power is declining. Another school opposes this view; they claim it is reviving. But whether we support the 'decline' theory or its opposite, the 'revivalist' theory, American cultural ascendancy appears unstoppable and irreversible. The United States may well be on the decline, but let us consider the example of the British Empire. After its collapse, its language, English, continues to flourish and spread.

The G-7 summit in London in July 1991 produced a photograph that neatly sums up my argument about the New World Order. It was the official, formal group photograph marking the conclusion in which the leaders of the G-7 nations lined up alongside Gorbachev. The photograph may well have been the straw that broke the camel's back and triggered the coup in Moscow in the next month. Gorbachev, begging bowl in hand, was thought by the conservatives to have sold out and humiliated his country. The English-speaking members of the group, the United States, the United Kingdom and Canada, formed a distinct group which provided the cultural lead; Italy, France and

Germany, the Europeans, were not always comfortable with this idea but went along with it; Japan, the seventh partner, was not only looking to the United States as Top Cat but also as a sparring partner for world trade. So, although Japan and Europe may be economic competitors of the United States, they are part of the same political and civil order.

The message to the planet was clear. These countries would direct and dominate the world order. Like stern teachers in a classroom they would keep a close eye on the turmoil in the Muslim world, the famine in Africa, the dictators in South America. A sharp slap on the wrist would be administered for errant behaviour (either the military blitz inflicted on Saddam Hussein early in 1991 or the media blitz on the Moscow coup-planners later in the year). They would guard their economic supremacy jealously, thereby reinforcing their pre-eminent political and cultural position.

The desire of the West to dominate the world can be explained largely in political and cultural terms, but there are also other compelling causes. In order to maintain the high standards of living in the West, the planet's resources must be diverted to it. Arab oil needs to be at the disposal of the West. For this purpose both the carrot and the stick are used. Hence we see the spectacle which causes so much anger and anguish in Asia and Africa of corrupt Arab rulers in collusion with equally corrupt people from the West. Similarly, global trade and financial markets must be dominated by the West to maintain its hegemony. There is thus an overlapping of economic, financial, social and cultural interests which explains the compulsive need of the West to assert itself over the globe.

The consequences are apparent. Two almost distinct species of homo sapiens appear to be evolving. Perhaps a visual image best illustrates this while raising deeply disturbing thoughts of the future. It would be difficult to explain to the proverbial Martian that those people living on the continent of Africa and those on that of north America belong to the same species. In wealth, facilities, life expectancy, health and ownership of property they diverge so much as to raise the question whether they can close the gap even by the end of the next century. The image is a clear signal of the triumph of the West. Although there are many in the West who are deeply concerned about these divisions – and let us not underestimate their goodwill and vision – there are far too many whose only response appears to be: Quick! Man the frontiers and close the borders, for we must not allow these foreigners over here.

The problem with this civilization is the hole where the heart should be, the vacuum inside; there is no moral philosophy or set of principles that drives it. What gives it its dynamic energy is individualism, the desire to dominate, the sheer drive to acquire material items, to hoard. Every technological development must be gathered into your home; it is the obsession to out-buy, out-eat and out-sex the Joneses next door. Not much of a philosophy, you would say. You would be right. Such frenetic energy keeps society moving, but all the evidence – presented by its own analysts – suggests dissatisfaction and despair.

For the African or Asian we met above, this civilization would, more likely than not, be seen as a kaleidoscopic jumble of caricatures and stereotypes (see 'The growth of occidentalism' in Chapter 4). In that light it would be apparent that the civilization does not have the answers for the planet; indeed, in its arsenal of nuclear weapons, its greedy destruction of the environment, its insatiable devouring of the world's resources, its philosophy of consumerism at all costs, it is set to terminate life on earth in the near future unless it can change its ways fundamentally. Although many of its citizens lead lives that are pleasant and free, many others do not. Those sleeping in cardboard boxes in the cities have a story to tell us. For those who do not belong to this culture – like people in Africa and Asia – there is little it can offer; it would even build an electric fence around its borders to prevent them from invading and contaminating it, to become 'Fortress United States' and 'Fortress Europe'. It still looks down on others as inferior on the basis of race and religion. So, as it dazzles the African and Asian with images of plenty, of a cornucopia, of *Dallas* and *Dynasty*, it withholds access to them. These tantalizing images are thus no more than dangerous illusions for the majority of the people on the planet. They cannot solve anything; but they can, through the envy and desire they spread, spoil a great deal of contentment, patience and balance – the virtues of traditional society which no longer have the power to soothe or mollify.

Much depends on those who can build bridges between the two civilizations. Unfortunately, intellectuals appear to have abandoned the role of objective commentators. Into the vacuum have stepped the prejudices and stereotypes of the media. Historians and social scientists, as Edward Said has so forcefully reminded us, have themselves fallen victim to them (also see Ahmed 1991f). Perhaps novelists could play their historical role of explaining and hence bringing people together. E.M. Forster's humanist credo, 'Only connect', is now more relevant than ever in the context of my arguments. But as Salman Rushdie – like Forster educated at King's College, Cambridge, though of another generation – has shown, the novelist can also disconnect, creating hatred and division.

The racial arrogance of Western civilization

Western civilization has a legitimate world-view on questions of race and identity, self and nationhood which are rooted in European history. The genealogy of this world-view is to be traced directly to Darwin, then, nimbly skipping past Christ, to the Greeks back to Achilles the warrior, Homer the poet and Plato the philosopher. At the time, and in the context of the stifling, church-dominated intellectual climate of Victorian England, which saw both society and the cosmos as harmonious and balanced and dominated by a benign divinity, Darwin appeared like an icono-clastic revolutionary. He too, however, was echoing the Greeks. Sparta had already arrived at the perfect method to ensure the selection of the fittest: frail babies were simply left outside to face the elements; their death was a testimony to Spartan philosophy.

This intellectual and cultural legacy set the tone for the smug and self-congratulatory questions that were embedded in the Western world-view. Were not these nations living evidence of the survival of the highest order? Were they not at the top of the world hierarchy and its natural leaders? Had not the most advanced industry and technology, the latest ideas of science and progress, gone into their successful breeding?

Inferior species in Africa and Asia, mostly seen as weak and sick, were doomed. Perhaps some, like the 'noble savage', evoked a romantic sympathy; he was duly acknowledged. But he too was doomed to extinction for he was a misfit in the world of science and technology. So there was no cause for tears. Nature was cruel but fair; only the deserving survived. The aggressive desire to domin-ate in every walk of life – tennis, sex, driving a car or commerce – may be so explained. In this civilization, superior technology, not morality, mattered. The Western geo-political world-view thus had a coherent, if questionable, scientific underpinning.

Marx's vision of a common humanity, at the heart of which lay the concern for the less privileged, was essentially in the Semitic tradition. But having once dismantled God and Christ, love and humility, care for *all* human beings, the way was open to Hiroshima. Hell was here on earth and it wore the face of the enemy; the way to heaven lay in its destruction.

This attitude explains the ambivalence to the economic and social suffering of those African and Asian societies on the verge of starvation or civil war. It explains the phrase used by the soldiers during the Gulf war: a 'turkey-shoot'. This not only reflected Achilles but also Darwin: the turkey was a clumsy bird which was neither strong nor able to fly; it was fit to be preserved only for the festive table. There is simply too little Christianity and too much of the Greeks in the Western world-view.

Muslims, harking back to the first two encounters with Christianity, and out of step with developments outside their world, suspect its hand in the present encounter. They are wrong. In this global civilization true Christians – those who follow Christ both in word and deed – are few and far between and certainly not in command of policy. Popular opinion defines a good Christian as one who goes to church on Sunday – there is little else expected, so minimal are the demands of religion nowadays – regardless of the fact that every commandment may be broken during the rest of the week. The majority of the population openly declare their disbelief and even mock the church. A Muslim visiting the West for the first time may hear the words 'Jesus' or 'Christ' frequently and be impressed. What he does not realize is that the name has been reduced to a swearword, an exclamation, and little more.

There are therefore major contradictions, deep flaws, in contemporary Western civilization (see Chapter 6, 'The demon and the disintegration of the family', for a fuller discussion). Its worst aspect is that it encourages ethnocentricity and arrogance towards 'others' and 'foreigners', and is intolerant of those that do not match its standards or conform to its values. Self-doubt and critical self-analysis, so central to the European intellectual tradition, are dismissed as leftist or liberal griping; the people of goodwill are thus marginalized.

Below we will examine the growing cancer of racism in society, which is an aspect of the European intellectual and cultural tradition. Because imperial colonization is only a generation away racial tensions lie just under the surface. The xenophobia is marked in the imperial popular novelists like Rider Haggard and Dornford Yates as well as contemporary ones like Kingsley Amis (see his *I Like it Here*, 1958). Colonel McNeile's Bulldog Drummond hated 'negroes, Jews, hunchbacks, dwarfs or other inferior beings', those who were not members of the 'Breed' (of Englishmen). John Buchan did not disguise his anti-Semitism in his most famous novel *The Thirty-nine Steps*.

However, there was also the likeable 'dusky nabob' in a Billy Bunter story, or the noble Pathan in a John Masters novel. Then there was E.M. Forster's Dr Aziz (*A Passage to India*, 1967). By depicting an Asian so successfully, Forster almost single-handedly demolishes the belief in Asia that Europeans cannot truly understand 'orientals'. Aziz is unique in his sympathetically accurate portrayal. Even the contradictions – dreaming of fighting alongside the Mughal Emperor Aurangzeb one minute and visiting the Calcutta brothels the next – only help to add to the vividness of his character. Underneath the noise, clash, bustle and confusion of the Anglo-Indian encounter we discern the message of a common humanity, of the equality of races. And Forster had matched his words to his actions: his book was dedicated to his friend Ross Masood (the grandson of Sir Sayyed whom we met in Chapter 1). All this is remarkable considering it was taking place during the high noon of Empire. It is a salutary lesson for those who view the confrontation of cultures simplistically.

In contemporary English literature there is no Empire as a reference point, no royal princes and chivalrous tribesmen to draw on. Dr Aziz in Britain, transplanted from his beloved India, would become the owner of the corner shop – the equivalent of the universally resented Indian stereotype, 'Mr Patel'. The transformation is a result of complex historical processes; these include the modern story of European imperialism, immigration from the colonies, racism in Europe and times of economic and political change. The Asian is an alien and threatening presence. No longer romantic and mysterious, he is contemptible and smelly. There is inane triumphalism and, lurking not too far underneath it, bigotry and racism:

> ... or in the case of the 'Golden Crescent', the laboratories of Pakistan from which heroin came into Europe. In [the policeman] Hodge's mind, small dark men, Pakis, Turks,

Iranians and Arabs, converged on Britain by donkey or container truck or the occasional ship: always at night, a black and sinister movement of the deadly opiates financed by men who lived in large houses and belonged to country clubs and had yachts.

(Sharpe 1985: 85)

But these issues lay dormant. They found a focus, a flash-point, in the Rushdie crisis, which exploded in the media. In that sense the crisis of *The Satanic Verses* in the 1980s in Britain was not only about literary ideas and freedom of expression. It was also about race and religion in British society. One of the major causes of the explosion of the British Muslims was the feeling of not being valued in the larger community. They had worked hard and long to create comfortable lives for themselves and generate wealth for the nation, but simmering resentments had grown over a generation, both within and without. It found expression in the Rushdie affair, a cry of identity, a need to be heard and understood.

A Muslim writer, commenting on anti-Semitism in the West, makes this chilling point while linking it to recent racist attacks on Muslims in the wake of the Rushdie affair:

I have come to think that anti-semitism, endemic in Western culture, has more or less been forced underground. Thankfully, and for good historical reason it is no longer easy to attack Jews publicly or depict them in fiction as unpleasant caricatures. But these salutary taboos do not extend to Muslims. I would even be so bold as to argue that there has been a transfer of contempt from Jews to Muslims in secular Western culture today. Many Muslims share this fear: indeed, one has written that 'the next time there are gas chambers in Europe, there is no doubt concerning who'll be inside them' (Shabbir Akhtar in *The Guardian*, 27 February 1989).

(Kabbani 1989: 11)

This may appear far-fetched, but a former Lord Mayor of Bradford, Mohammad Ajeeb, has actually received abusive letters saying, 'What you deserve is the gas chambers' (Webster 1990: 107). There is disturbing evidence of widespread racist hatred breaking into physical violence against Muslims. The following account of the senseless shooting of a young Pakistani boy in England confirms this:

Last summer 19-year-old Stephen Lamb stole a car and rifle and drove round Oldham taking potshots at random. He hit a black man, a white man and an Asian schoolboy, Tahir Akram, who bled to death. Mohammad Akram's grief for his firstborn son was a timeless lamentation: 'Everywhere I go my son used to be with me. Tahir. . . . Therefore I don't feel like going to friends because I miss him a lot. Everywhere I go brings these memories back and that's why everybody thinks I'm a bit changed. To be honest, all is dark for me now, I can't find the way out. There is something that is squeezing my heart all the time. I loved him so much.' O Absalom my son, my son Absalom . . . 'There were two coloured guys and one of the people in front said "He'll do". He didn't expect it. His face was really hilarious. We were all laughing at it. He was so shocked. That's all Stephen went up for, to shake them. We saw a lickle Paki family and they was walking and the next thing we knew another shot were fired. Stephen was saying the lickle boy had fell but we were still laughing at the face on the coloured boys, we weren't really interested in the lickle Paki boy. . . . Next day, when we heard he was dead, he said, "He's only a Paki anyway".'

(Banks-Smith, discussing the documentary *First Tuesday*, Yorkshire TV, 1990 in *The Guardian* 5 September).

The young 'Paki' boy is not an uncommon victim. In this account the victim is a father, the working head of a household:

Asrof Ali was watching cricket on television with his five children in his council flat in Chingford, east London, when there was a banging at the door. . . . 'I went to see what was happening and they said "You fucking black bastard, why don't you go back to your own country?" Then they hit me'. . . . His neighbours left him lying on the floor in front of his terrified children with a broken nose, cut face and mouth. It was the third attack apart from regular abuse about 'smelly food'. The next day the neighbour warned his children: 'If your father tells the police, we'll shoot him.' . . . 'I don't mind if they kill me,' says Mr Ali, 'but I have five children between the ages of three and 11 and I worry about my wife and family.' . . . He does not finish work until midnight and returns to a dimly lit car park with racist graffiti on the walls. Mr Ali has had his own door daubed with 'KKK' accompanied by the swastika. He says he approaches his flat 'like a cat' because he does not want to alert the neighbour who lives nearby.

(Campbell 1990)

There is no end in sight to these incidents (see 'Stephen Cook reports on an estate in East London where Bengalis are trapped in their homes by violence and a housing shortage' in *The Guardian*, 12 September 1991).

A major report concluded that Asian families seal their letter-boxes to prevent arson attacks, 5-year-old children are spat at on their way to school and women are forced to shop together for self-protection (Waltham Forest Council 1990; also see Green 1990). The report, 'Beneath the surface, an inquiry into racial harassment in the London Borough of Waltham Forest', is the most extensive concerning a borough. It took two years to compile and catalogues everything from murder to constant verbal abuse. The report cites the case of Parveen Khan and her three children, who were all burnt to death after the family's home was set alight in 1981. Her husband, Yunus, has since died of a heart attack. No one has been prosecuted for the murders. As the report said: 'There was an almost fatalistic acknowledgement of racial harassment as a fairly common occurrence. Perpetrators are confident nothing will happen to them' (ibid.).

Rushdie, unreliable on Islam, is worth citing on racism. He knows the former second-hand, mainly through reading orientalist literature, much of it tainted by colonial and racial prejudice – but he has experienced the latter first-hand in Britain:

Four hundred years of conquest and looting, four centuries of being told that you are superior to the Fuzzy-Wuzzies and the wogs, leave their stain. This stain has seeped into every part of the culture, the language and daily life; and nothing much has been done to wash it out.

For proof of the existence of this stain, we can look, for instance, at the huge, undiminished appetite of white Britons for television series, films, plays and books all filled with nostalgia for the Great Pink Age. Or think about the ease with which the English language allows the terms of racial abuse to be coined: wog, frog, kraut, dago, spic, yid, coon, nigger, Argie. Can there be another language with so wide-ranging a vocabulary of racist denigration?

(Rushdie 1991: 130)

Rushdie is unfair to England. The same winds of racism blow across other lands. Le Pen talks of the 'smell and noise' of the immigrants; even the lofty office of the Prime Minister of France echoes this crude racist sentiment. And after the reunification of Germany the Nazi ghost, re-arisen, stalks the land, terrorizing immigrants. The war-cries, *'Ausländer Raus'*, 'Foreigners Out' and *'Juden Raus'*, 'Jews Out', reverberate throughout Germany. The Afro-Asian immigrant community in Europe is in danger of becoming increasingly isolated, increasingly the butt of European racism, as once were the Jews:

> Harlem Desir, founder of the French anti-apartheid move-ment, SOS Racisme, warns of aggression against ethnic minorities in the 1990s in Europe. 'In France, these com-munities, scorned and treated like second-class citizens, turn in on themselves and breed hatred', he has said. 'Western Europe is now the biggest recipient of immigrants. Yet unlike the US, it does not have the immigration culture of a melting pot. We need a new social contract which takes no notice of ethnic origin. There is a new wall around Europe and it passes through the Mediterranean,' said Desir.

(Bunting 1990)

No institution, however sacrosanct, is immune to these dangerous winds stirring across Europe. Even Cambridge University, that ancient and honourable institution, idyllic home of so many foreign students, was touched by the prevalent strain of racism in British society. A porter was reported to have turned away a top reggae band from his college with the words, 'Who wants to hear a bunch of nig-nogs playing anyway?' (*Varsity*, on 23 February 1990, reported the matter as a front-page story with the headline, 'Racism Row at Queen's Gig'). When pressed for an explanation, the porter placed his feelings on record: 'Well, I'm a racist bastard – what about it?' The matter died down after apologies were offered all round and accepted. But the porter's sentiments revealed faithfully the mood of a growing section of society at large (as we will also see in the next chapter).

The emergence of racism's focus on Muslims – 'He's only a Paki anyway' – is a major challenge to Europe's notions of humanism and its self-image as a civilized society, but, however fascinating the discussion, it must lie outside the scope of my arguments. Nonethe-less, it is clear that racism threatens more than Muslim immigrants.

What can Islam give to the global civilization?

In the main, Muslim civilization appears to be at variance with Western civilization. The lives of individuals in urban areas or small groups living in the West are exceptions. In its attitude to the deepest values – democracy and the position of women – Muslim societies have been sharply faulted by the West. In particular, Muslim politics are in flux. Most of the Muslim nations are ruled by authoritarian figures in or out of uniform, often employing an Islamic idiom to support their rule. Corruption is endemic, and law and order constantly threatens to collapse. The picture for Muslim education is also bleak. An uninspiring, stifling mediocrity hangs over intellectual endeavour. Limited incentives for innovative work, bureaucratic interference, low salaries, political pressure and departmental jealousies discourage the movement toward excellence. The average person in Western countries lives about one-third longer than his Muslim counterpart, his life is healthier and freer of tyrannical rulers and political instability. The scientific discoverers, the Nobel Prizewinners, are mostly to be found in Western civilization. When a Muslim learns science and technology, he is usually lured by the more congenial conditions to live in the West, and no longer contributes to his own society.

In its uncontrolled population growth – at 3 per cent the highest in the world – its appalling education standards, its general poverty, its horrifying treatment of political prisoners, its coups and its intolerance of academic excellence, the Muslim world appears to have little to offer. It is no wonder that one of the Arab reformers, Abduh, lamented in Europe, 'I saw no Islam but many Muslims', and, at home, he declared, 'I saw Islam but no Muslims'. But most of these ills of Muslim society are self-created. These are Muslim lapses, a sign of social decay, not Islamic features.

On the threshold of the twenty-first century, what can Islamic civilization contribute to the world? The answer is, a great deal. Its notion of a balance between *din*, religion, and *dunya*, the world, is a worthy one. It can provide a corrective and a check to the materialism that characterizes much of contemporary civilization, offering instead compassion, piety and a sense of humility. The philoprogenitivity of Muslims is a social fact. The qualities mentioned above underline the moral content of human existence, they suggest security and stability in family life, in marriage and in the care for the aged. Recent signs in Western societies indicate that perhaps the time is ripe to re-admit care and compassion into human relations; here, too, postmodernist sensibilities can help.

In its abjuration of materialism, Sufism provides a balance to the dominant values of Western civilization, although many see the impact of Sufism as limited in our world (see the next chapter). Especially in the Sufistic message of *sulh-i-kul* (peace with all), Islam has a positive message of peace and brotherhood to preach. This message is irrespective of colour or creed and has stood the test of time. Not surprisingly, Sufistic Islam has made significant inroads in the West, especially among European converts.

Islam places knowledge at the highest level of human endeavour. Repeatedly the Quran and the sayings of the Prophet urge the acquisition of knowledge. Indeed, the word knowledge, *ilm*, is the most used after the name of God in the Quran. The Prophet urged his followers to 'seek knowledge, even unto China'. Human beings are asked in the Quran to think of and marvel at the variety confronting them: 'And among His signs is the creation of the heavens and the earth, and the variations in your languages and your colours' (Surah 30: 22).

Change and re-interpretation are embedded in Islamic history and text. The following discourse between the Prophet and Muadh ibn Jabal, a judge, on his way to the Yemen clearly indicates the principle:

Prophet: How will you decide a problem?
Muadh: According to the Quran.
Prophet: If it is not in it?
Muadh: According to the *sunna* [Islamic custom].
Prophet: If it is not in that either?
Muadh: Then I will use my own reasoning.

The Islamic principles which encourage flexibility and rational choice are reflected in the exchange: *ijtihad*, independent judgement; *shura*, consultation; and *ijma*, consensus. Clearly, rationality and man's own judgement play a part in arriving at decisions.

The Greens: Western gift or global philosophy?

It is the ambivalent love–hate relationship of the Afro-Asian world with the West that ensures suspicion and even rejection of ideas emanating from the latter, however worthy or mutually beneficial. Take the new religion of the Greens, which will grow in strength into the twenty-first century (for some recent literature, see Allaby 1989; Hecht and Cockburn 1989; Kemp and Wall 1990; K. Lee 1989; McKibben 1990; Oppenheimer and Boyle 1990; Pearce, Markandya and Barbier 1989; Ponting 1991; M. Robinson 1989; Weiner 1991; also see Ahmed 1990e).

It is believed that the ecological damage to the planet is becoming irreparable. We face cataclysm unless purification begins now; the dangers of CFCs, depletion of the ozone layer, deforestation and pollution, the greenhouse effect – also buzz words – are common knowledge. Every day new additions are made to the list of horrors.

The green religion has its prophets and high priests, its loony fringe and fanatical fundamentalists. The main weapon in its armoury is the media. Stars like Jane Fonda and Robert Redford advertise its aims and speak on its behalf. 'Looking good' is an intrinsic part of its projection. And the media message works. But away from the hype the movement's philosophy deserves the support of every right-minded person. Perhaps it is already too late; perhaps the process is already irreversible. The modernist complacency and trust in progress must change. This religion is assuming a central intellectual position in the global civilization that we identified earlier as beginning to dominate the world.

I grew up in Abbottabad, named after its first British Deputy Commissioner, Abbott, and a popular colonial hill station, in Hazara, northern Pakistan. This was in the early 1950s. The thick forests of juniper, fir and pine, the babbling streams and the quiet, slow pace of life were enchanting. The air was intoxicating with the scent of fruit and flowers in spring. The colonial British called Hazara the district made by nature for them in the Gazetteer of 1907, still the best authority for the area.

Now the forests of Hazara are devastated, its streams blocked for ill-planned housing schemes, and small shops and industrial units have sprung up haphazardly. The politicians have cut down the forests mercilessly. The common people, always wise, call their politicians *jungle chor*, the forest thieves. It is an apt title.

Trees mean money, money means buying votes, votes mean office and the capacity to cut forests with impunity and to build shops and houses. It is a devastating cycle of greed and destruction familiar in most parts of the world.

Traditional civilizations and philosophies have much to teach us. Islam's very colour is green and its concept of the good life, Paradise, is replete with gardens, orchards and rivers. Like Coleridge's Kubla Khan who made the pleasure-dome 'Enfolding sunny spots of greenery', Muslims were always enthusiastic garden builders. The first thing that any sensible king did on accession was to lay out gardens and running streams. One has only to think of Shalimar in Kashmir, at one end of the Muslim world, and Granada in Spain, at the other. References to Paradise – of pure and clean water, milk and honey – litter the Quran. Balance and symmetry, austerity and humility, are constantly emphasized. A good Muslim is a tenant, not owner, of the earth; he must tread it softly.

The non-Western world is cynical, therefore, about this new present or 'gift' from the West. It recalls earlier dealings, like the business about the Opium wars in China during European imperialism. The West labelled the Chinese 'opium eaters'. The irony was it had introduced opium to them, pressed the Chinese to buy it, forced the Indians to grow it through punitive taxation systems, then sold it to the Chinese. This cynical imperial cycle may be mythical but it is widely believed in Asia. The Chinese have cause to snigger at the Western suggestion that they forgo the convenience of the fridge to save the ozone layer.

Earth Day Special, the one-and-a-half-hour American television extravaganza, was illustrative of the postmodernist media's treatment of green issues (shown on BBC1 on 27 May 1990). It was hyped as a 'multi-media celebration'. A lot of it was schlock, but the message was important. So was the confirmation of the spokesmen, all media stars, including ET and Bugs Bunny. It is significant that politicians and academics were conspicuous by their absence; Carl Sagan, who appeared, is as much a media star as an academic. This civilization wants slickly packaged and simplified ideas, not inaccessible tomes, however worthy. It only wishes to see and hear the beautiful and the glamorous, and not even that for long. The time span of its attention is less than a minute on television. What were also conspicuous by their absence were voices from Africa and Asia. Here was cultural ethnocentricity at its height. Once again the prophets of the West were speaking at, not to, the non-Western world. Once again the latter will be wary of what they offer. It is perhaps this which explains why the full impact of the horror of what is probably the world's greatest ecological disaster, the burning oil wells in Kuwait in 1991, is not appreciated in the Muslim world.

THE CONTINUING IMPACT OF THE EUROPEAN COLONIAL LEGACY

When the Europeans abandoned their colonies after the Second World War, they left behind permanent, continuing influences. Some of these were beneficial, other parts were not. In both aspects, for the purposes of our argument, the postmodernist factor is crucial. The dominant global civilization of the West also encourages the survival of many features from the colonial past in these societies but it is the age of postmodernism which allows certain cultural and political features which lay dormant until a decade ago to surface.

Macaulay's chickens: the Anglo-Indian encounter

In order to appreciate the cultural aspect of the European legacy in South Asia let us first look at the celebrated Anglo-Indian encounter. One important strand of the encounter can be traced back to Macaulay and nineteenth-century India. Lord Thomas Babington Macaulay was one of those extraordinary Victorian savants, a high priest of European humanism. Through his famous Minute on Education in 1835 he helped to change the course of Indian history. Britain was to create an Indian élite, junior allies in imperial progress: 'a class of persons, Indian in blood and colour but English in taste, in opinions, in morals and in intellect'. The élite, in turn, would assist in guiding India to a better future. It was a bold and clear-headed vision. In one move, native languages and values were made redundant. Simply put, the more like an Englishman an Indian thought and behaved the higher he scored on Macaulay's scale. A paradox lies at the heart of the matter: the more English the Indian becomes, the more alienated he is from his own people and the culture which he is meant to represent.

The Minute set the stage for an Indian response. It came in the uprisings in 1857. However, the fury did not last and that year was a decisive turning point in the Anglo-Indian encounter. British rule began in earnest; the Mughal Emperor was banished from India, the Mughal Empire ceased to exist and English now became the undisputed lingua franca of the subcontinent. The Crown took over the Indian administration from the East India Company, the Indian Civil Service exams were instituted, and schools and colleges modelled after English ones were started. Of the public schools Aitchison is known as the Eton of Pakistan and, in India, Doon School and St Paul's are just two of the many well-known ones. These institutions survived after the colonial period was over, although changed in style and spirit. Above all a new political culture developed, emphasizing liberal and humanist values.

The impact of the synthesis of cultures was far-reaching in three fields: politics, language (English), and sports, especially cricket. In politics, the founding fathers of India and Pakistan – Gandhi, Nehru, Radhakrishnan, Jinnah, Liaqat – best symbolize the Anglo-Indian encounter. Although they opposed the colonial British, they nonetheless score high on Macaulay's scale, with their Oxbridge and London education. Their written work, even their thinking, would be in English and their political inspiration would come from Westminster. Indeed, to critics in their community they were more English than native. Nehru's enchantment with Keats and Jinnah's with Shakespeare would survive their entrance into the hurly-burly of Indian politics.

The three activities encouraged a link with global networks, common points of reference – and there was a defined geographical and spatial centre in the imperial city of London. They allowed a common sense of humanity, of belonging, which at certain points transcended the real differences in race, religion and nationality. Black or brown – Nehru in politics, West Indian cricketers, writers of Indian origin like V.S. Naipaul – they would be known and acknowledged throughout the English-speaking world.

Conversely, those high on the scale were seen as selling out and therefore were reprimanded by traditional elements: the *ulema* called Sir Sayyed and Mr Jinnah *kafir*; the Bharatiya Janata Party (BJP) in India denounced Nehru – in retrospect – for not being a good Hindu, as too Anglicized; Imran Khan has been publicly warned in Pakistan not to rub the ball the way he does so near the groin as it is provocative and may inflame female passion.

Well after independence from the British in 1947 Macaulay's

impact would be visible. The person of Field Marshal Ayub Khan of Pakistan, with his Sandhurst training, golf and *shikar* (hunting), clipped moustache and British bearing typifies it. The Foreign Office in London would benignly explain away his martial law as 'benevolent dictatorship'. In the 1960s the Western press would affectionately describe him as 'barrel-chested and Sandhurst trained'. It is with Idi Amin that the image of barrel-chested Field Marshals trained by the British took a knock. Military dictatorship was one thing but stocking human heads in the fridge quite another matter.

There was no escape from Macaulay in South Asia. All of us were affected in varying degrees. Of his legacy, I enjoy cricket, believe that the only method of conducting sensible politics is through parliamentary democracy and enjoy the English language through which I was allowed access to the literature of the world. It was an escape from the isolation often imposed on me by my postings in some of the most remote corners of Pakistan. A collection of Shakespeare plays, the essays of E.M. Forster and those of George Orwell, P.G. Wodehouse stories, an Oxford selection of English verse – battered copies of these were invariably to be found in my baggage and I was grateful. The books were congenial company, trusted friends. Engaging with writers in other societies also helped me to understand my own culture and tradition better; it helped to reaffirm my own faith. Perhaps because of this I was able to appreciate critically the beneficial impact of the West. There was also an unexpected bonus. Because of their English translation from the original I was able to read Babar's memoirs, Ibn Battuta's travels and Ibn Khaldun's ideas (see Chapter 4). I had to thank the English language for helping me to discover the richness of my own Islamic cultural legacy.

English in South Asia has produced a significantly rich literary harvest (see Hobson-Jobson, the legendary dictionary of British India for mutual linguistic interaction). As early as 1913 an Indian, Tagore, whose work was a synthesis of Indian languages and English, won a Nobel Prize for Literature; other Indians would win it too. The literary sophistication of South Asians has touched new heights in the writing of V.S. Naipaul and Nirad Chaudhuri. True to the end these two committed Anglophiles have retired to write in rural England, the latter in Oxford. Writers like Ruth Jhabvala and Anita Desai, with film-makers like

James Ivory and Ismail Merchant, have produced popular films
for international audiences based on their work. English, however
uneven its quality, remains a major language in South Asia.
Indeed, so high was considered the standard of English in Madras
that a common joke had Shakespeare reappearing from the next
world to sit – and fail – the Shakespeare paper in the MA exam. It
is possible, even in the remotest areas, to be asked who one
prefers, Milton or Shakespeare.

In sports, especially in that quintessential English game,
cricket, many figures gained international reputations. 'Cricket',
Nandy began his book on cricket, 'is an Indian game accidentally
discovered by the English' (Nandy 1989: 1). Some South Asians
became legends, like Ranjitsinhji, known in cricket as Ranji (ibid.:
57). Others, also Oxbridge, like Ranji's nephew, Duleep, Kardar,
Pataudi and Imran Khan, would also be high on Macaulay's scale.

However jolly and convivial the atmosphere at the cricket club,
questions of race and colour were never far from the game. This
is perfectly illustrated by a well-known story of Ranji. The great
cricketer was playing for England against Australia and had just
hit a magnificent six. 'He is a prince, you know', said an English
spectator to the Australian sitting next to him. 'Do you have a
prince in your team?' he asked in triumph. The very next ball
Ranji was clean bowled. The English fan was quick to change his
opinion. 'Bloody nigger', he muttered.

It is in the three critical areas we have identified – alone, or as
a combination – that other groups like the Arabs or the Afghans
are found wanting. Though both are obsessed with horses,
another primordial English cultural streak, they neither had the
educational network of India nor were familiar with the English
language. Westminster meant nothing to them and they did not
play cricket. It was a complete lack of cultural communication.
Try explaining a Chinaman or silly mid-off to an Arab or Afghan.
Bedouin robes may look impressive billowing on camels in
extravaganzas like *Lawrence of Arabia* but would inhibit the fast
bowler in his delivery; the shifting sand is not much good for
cricket pitches or grounds either; and the BBC television revival
of the film revealed how much it depended on the costumes and
desert scenery. Even when cricket matches have been successfully
organized, as at Sharjah, the teams have been foreign.

Arabs themselves are conscious of these features. The Iraqi
ambassador to Paris, Dr Abdul Razak al-Hashimi, who was thrown

into world prominence during the Kuwait crisis in 1990–91, declared, "Iraq's strength is in part derived from its refusal to swallow afternoon tea and other legacies of British colonial rule" (Wavell 1990). '"Pakistan, India, Hong Kong and Sri Lanka all have afternoon tea, rugby, and . . . what is that game?" said the ambassador miming a bowling action. "We do not have cricket in Iraq", he said with satisfaction' (ibid.).

The Afghans, in spite of – perhaps because of – three full-scale wars with the British, never took to cricket. Their national game was *buzkashi*. In it fierce horsemen, kicking and beating rivals, gallop after the prize, a bloody and decapitated calf. It is not difficult to imagine what Macaulay would have thought of this.

For the British, Arabs are 'towel-heads' (the expression Taki uses for them in his column in *The Spectator*), for the Americans, 'hankie-heads' (O'Rourke 1991); they are men in robes losing easy money in London casinos, women torturing Filipino maid-servants in their London flats. But this is to caricature a whole race on the basis of the actions of a few. The Arab writers, mystics and poets and their centres of learning, like Al-Azhar, are blotted out by such images. Mahfouz's recent Nobel Prize for Literature is a reminder of that rich civilization. But Macaulay, in any case, had dismissed Arabic and Sanskrit learning as worthless. For him the ideal was based in classical Greek culture.

It is significant that not one South Asian would feature on any popular Western list of the most hated Afro-Asian leaders. The usual choices – blown up by the Western media into mythological proportions – are Gaddafi, Arafat, Khomeini and, in 1990–91, Saddam. Not a single British university spire was visible in their educational past. In sharp contrast South Asians like Gandhi and Nehru are prominent among the most durably popular; here 'one-off' figures like Mandela do not affect the argument.

There is something characteristically Anglo-Indian in the revealing autobiographical material gathered by Zerbanoo Gifford of Asian lives in Britain (1990). All the contributors appear to want is recognition by the white folk that underneath their dark skins they, too, are English. Through clumsy hints of family connec-tions, élite British education and political loyalties they wish to be accepted. This is also revealed in the photograph selected from a lifetime of activity to accompany their contribution. It is typified by the group photograph of a Pakistani standing in a room with the Queen on a visit to a Cambridge college; this is the high point of the Asian's life: the one image that sums it up. In that moment she is sublimated and Macaulay vindicated.

Yet the colour of Gifford's guests is all wrong. However practised the accent, the colour is unacceptable to the majority; it is the final diacritical factor that will keep them apart. In the meantime, they have drifted away from their own roots. Local culture means the Kashmiri shawl, the Sindhi pottery, the occasional Indian curry; little more. The Macaulay syndrome has ensured that this group appears to live on a different planet from their compatriots in Bradford or Birmingham.

'In common with many Bombay-raised middle-class children of my generation, I grew up with an intimate knowledge of, and even sense of friendship with, a certain kind of England', ruminates Rushdie, describing the Macaulay syndrome (1991: 18). It was

> a dream-England composed of Test Matches at Lord's presided over by the voice of John Arlott, at which Freddie Trueman bowled unceasingly and without success at Polly Umrigar; of Enid Blyton and Billy Bunter, in which we were even prepared to smile indulgently at portraits such as 'Hurree Jamset Ram Singh', 'the dusky nabob of Bhanipur'. I wanted to come to England. I couldn't wait. And to be fair, England has done all right by me; but I find it a little difficult to be properly grateful. I can't escape the view that my relatively easy ride is not the result of the dream-England's famous sense of tolerance and fair play, but of my social class, my freak fair skin and my 'English' English accent. Take away any of these, and the story would have been very different. Because of course the dream-England is no more than a dream.
>
> (ibid.)

Almost inevitably, as Rushdie frankly admits, Macaulay's youth revolted against their own cultural and spiritual roots:

> God, Satan, Paradise and Hell all vanished one day in my fifteenth year, when I quite abruptly lost my faith. I recall it vividly. I was at school in England by then. The moment of awakening happened, in fact, during a Latin lesson, and afterwards, to prove my new-found atheism, I bought myself a rather tasteless ham sandwich, and so partook for the first time of the forbidden flesh of the swine. No thunderbolt arrived to

strike me down. I remember feeling that my survival confirmed the correctness of my new position. I did slightly regret the loss of Paradise, though.

(ibid.: 377)

Consider Kureishi, with his new novel in 1990, the darling of the British literary establishment. His almost perfect mimicry makes him noteworthy. The humour, cynicism, lively language, exaggerated priapism, and a pace that never lets up – making depth and insight difficult – reflect popular English taste. His anarchic vision of inner-city life and cloacal obsessions – in his films and novel – repeat well-trodden literary themes. A host of writers, from the younger Amis to Burchill, testify to this. It is the characteristic South Asian overkill which ensures the excess of bums and testicles in Kureishi's work. His novel's protagonist's testicles, powdered, are like Turkish delight; the white racist would remind us that Turkey borders the Black Sea in which Asians are dipped *en route* to England. Now that the British media, satiated with sex, appears to have discovered the fart (entire television episodes of Ben Elton, Dave Allen and Victoria Wood are woven around it), his next work may well be *My Beautiful Fart*.

Always mimetic, Tariq Ali, too, in this cultural milieu discovered the penis at the age of 50. A *Sunday Times* reviewer was agog: 'It is unusual, outside the pages of pornography or specialised medical textbooks, to find a publication quite so prominently bedecked with male genitals as Tariq Ali's *Redemption*' (Peter Kemp 1990; also see the equally devastating 'Profile' in *The Independent*, 29 September 1990). Tariq's discovery of the penis and its noisy announcement to the world meant that gone was the unrelieved tedium of his earlier Marxist jargon. As he never does things in half-measure bombs have become bums, semen has replaced sweat, and sex is substituted for socialism in his recent writing. This was one Marxist who had converted to postmodernist expression with little regret.

In the 1980s the work of Salman Rushdie and Hanif Kureishi became symbolic of the literary trends in postmodernism: eclectic, satirical, iconoclastic and irreverent. They would be the most extreme examples of the success of Macaulay. But, for the white racist, no Asian is acceptable, however Anglicized. For some Asians, Rushdie, with his Booker Prize, became the symbol of success, for others he was a cultural mutant. Most, until *The Satanic*

Verses affair, would never have heard of him (see pages 169–77, '*The Satanic Verses* affair'). Western wives, black-tie appearances and a celebrity life-style only appeared to mock his claim to speak on their behalf. The revulsion partly explains the intensity of the South Asian response to Rushdie: in a sense they were rejecting absorption into British culture.

For the majority of Asian immigrants life is a constant struggle to cling to their own cultures. Arriving after the Second World War, they worked long and hard to build comfortable nests. By burning Rushdie's book they plummeted on Macaulay's register; they were negating the work of a century and a half. They were also rejecting postmodernist expressions of culture as manifested by their own kind.

A British Muslim scholar explains the causes of Westernization among Muslims:

> Whatever the case may be, the income and education factors in British context may lead Asian Muslims into Westernized lifestyles and Western value systems. The income factor gives the buying power of lifestyles with the attendant trappings of the indigenous class symbols. Since they cannot be assimilated into the indigenous class system they can ape it. Similarly the education factor can also brainwash the individual into the indigenous class customs of British culture. The value system of Asian Muslims may have become secular and rooted in the secular ideologies of Britain.
>
> (Raza 1991: 8–9)

But even those Muslims who become Westernized are not fully accepted in the West:

> Asian Muslims may drink, go to discos, have pre-marital and extramarital relations and some even eat pork. By becoming Westernized they may ape Western class customs and mannerisms but cannot assimilate with ease as they are not accepted. . . . Some rich Muslims may even pay for the building of the mosques. Others may go for *Hajj* and think that by doing this they have done their duty to Islam. Another may even legitimize their drinking by saying: 'I don't serve alcohol in my home. But if I am called upon to toast the Queen in champagne, I don't hesitate. What it says, in the Koran is don't drink and pray, not don't drink at all.' There are others who

consider themselves British, sell wine and whisky and consider it risky to invest in Pakistan. They are married to English women and reside in spacious houses.

(ibid.)

British commentators on the Rushdie affair had, overnight, become anthropologists, tracing the genealogical links of the protestors to South Asia (Ruthven 1990). That was sensible with the continuing close links to ancestral homes, but they would have done well to push deeper into the past in order to locate the roots of the dilemma. The exercise would have led to Macaulay's Minute.

It is also well to remember that not only South Asian Muslims are involved in this process. Hindu groups in the United Kingdom threatened a distinguished academic compatriot, Bhikhu Parekh, at an English university, for his biography of Gandhi (Parekh 1989). It was read as casting a slur on the Mahatma's sex life. The matter made it to the national press but was drowned by the din of the Rushdie affair, which in some ways it imitated. Perhaps Buddhist groups will protest against the title of Kureishi's novel, *The Buddha of Suburbia* (1990). The images of Bradford book-burners may well be replaced by suicidal Buddhist monks.

Macaulay, with his notions of ideal culture, might not have approved of some of these developments but he would have marvelled at the logical limits to which his Minute had taken the 'Indian'. (We will also consider this point in the next chapter in our discussion of Muslim scholarship.) Bradford book-burner or Booker Prize winner, his chickens had come home to roost.

THE TYRANNY OF THE NATION-STATE

In Chapter 1 we pointed out the modernist impulses in post-colonial states. However, because it encourages the rejection of centres and systems, engenders the growth of local identity, makes available information and thus teaches people to demand their rights, and fosters ideas of freedom and eclecticism, postmodernism challenges the state. The relatively recently formed and weak nation-states of Africa and Asia are thereby shaken to the core. The intensity of political demands is given its fullest expression because of the postmodernist era.

Arguably, one of the worst legacies of European modernism is the nation-state, at least in the manner in which it is found in Africa and Asia. It is in these continents that the Muslim lands lie. The nation-state, in its monolithic power, its desire to centralize, corrupt and control, its security apparatus characterized by unlimited power and limited imagination, is often an unmitigated disaster for the less privileged, in particular the minorities. Entire tribes and districts were cut in two or forced to migrate *en masse* as post-colonial borders were drawn by Europeans preoccupied with the thought of returning home. Many of the present political tensions can be traced to the ill-informed nation-building exercises of the departing Europeans. Kashmir, in South Asia, is one example (see the next section).

Typical of issues confronting post-colonial states is the perverted relationship between the state and its component parts. In many post-colonial states, the majority is based not on ideology, but on the preponderance of the religious or ethnic population. We thus witness the tyranny of the majority, using democracy as its vehicle.

In South Asia the tyranny concerns the overwhelming number of the majority group and its determination to dominate the minority: Hindus in India, Punjabis in Pakistan, Bengalis in Bangladesh and Sinhalese in Sri Lanka. In what was one of the most tranquil areas of the region, Sri Lanka, ethnic conflict has claimed about 30,000 people in recent years in the fighting between the majority Sinhalese and the minority Tamils. This was the Serendip of legend, dominated by one of the most peaceful religions of the world, Buddhism.

For the majority, as long as they stay united along sectarian or ethnic lines, democracy could mean perpetual rule. Because the majority orders economic decisions, eternal monopolization of the national cake is thus guaranteed for them. For the minorities there is no escape from the logic of numbers. The increasing violence of their responses is as much a sign of despair as evidence of this logic. It is the irresistible force of cultural particularism meeting the immovable object called the state.

Due to obsessive jealousy regarding its powers and prerogatives, and usually lacking imagination in its bureaucratic responses, the state exhibits a poor record of communication with its minorities. Because the state lacks compassion, in the form of cultural tolerance and fairness, in that of constitutional safeguards, its minorities feel vulnerable. Over the decades, their patience exhausted, they have one option to exercise: that of rejecting the state. This may be in the shape of a full-blown secessionist movement, acts of sabotage, burning the symbols of the state such as the flag or sullen disengagement from them.

The modern state itself is a recent invention, its roots relatively weak. In the summer of 1947 in Delhi, an Englishman signed into creation, with one stroke, two nations, India and Pakistan. Although various concepts of a united land were embedded in history, the reality was that of diversity. Over 500 states and thousands of villages, often as different as chalk and cheese – encompassing 200 languages, different customs, culture and history – were to be defined, henceforth, as the state of India. Pakistan constituted two halves divided by a thousand miles of India and the language, the culture and society of its two populations were dissimilar. The one link, religion, was snapped by an ethnic tidal wave in 1971.

Once in power, the first priority of the nationalist leaders, understandably enough, was to consolidate the state. In the early years the nation rallied round the nationalist leaders, the minorities swept along in the enthusiasm. In many cases, the world was still seen through colonial eyes by those sitting in the old colonial secretariats, in the still-warm colonial chairs. The idiom and the responses were thus pre-determined. Groups demanding rights became 'miscreants', 'secessionists' and 'trouble-makers', to be dealt with firmly. To the authority of the state was added the arrogance of the parvenu. Dissent was not to be tolerated, and the steamroller – or the bribe – was employed to silence it.

The harshness of the native ruler to the native ruled was the paradox of the post-colonial world. The harshness must be understood in the context of the post-colonial culture of violence in South Asia. The revolution of independence fed on its own children: two of the founding fathers – M.K. Gandhi and Mujib – were assassinated, and a third – Jinnah – escaped several attempts. Two Indian Prime Ministers, Indira and her son Rajiv, were also assassinated. The first Prime Minister of Pakistan, Liaqat, was shot, and the first popularly elected one, Bhutto, hanged. The last President, Zia, was blown up in the air with a large party of senior generals. Countless leaders have been shot and killed in Bangladesh. But not only the palaces of the nation's capitals are targets. From the time of independence in 1947, when a mad orgy of sectarian killings gripped the entire land, to the present, hundreds of thousands have died in numberless villages and anonymous streets, and for what?

Rational discourse becomes difficult with this background. It is naturally easy to think and behave like the group. Obduracy and arrogance in the majority, rebelliousness and despair in the minority are encouraged. Where once, before Independence, Indian troops fired into Punjabi crowds demonstrating in favour of self-determination in Jallianwala Bagh, they now shoot to blot out Sikh expressions of ethnic identity. Where Frontier Force regiments once exchanged fire with tribesmen across the Indus, in Pakistan they now do so against the Bengalis (in 1971), the Baluch (in the 1970s) and the Sindhis (in the 1980s). The use of troops extends beyond the borders. Indian soldiers patrol the forests of Sri Lanka, others the mountain passes of Nepal, yet others the Maldives, to impose the Delhi vision of *pax indica*.

The noble savage at bay

The nature of the post-colonial Afro-Asian state, the fragility of its international borders and its centralized, tense and depersonalized authority offer us some important clues, a paradigm, about its relationship with tribal or nomadic peoples, and their inevitable exploitation by 'outside' powers. Boxed into administrative districts and agencies, often in politically sensitive zones, the problem of these groups in the 1990s will judder many states, even threaten their very existence. All the South Asian countries face – or have faced – serious tribal problems in the form of movements for autonomy or outright independence: India in Assam (and although the Sikhs and Kashmiris are not strictly tribal in the sense we use the term, the articulation of their politics is); Pakistan with its Baluch and Pathan tribes and Bangladesh with the tribes of the Chittagong Hill Tracts.

In *Resistance and Control in Pakistan* (1991a) I discuss precisely this problem, raising the issue of a 'district paradigm'. The emergence of a religious or ethnic leader, around whom the tribe rallies, the idiom of 'holy war', the manipulation of tribal identity, the problem of straddling international borders and the brutal response of the modern state are described through an actual case which took place in the North-West Frontier Province. The paradigm relates to questions of ethnicity and tribalism in the modern world.

The Afro-Asian state has often meant cruel partition for tribesmen as borders split villages and tribes in two. The Pathans, divided between Afghanistan and Pakistan, are a good example; so, too, to cite a topical and relevant example not in South Asia, are that ancient, noble but tragic people, the Kurds, split between half a dozen nations. Muslim tribesmen have good cause to blame Western powers for their clumsy border-making exercises. The Arabs attribute, albeit simplistically, almost all their political problems in the Middle East to this.

Unlike the agricultural peasants, vulnerable on their open farms and fields, who saw the state as a continuation of earlier despotic rule and learned to adjust accordingly, the tribesmen cannot cope with rigid structures. Nomadic and pastoral, they move with the seasons and recognize no borders. And that is where the modern state comes in. Once the rebellious Baluch – or Kurd – could disappear into their mountains, or the tribesmen of Chittagong into their jungles. Now the helicopter gunships and fast-moving armoured vehicles can penetrate their most inaccessible areas. To make matters worse their very values of honour, bravery, chivalry – the core of the tribal code – are assaulted, almost certainly irreversibly, by the VCR and television. New ideas and values flood their homes and challenge their ancestral ones.

These people are trapped by their own self-perception. They are dominated by the ethos of defined codes, unchanged for centuries. They have lived in demarcated areas corresponding to clans and segments infused with a spirit of egalitarianism ('such as would excite the envy of an Athenian demagogue', noted a British political officer early this century – Ahmed 1991a: 171 note 14). The tribes proudly retain ancient memories from their pre-Islamic past. The Pathans gave a tough time to Alexander in the passes when he crossed into India, a fact noted by the Greeks; the Kurds have not forgotten that Xenophon's *Anabasis*, or *The Return of the Ten Thousand*, portrays the ancestors of the Kurds as brave warriors who fought the Greek armies on their way home from Persia.

The reply in public from Wali Khan, the symbol and leader of Pathan identity, when asked about his identity, sums it up. 'First', he said, 'I am a Pathan because I have been so for thousands of years; then I am a Muslim, which I have been for about 1300 years and, third, I am a Pakistani, which I have been only for the last 40 years or so'. Ethnicity, religion and nationality – in that order; the chronological sequences of his identity are thus summed up. They also hint at the inherent tensions facing Muslim tribesmen in today's Muslim state. It is, therefore, for this reason that they are not easily swayed either by Arab nationalism or Islamic revivalism.

But the modern state has sapped the tribal system of its vitality. It has lost its élan. Indolence and fatalism have taken its place. The modern state has usually meant exploitation, displacement, disease and drugs for tribal people. Nothing disintegrates tribalism as much as the arrival of the first electric pole or the first government-controlled school. Tribalism exists as a whole or not at all (see 'The myth of the noble savage: Muslim tribesman', chapter 7, Ahmed 1988).

In the European colonial tapestry there was one bold and colourful strand which appealed to many of them both intellectually and emotionally: Rousseau's notion of the 'noble savage'. For the French, the Berber in North Africa, and, for the British, the Pathans of the North-West Frontier Province of India were invested with this idea. They embodied simplicity, courage and good humour. This romantic notion has not died out entirely.

It partly explains the continued fascination with figures like Lawrence of Arabia. It explains why Sean Connery, perhaps the most romantic of contemporary film heroes, played the part of a Berber chief in *The Wind and the Lion* with such successful flourish. It partly explains the continued sympathy in the West for the plight of the tribesmen confronting the wrath of the modern state: in the 1980s, the Afghans against a Russian-backed government and, in 1991, the Kurds against Saddam's state. It is apparent in the moving accounts of the Kurds by writers like Martin Woollacott reporting from north Iraq in *The Guardian*.

It is also confirmed by the Western responses to the post-war situation in Iraq. There was a cautious wait-and-see approach to the Shia rebellion against Saddam in the south, memories of the Shia revolution in Iran being still fresh. The last thing the West wanted was another Islamic revolution to succeed. In contrast, there was also the unrestrained support for the Kurds in the north, although both groups were victims of Saddam's guns.

There is, however, nothing romantic about the tribesman in the modern state, whether India, Pakistan, Bangladesh – or indeed Iraq, Egypt or Iran. Intellectuals and leaders, usually from the urban areas, talk of 'modernization', which has no place in tribal life. The education and civil and defence service structures, based on familiarity with state networks and nepotism, discourage the absorption of tribesmen and view them as backward. In Muslim countries, to the orthodox *ulema*, the religious scholars, the tribesman is still an incomplete Muslim in need of formal training. The climate for the tribesman is one of indifference at best, as in Jordan where the Bedouin are allowed to exist in their own ways, and open hostility at worst, as in the Shah's Iran when the Baluch and Kurd were actively persecuted.

Saddam's own answer to the issue of Kurd identity was typical of his attitude. He used the sledge-hammer, with the knowledge of those very powers in the West who condemned him in 1990–1. In one horrific action, 5,000 people died in the poison gas attack on Halabja in March 1988. The thriving market town on the border with Iran was converted into a ghost town and has become a symbol of death. Because of the loathing that Saddam's name evokes in the world, we hear so much of Halabja. But there is little doubt that other Halabjas exist among other tribal groups elsewhere in the world.

If the problem is reversed, if tribesmen take over the state, how do they fare? Saudi Arabia (named after the al-Saud tribe) and Kuwait (for all purposes the state of the al-Sabah) are such examples. While the state ensures employment and privileges for those connected to the ruling lineages, it also illustrates the limitations of tribalism. Here the tribe is capable of assuming some of the worst aspects and excesses of the modern state. While power and privilege wait on the tribal leaders, those who do not belong to the proper lineage have few rights. A minor breach of rules can mean years in a jail which is often a hole in the ground; a whisper against injustice could mean instant expulsion. Once again the modern state is little understood and poorly served.

Indeed, the modern state appears to be an unmitigated European disaster imposed upon these tribesmen. It may offer much, but it also takes away far too much. The crisis of the Kurds that we witnessed in Iraq in 1991 was not only the failure of one leader to resolve the tribal problem, but also the larger question of the legitimacy of the state itself and its failure to deal with ethnic identity.

We therefore need more understanding of ethnicity – language, customs, culture, lineage. How do groups identify themselves and what activates their sense of ethnic identity and pride? How best can the state accommodate it? The answers will also help those looking for clues to the events in the USSR and East Europe.

Unfortunately, during 1990–1, we have heard little from the experts. We did see on the television panels an eerie, bloodless exposition: the military men triumphantly, mechanically, reeling off statistics that spoke of the success of the allied air strikes with no relationship to the death and suffering below; the political scientists talked airily about abstract ideas, trapped in 'left' versus 'right' arguments which are, in any case, almost irrelevant to tribal groups.

What we did not hear, with some honourable exceptions, were the Middle East experts, many of whom, having spent considerable time in these areas, were in an ideal position to explain them to us (see discussion in Chapter 4). Culture, custom and ethnicity were allowed to remain a blank by people who, it must be said, depend for their bread and butter on studying the Middle East. Partly to redress this, the Royal Anthropological Institute sponsored its first major conference on the Gulf war in April 1991, at the London School of Economics.

Some of us had pointed out, through the media, the complexity of Middle East society, warning of rushing in where sensible angels would fear to tread, but had been drowned out by the rampant gung-ho jingoism. The wailing for the Kurds of many who supported the war sounded hollow in its aftermath. They have failed to establish a link between cause and effect. The incomplete victory against Saddam unleashed a ferocity, unprecedented even by Iraqi standards, on the Kurds and Shias; the war, and the way it ended, was the direct cause.

Among the Kurds George Bush, for a few weeks after the war, had become the representative of freedom and liberty. He was even absorbed into tribal mythology and local idiom conferred on him the title 'haji', reserved for those Muslims who perform the haj, the pilgrimage in Saudi Arabia. Signals were given – or at least so interpreted – indicating recognition of Kurdish identity. Then Saddam moved to crush them. Kurdish cries soon went unheeded as the haji concentrated on his golf and boating. The war with Saddam, his athletic frenzy implied, was over; the Kurds were Iraq's 'internal' problem once again, they had served their geo-political purpose.

In this particular case he is wrong, for the Kurds have no defence against Iraqi gunships, but in another sense he may be right. The problem is internal, and it is essentially the inability of

the modern state to come to terms with the post-colonial paradigm, to allow fair play and justice, a civil society, to develop. What
we are witnessing with the Kurds is the last gasp not only of an
entire people – a Muslim holocaust in the making – but the
post-colonial paradigm at terrible play. Turbulent times are
predicted. African and Asian cynics would say this is what the West
wants: permanent strife in the Middle East and South Asia,
nations perpetually off balance and internally bleeding.

There are no easy answers. The irresistible power of the state
will continue to meet the immovable pride of ethnicity and the
cost will be heavy. It is the reason why many states who opposed
Saddam in the Middle East, with their own tribal problems
simmering, quietly looked away. Perhaps that other Western
concept, democracy, needs to be given a proper chance. It is the
only hope. All else, including higher standards of living, of
education etc., is secondary. But the ballot-box poses a terrible
dilemma. It may – as Gorbachev in the USSR knew so well – also
prove the greatest threat to the state itself: it could well declare its
own demise in a free vote. The hierarchy of identity so succinctly
expressed by Wali Khan haunts every South Asian government
with a tribal population in search of its identity.

The fading vision of the founding fathers

In retrospect, we note how much the generation of South Asian
founding fathers owed to the Anglo-Indian encounter (discussed
above). The synthesis went deeper than Nehru enjoying Keats or
Jinnah reading Shakespeare; deeper even than studying at
Cambridge or in Lincoln's Inn, London, respectively. The
European liberal-humanist ethos was reflected in the work of the
intellectual giants: Radhakrishnan, Tagore and Iqbal. It was
reflected in the speeches and vision of the future. Independence
was to be, in Nehru's famous words, a 'tryst with destiny'. India
would awake to an ideal, Utopian future at Independence, at the
stroke of the 'midnight hour'. (The phrase gave Rushdie the title
for his Booker Prize-winning novel, *Midnight's Children*, 1981.)

There was a sense that a meeting point between the inherited
wisdom of the great Asian religions and European humanism
existed. It brought together such unlikely pairs as Gandhi, a
devout Hindu, and Azad, a devout Muslim; Nehru, the leader of
the nationalist movement against the Raj, and Mountbatten, the

Viceroy of the Raj. That meeting point has disintegrated, leaving a hole in the heart of South Asia.

For all the debunking of his critics, Gandhi represented a moral position. Although accused by many Muslims of being a Hindu, as opposed to an Indian, leader he fasted to stop their slaughter by Hindus. He also fasted to force India to release the assets due to the newly formed and bankrupt government of Pakistan. This may have been political theatre but it also reflected a concern with larger issues such as suffering and truth. In the present climate it appears there is no South Asian leader capable of such acts nor, possibly, of understanding their humanist base.

There has been progress: repeated attempts to involve the widest number in the democratic process, especially noteworthy is India, where, in spite of its problems, democracy has survived. This process has widened the base of and access to wealth and privilege. Incomes per capita, between $200 and $400, are low, but distinctly better than a generation ago. Journalism, arts and crafts are vigorous, almost exuberant; English, once the preserve of the élite, is now widely used for commerce and education (although there is little Shakespeare and almost no Keats). Areas of economic prosperity have been produced, like the Sikh districts before the political troubles. The introduction of technology is irreversible with computers and fax machines becoming common in cities. But the progress is vitiated by the savage, large-scale killings, the widespread corruption, the appallingly low standards of education overall and the general despair. The queues for migration abroad are long and unending.

The results are disappointing, not only because they cannot live up to the rhetoric of the founding fathers, but also to their own historical past. This was, after all, the land that produced ancient cities like Moenjodaro and the grandeur of empires like those of the Mauryas and the Mughals, the architectural and artistic wonders of the Ajanta caves, the Chola temples, the Shalimar gardens in Kashmir and the Taj Mahal in Agra.

Moving towards dissolution

Once Gandhi, contemplating the West and its technology, could say, 'They are children playing with razors', a thought also expressed by Iqbal. Now, however, there is a scramble to acquire Western technology in contemporary South Asia. The region, it appears, shorn of humanism, devoid of its sense of destiny, cannot resist. At best it can imitate. It is the period of amoral whiz-kids, computer experts and statistics. Where commentators were once impressed with Mahatma Gandhi's moral stature, it is India's armed forces, the fourth largest in the world, that, if anything, impresses them now.

The links with the past are not entirely broken: Rajiv, like his grandfather, was a Trinity man; Benazir Bhutto, like her father, went to Oxford; Iqbal's grandson was in Cambridge in 1990. (The frequent mention of Oxbridge in the text may suggest I am an over-impressed South Asian. It is in fact an anthropological reflex. Although the importance of Oxbridge has considerably diminished in British life – even the Prime Minister is no longer required to have been to Oxbridge as part of the qualification for the job – the traditional South Asian perspective, inherited as part of the colonial legacy, still remains. It is useful to recall that the author of the 1835 Minute, Lord Macaulay, was himself a Cambridge man. Though there are signs of change in South Asia, Oxbridge is widely perceived as representing the best of Western education and also, reflecting the pervasive caste-consciousness in the region, the top of the social hierarchy. These South Asians would wistfully concur with the Victorian, Leigh Hunt, that Oxford and Cambridge

> are divine places, both; full of grace, and beauty, and scholarship; of reverend antiquity, and ever-young nature and hope.
>
> (Hunt 1988: 43)

Links with Oxbridge are therefore diligently cultivated, often expressing themselves in the most idiosyncratic forms. A class-fellow of mine in Karachi, a stone's throw from the Bhutto residence, still maintains with spit and polish the E-Type Jaguar he bought in Cambridge thirty years ago, although spare parts are difficult to come by and it is off the road most of the time. Like a hallowed relic from the past, through the upheavals in his life and the turmoil in the city, it remains for him a visible proof of his worth, an expression of his identity and a tangible memory of an idealized Elysian past.)

But Europe, nurturer of humanism, has changed. Its humanism is assumed, but in danger of being mutated beyond recognition as it adopts materialism. The Thatcherism of the

1980s is but one sample of this mutation. If South Asia has no Jinnah or Gandhi, England does not have a Churchill nor France a de Gaulle either. Unless South Asians are able to create the vestiges of humanism – a climate of tolerance, a respect for the minorities and those less privileged, a rule of law, an atmosphere of integrity – the future may be painted with Lebanese hues.

South Asia appears to be moving inexorably in the opposite direction to Europe; whereas European countries, in spite of the local resurgence of identity, have been heading for unity, South Asia exhibits centrifugal tendencies. European conflicts have been recorded for centuries, culminating in the two world wars costing millions of lives. But, after the devastation of the last war, traditional foes like France and Germany are joined. Visas have vanished, passports will soon no longer be necessary and the frontiers are dissolving. East and West Germany are one again. Economic prosperity and social progress are a consequence, making Europe one of the world's most stable and prosperous regions.

In contrast, South Asia, often united for centuries in one form or another, is falling apart: Pakistan split from India in 1947, Bangladesh from Pakistan in 1971, and there have been numerous ongoing 'independence' movements of varying intensity and violence. Wars between the South Asian countries have been frequent, and tension remains high. To obtain a visa is difficult and time-consuming; the frontiers are being reinforced with concrete and armed posts. The consequence is one of the world's most unstable and poorest regions.

Unless awareness dawns and their fears are soothed, the people of South Asia, enmeshed and interlocked in religious and ethnic passions, will dissipate whatever energy they have while devouring one another. Recent South Asian history tends to blame all of its ills on foreign invaders and dynasties; perhaps for the first time it can lay the blame squarely on itself. Religious and political hatreds translate into massive budgets for the military and para-military forces, thus keeping social and economic levels of growth down. Educational, law and order and economic standards that hover around those of Central Africa negate and mock the glorious history of India – from the Mauryas to the Mughals. Unless sense prevails among leaders and those who form public opinion, Muslims and non-Muslims alike, the prognosis is not a happy or auspicious one for a South Asia preparing to enter the next century. At the heart of the matter remains the question of self-determination, self-identity and self-respect. This leads us to a discussion of Kashmir, which has been the subject of conflict between India and Pakistan since 1947.

KASHMIR: A PARADIGMATIC POSTMODERNIST MUSLIM MOVEMENT?

The central aim of this section is to identify the main elements of a contemporary postmodernist Muslim movement. An analysis of the contemporary Kashmiri expression of independence will allow us to raise the broader question of whether it is part of a global Islamic pattern or yet another temporary reaction to a regional, localized provocation (also see Ahmed 1990a and 1990b, 1991b and 1991e; Gandhi 1987; Hasan 1990; Naipaul 1990; and the previous section, 'The tyranny of the nation-state'. For a clear historical account of the Kashmir problem see *Kashmir: A Disputed Legacy 1846–1990*, A. Lamb 1991). We ask whether there is a link, not perhaps a direct political one but a conceptual one, to other Muslim movements, like those in the uprisings in Israel and the Muslim Central Asian Republics of the USSR? What are the unifying principles, the structural similarities, to be identified in these movements? How are they different from earlier Muslim reactions?

In an analysis of Muslims living as a minority in a non-Muslim state, I have suggested that the historical Muslim solutions of *hijra*, migration, and *jihad*, holy war, to unsatisfactory circumstances were no longer possible in the modern era (Ahmed 1988). A third choice appeared to have been developing after independence from the colonial powers, that of accommodation to the status of a minority in the modern state.

In the late 1980s Muslim movements in different parts of the world have challenged this assertion, suggesting a pattern for the future. They suggest a qualitatively different kind of socio-political response to state tyranny from that in the past. It is different in its total rejection of central authority, of the meta-ideology of the nation, indeed of the nation-state itself; in its re-formulation of local identity, its apocalyptic fervour, the violence it engenders, its bitterness for the broken promises in the past and its hopes for the future. It is what we may tentatively term a postmodern movement – the tentative nature of the discussion accounts for the question mark in the section heading.

The problem of Muslims as minorities is not marginal as they constitute about a quarter of the total Muslim global population. By examining Kashmir in India we will thus be able to throw light on Muslims in Israel and the USSR – which will partly explain the events of 1991 which set them on the path to freedom in Central Asia. We may identify the familiar topoi running through the Muslim movements. Seven features are pointed out:

One: A deep and simmering sense of deprivation among Muslims. A feeling of social, economic and political frustration exists among Muslims in these countries. There is little industry, growth or economic opportunity for them. The stagnant economic picture is related to the feeling of being deliberately neglected – or discriminated against – by the central government.

All the statistics in India support this argument. Muslims do not get a fair share according to demographic and constitutional rights. Although 12 per cent of the total Indian population of around 850 million, Muslims have less than 3 per cent of government jobs; percentages in education and industry are even worse. The paradox of Hindu fundamentalists claiming that Muslims are pampered by government is thus highlighted by these statistics. For Muslims the tyranny of both the majority and the state – and their overlapping ideology – reinforces their sense of deprivation and injustice. (Anita Desai's *In Custody* portrays allegorically – and with perception – the decline of Urdu and Muslim culture in India.)

Kashmir, the one Muslim majority Indian state, has virtually no major industrial unit. Tourism, during the 'season', is its only source of income. The Kashmiri language and culture have been allowed to atrophy. Politically, Kashmiris have incessantly complained that their state is almost unique in India for not having had – or almost never having had – fair and free elections since Independence. Its own local government is seen as corrupt and inefficient, imposed on them by Delhi. Promises of a plebiscite, from those of Mountbatten to those of Nehru, have been ignored and forgotten. These grievances bring together the disparate Muslim ethnic groups in Kashmir, including Ladakhi Muslim and Jammu ones, although their political positions may be different. The concept of 'Kashmiriat' as a distinct, local culture is thus fuelled.

Two: The central governments in each case have clearly shown their bankruptcy of ideas in their dealings with these movements. Failed methods, exhausted ideas and cultural stereotypes emanate from government. The bankruptcy of ideas has ensured the over-reaction. The government has understood neither the mood nor its causes. The problem is seen in simplistic terms, as one of law and order, one linked to terrorism, one created by fanatics, 'fundamentalists'. Bullets and batons have been too frequently used. Stories of torture and rape are too commonly cited.

The impatient and aggressive reaction of government reflects its fear of foreign involvement and possible international complications. All three Muslim areas are situated on sensitive international borders which have been formed only this century. The legaiity of their absorption into the larger state has always been a source of political controversy. The state simply cannot compromise on these areas without a genuine possibility and fear of unravelling its own fabric. The USSR historically feared that its Islamic republics might one day break away; Israel is concerned about a separate Palestinian state; and India about Kashmir joining Pakistan or even becoming independent. The impact of Kashmir breaking away from India would be devastating for the more than 100 million Muslims elsewhere in the country. To parties like the BJP, it would confirm their argument that Muslims cannot be trusted and must either 'Hinduize' or leave the country. Four decades after independence, Muslims in India again face uncertainty, the old wounds having been opened. Religion, politics and communalism are inextricably mingled in India, affecting every aspect of life, even the popular cinema (see Ahmed 1991b).

Such fears engender extraordinarily harsh measures by the state. In the late 1980s the brutal handling by Moscow of the Azerbaijanis is contrasted with its initial gentleness towards the Lithuanians; in one place tanks and killing, in the other, talks and promises of concessions. The Israelis have lost considerable support among their traditional allies in the West for their repressive handling of the Palestinian *intifada*. The Indian government is criticized, even by many Indians, for its unprecedented heavy-handedness in Kashmir. The point is not whether government-inspired agencies did or did not kill Mir Waiz, the popular spokesman of Kashmir; it is that the people in Kashmir believe he was killed. Unending curfew, total disruption of life, escalating violence and reports of rape and torture are reported (see Bose *et al.* 1990; also see 'Kashmiri villages tell of torture by Indian troops', by R. Whittaker, *The Independent*, 6 June

1990; both Whittaker for his paper and Derek Brown for *The Guardian* sent in similarly disturbing accounts throughout 1990–91).

Again, let us not isolate events in Kashmir from those in the rest of India. The last years have seen an increase in violence, whether caste or communal (Akbar 1985, 1988; Bonner 1990; Brass 1984; Naipaul 1990; Tully 1991; also BBC2's *Assignment* by Mark Tully, first shown in Britain on 11 December 1990, and another *Assignment*, titled 'Awakening of the Godmen', reported by Brian Barron on BBC2, 14 May 1991). 'In Aligarh, a man has his eyes put out and his penis cut off by the mob', began a report from mainland India under the title, 'The terror' by Derek Brown (*Weekend Guardian*, 15–16 December 1990).

The brutal administrative actions of the Indian government in Kashmir must not be seen as specifically designed for Muslims alone. The response to Sikh assertion of independence was, and is, similarly harsh (see special issue, 'Politics in the Punjab', *Pacific Affairs* 1987). It is subsumed in the central government's deep-rooted nightmare of disintegration, which leads back to the events of 1947. The only reaction to assertion of identity is suppression: 'Pakistan' must never be allowed to happen again.

The state is paying a heavy ideological and psychological price. The brutality challenges its very base. India has always prided itself on its secular, humanist and liberal ideological foundations. Non-violence is part of its self-image and mythology. Mahatma Gandhi and Nehru, because of their ideas of human dignity and suffering, would have been appalled at the handling of the present crisis.

We saw how a Sikh bodyguard violated every South Asian tradition, including the highly developed sense of honour among the Sikhs, by assassinating the very person who was to be protected, the Prime Minister of India. Something had snapped for the assassins. To the Sikhs Indira Gandhi had become a symbol of the repressive state. Similar tensions are now being created among Muslims. The long-term effects will be devastating. They suggest a change of self-perception at all levels of Indian society.

Take the Indian military and para-military forces, one of the largest in the world, with more than 2 million soldiers. What matters in the context of our argument is its introduction to long and involved bouts of civil administration. Sustained and final authority to administer civilian populations, with the inevitable stories of torture and rape, break down the essential core of discipline and self-image of a professional fighting force. Morale, that mystical quality sustaining *esprit de corps*, is damaged. It is the difference dividing a disciplined body from a mob or rabble. In Sri Lanka stories of rape and torture were rife; they are also in circulation in Kashmir (for example, the account of 800 soldiers raping about sixty women in February 1991; see 'Indian villagers tell of mass rape by soldiers', in *The Independent*, 19 March 1991, by McGirk and Kupwara).

'The files of human rights monitors in Srinagar bulge with accounts of inhuman depravity inflicted on the Kashmiris', writes Tony Allen-Mills ('Delhi's sledgehammer turns paradise into hell', in *The Sunday Times*, 2 June 1991). 'One man has holes in his buttocks, inflicted by an electric drill during interrogation by paramilitary police. Another was thrown in a bath full of water carrying a live electric current. Another had his genitals cut with a knife' (ibid.).

Another report concludes: 'And the greatest recruiting sergeants for this insurrection have not been Allah or the prophet Muhammad but the broken promises of history, years of discrimination against the Muslim majority of Kashmir, and, most critically in recent times, the ferocity of Indian army repression' (Bob Wylie, 'Valley on fire', in *Weekend Guardian*, 3–4 August 1991).

These are not the same Indian regiments that accumulated honours on the battlefield against other honourable soldiers; for those who still revere that military tradition, something fundamentally disturbing is taking place in Kashmir.

Even in Muzaffarabad that reality is unavoidable. Faisal Rahman is 30 but he looks at least 10 years older. He used to be the muezzin, the one who called the faithful to prayer, at the mosque of Said Bora, a village just over the border. Now he is one of the 3,000 or so Kashmiri refugees living near Muzaffarabad. In April last year, he was taken to the local Indian army interrogation centre for the third time and accused of helping mujahedin militants to cross the border. He denied the charge for the third time. He says that three soldiers then held him down while another amputated his left leg below the knee. He says he used the cord of his pyjama-style shalwar trousers to make a tourniquet, before he crawled to his house. 'It took one blow', he says, 'the way they cut a sheep's head. Let them slaughter us, still they will not silence our fight for freedom'.

(ibid.)

Since Independence the Indian army has maintained the reputation of a professional fighting force, not least because it has avoided involvement in administration and politics. The actions of the army in Pakistan and Bangladesh have provided salutary examples. The Indian army is the pride and joy of a secular India. Members from the minority communities have headed the army with professional competence and confidence. But its soldiers are sons of the South Asian soil. Their actions in Kashmir are taking them into dangerous waters; they do not augur well for the army's professional stance and future (see 'The generals get jittery as Delhi's democracy falters', by Tony Allen-Mills, in *The Sunday Times*, 19 May 1991. We have already heard the agony of the Israeli soldier guarding Arab civilian prisoners in Chapter 2; Shavit 1991).

It is also relevant to raise the issue of another powerful force that has, of late, assumed an important role in South Asian affairs: the 'intelligence services'. There is little literature on this, but for a detailed account of the role of the Israeli intelligence agencies see Black and Morris 1991. Their vast powers and wide influence are a phenomenon worthy of serious study. They have their own autonomous organization, ethos, leaders and methods of working. With stories of mayhem, terrorism and assassination spilling out of their dirty-tricks' bag they pose a challenge to notions of liberalism, humanism and tolerance. Habeas corpus is invariably the first victim of their activity. Anonymous hit-men operating from numberless 'safe houses' are neither accountable to the public nor discriminating in their victims. They need to learn lessons from the toppling of the statue of the founder of the Soviet secret police, Felix Dzerzhinsky, in Moscow.

These agencies are known to be active beyond their borders, sometimes acting on their own volition: in 1990 both Benazir Bhutto and V.P. Singh, as the respective Prime Ministers of Pakistan and India, complained of this publicly. Their definitions of loyalty to the state and of who should be on their hit-lists are not necessarily shared by the civilian government. Events in Kashmir, in Indian Punjab and in Pakistani Sind are commonly assumed to be influenced by these agencies. Pakistani agencies are seen as supporting the JKLF in Kashmir by Indians; India's are believed to be master-minding the turmoil in Sind by Pakistanis. Their involvement in daily life and stories of brutality feed and explain the bitter and sustained nature of the movements.

Three: Major internal social and political changes are taking place in each of these three countries. It is a period of transition, coalition and weak governments, of leaders with uncertain futures. Internally, the law and order in many districts, right across the land, appear to have collapsed, with horrific stories being reported in the press. A vocal, restless younger generation adds fat to the fire, being all too ready to bring out processions and damage property or people. Materialism is the current ideology, and possession of television and a fridge every house-owner's ambition. Urban groups dream of life-styles inspired by American television soaps and among them the most popular video cassettes are *Dallas* and *Dynasty* (Tully 1991: 149). There are high political and economic expectations and the growth of a large and vocal middle class.

India's middle class, numbering between 100 and 150 million, has emerged over the last decade to make its presence felt. This class contrasts with the underclass whose 350–400 million people flounder in a semi-permanent condition of deprivation. The middle class explicitly identifies with a particular style of post-Gandhian Hinduism, which has, therefore, become part of the dominant culture of India in a manner it never was a generation ago. This class provides a fertile breeding ground for communalism. From it come the scuppies: saffron-clad urban professionals. From it come also the fire-brands who, by burning themselves, in 1990 rocked India to prevent the lower castes being given more government reserved seats. It is the class of bride-burners and, now, after the protests against the lower castes, self-burners.

The middle class, cosy and smug in its beliefs, would by definition encourage the status quo, aspiring only to the good life. Bright young men and women mostly from this class, join service not to 'serve the people' – a cliché from the past – but to lead better lives, often making money illegally. Corruption is widespread. The wishes of this class dictate cultural trends, its ideas political developments.

Although not exclusively Hindu the ethos of Hinduism pervades the middle class. It revels in the triumph of Hindu fundamentalism in India, which was illustrated by the spectacular rise of the BJP, the Hindu communalist party. From two seats in parliament in the previous session it won eighty-eight in 1989; it went on to add about thirty more to this number in 1991. With a weak coalition central government based on shifting alliances it emerged as the dominant factor in Indian politics. Its main platform is Hindu unity against Muslim domination and exploitation. This, as noted above, is not borne out by the facts, but it has proved an irresistible political and cultural rallying point. For the BJP the founding fathers we mentioned above are seen as villains: Jinnah for creating Pakistan, Nehru and Gandhi for conceding it.

The Indian middle class tends to simplify issues dangerously. Its sentiments about Muslims will no doubt be recognized in its counterpart in Israel or the USSR:

> In Delhi drawing-rooms fascism has become fashionable: educated people will tell you without embarrassment that it is about time the Muslims were disciplined – that they have got away with too much for too long, that they are dirty and fanatical, that they breed like rabbits. While the chattering classes chatter, others take direct action. As I write, Old Delhi is in flames as Hindus and Muslims battle it out in the streets of the Chandni Chowk and the Sardar Bazaar.
>
> (Dalrymple 1990: 11)

The movement to demolish the Babri Masjid at Ayodhya and build a temple to the Hindu god Rama on the site acted as a flash-point, creating communal havoc across India late in 1990. 'Hindu threat to raze 3,000 mosques', proclaimed the headline of Derek Brown's story in *The Guardian* on 6 November 1990; 'India's "hour of peril" ends in days of slaughter', headlined Peter Hillmore in the *Observer* (4 November 1990). Reality and illusion, mythology and political action had fused in the *Glaubenskrieg* against Muslims (Ahmed 1990b).

The BJP leader embodied the communal hatred now widespread in the land:

> Advani finally reached Ayodhya in the last week of November. There he made one of his most extreme speeches to date: 'Only a government which respects Ram can function in India,' he raved. 'We will change the history of India and open a new chapter. . . .' Even as Advani was speaking, another Hindu

organization was releasing plans to destroy 3,000 other Indian mosques occupying Hindu holy sites: 'Not only the Ram Janmabhoomi [the Ayodhya mosque] will be liberated but hundreds of other places of faith will be repossessed. It is the rightful duty of all Hindus to eliminate every mark of their slavery at the hands of the Muslims.'

(Dalrymple 1990: 11)

Yet the political commentators ought not to have been surprised. The almost spiritual response to the widely popular television series *Mahabharat* should have warned them. When episodes were broadcast the nation came to a standstill and television sets were garlanded:

The 93-episode *Mahabharat* in particular became a national obsession. Viewing figures never sank beneath 75 per cent, and programmers claimed that they rose to 95 per cent (an audience of some 600 million) for two episodes. All over India villagers prostrated themselves before the gods on their new television screens. Suddenly the country became aware of its ancient Hindu heritage; and with that awareness came an aggressive assertion of Hindu religious identity. All over Delhi graffiti sprang up: *gaurav se kaho ham Hindu hain* – say with pride that we are Hindus.

(ibid.)

The above elements have created a national neurosis which explains the 'fortress' mentality of India. Thus the most incongruous and wild accusations blame Pakistan for everything from crop failure to political crises. 'Fortress' India must be defended from the enemy who is all around and minatory. This in part explains the extreme response in Kashmir, which is seen as a weak spot in the fortress.

Four: These movements are a sustained and total response over a period of time and involve the entire population against the larger state. They are not the usual one-day peaceful strike organized by certain groups or leaders against certain policies of central government in one part of town. It is a final rejection; a complete breakdown of communication. Hurt pride, unheeded grievances, a desperation, have exploded into the movement. It explains the readiness to risk all. Commentators have been surprised that the traditionally gentle and tolerant Kashmiris have been so agitated this time. They point to the syncretic nature of Kashmiri Muslims. It is a remarkable fact to contemplate now that during the sectarian violence of 1947 between Hindu and Muslim throughout India, Kashmir saw no communal killing.

Five: The movements remain acephalous. This is another term from anthropology, meaning a tribe without a chief or leader. Along with the intelligence agencies of the central government, we look in vain for the leaders of the movement. There is no Ayatollah Khomeini to rally people, not even a Sheikh Abdullah, the former leader of Kashmir. The Sheikh's family, reflecting the dynastic principle of politics in South Asia, has been overtaken by events. Unknown names, faceless spokesmen, express the revolt. It is the expression of the entire community. The student, the trader, the housewife, the peasant and the politician are all one this time. There is thus a populist element to these movements; an element which generates the uncontrolled anarchy. It is this which ensures the extremism and savage violence. The Kashmiri killing of a Muslim Vice-Chancellor was a sign of the times. The message was clear for Muslims: you were either with us or against us. The time for sitting on the fence was over for Muslims. This is where Islam comes in.

Six: Islam provides a viable reference, an appropriate frame of identity, for the movement. The Islamic sense of identity is dominant among other conflicting ideologies in these movements. We must first make clear our definition of Islam. By an Islamic identity, I mean a general awareness of being Muslim, whether in politics, clothes or customs, not necessarily in terms of religious orthodoxy. This is a recent development, for large parts of these communities were neutral regarding their Islamic identity over the last decades. Many had perhaps felt it prudent consciously to set aside Islam. They had become secular Soviets, Palestinians or Indians, good citizens, loyal nationals. But, in the end, they also faced the tanks and bullets of the state. They were labelled, *en bloc*, Muslim rebels. No 'ism' – Marxism or secularism – could protect them. With others, they had little to fall back on except the Islamic identity. *Allah-u-Akbar*, God is most great, became the universal cry of identity and defiance. Besides, once the momentum picked up, the only support they received was from other Islamic groups, whether Iranians supporting the Soviet Muslims, the Arabs the Palestinians or the Pakistanis the Kashmiris. Muslim leaders have always had a constituency in Kashmiri hearts. When those in

Pakistan die, whether of the left, like Bhutto, or the right, like Zia, there is widespread mourning, a generalized sense of loss.

It is also important to point out that, though Pakistan appears as a champion of Kashmir and has gone to war, twice at least, with India over its future, this time Kashmiris appear to be demanding their own future. Many would prefer an independent Kashmir, free of both India and Pakistan. The slogans of *azadi*, independence, in Kashmir exclude both Delhi and Islamabad.

The Islamic label is also a convenient one for the Western media. The mosque and mullah appear as easily recognized symbols of 'Muslim fundamentalism' in the West. A rally after the Friday prayer, a man with a beard arguing for rights, a youth with a gun, all are projected as Muslim fanatics ('Militants of Kashmir show their hand', reads a lengthy report in *The Independent* by R. Whittaker, 8 June 1990, with a large photograph of two young men with guns and covered faces). It is, therefore, easy to see these movements as 'Islamic'. Unfortunately, this also ensures indifference to the plight of these communities in the West. The last thing the West wants is more Muslim fundamentalism. So the deaths in these three areas, over 1,000 in 1990, made little impact internationally. In contrast, threats of cutting off gas to Lithuania by Moscow in 1990 were discussed on the front pages of the newspapers and during the main television news. Perhaps there is a racist dimension to this too.

However, the media are notoriously like a double-edged weapon. Pictures of Muslims standing up for their rights, facing tanks and bullets, in different parts of the world on television or in newspapers inspire Muslims elsewhere. An apocalyptic mood is created and enhanced. 'If my "brother" can face Israeli soldiers on the West Bank, why can't I face Indian ones in Kashmir?' they ask.

Last, though certainly not least, is the importance of the universal ideas of self, dignity, freedom and identity which characterize our times. The contemporary climate that has generated these ideas is a European one juddering communist states (provoking *The Economist* to ask in a lead article, 'Goodbye to the nation-state?' 23 June 1990). Reporters in Kashmir, like Raymond Whittaker, note the constant reference in conversations to 'Lithuania' as a potent symbol of the times and mood. Kashmiris say that if freedom can be demanded as a right by Europeans, why must they be denied it? There is thus, in these movements, a resonance of a larger global pattern.

The postmodernist spirit, easily noted in Kashmir, is a combination of cultural *jouissance* and nostalgia, of schizophrenia, of challenge to central authority and accepted traditional notions of modernity such as 'progress', 'economic development', 'the needs of the nation-state', 'central planning'. But South Asian political figures and bureaucrats appear well fortified against the postmodernist winds blowing in the world. Because they do not comprehend the new universal spirit, they cannot concede its cultural and political implications.

We may, therefore, sum up this discussion with the observation that the Muslim movements reflect a combination of external and internal factors. There is little doubt that they are substantially different from earlier expressions of identity. In this case, the desperation and determination appear extreme, sustaining the movement against the full and heavy-handed might of the state. Islamic revivalism is part of the explanation for the movements, deprivation and distrust the other parts. The clumsy handling by government ensures the continuation of the movement. The men in power are out of tune with the times. Where compassion and imagination are required, we note violence and suspicion. The lack of charity is compounded with absence of judgement.

Political expression in our world is characterized by changing, fragmented and cacophonous noises. The Muslim movements do not appeal only to ideas but also to emotion; not only to religious idealism but also to political realities; and they do not depict one monolithic, central position. More than the Resolutions of the United Nations, more than the speeches of the diplomats, the railing of the politicians and the arguments of the lawyers, the Muslim mood may be summed up best in a verse of Mirza Ghalib, the greatest of the Urdu poets of Delhi:

> I have seen her annoyed many times
> But this time it is something more serious.

> *Barha dekhin hein onki ranjshein*
> *Par koch abkay sargrani our hey.*

In this chapter we have indicated that the historical disruptions and developments which Muslims are living through, like the ongoing encounter with the West, affect all aspects of their life. We have also highlighted the complicated nature of the European inheritance in post-colonial societies. The tyranny of the post-colonial state and the bankruptcy of its rulers have also been emphasized. It is time to move away from the hurly-burly of politics and look at the scholars and writers who are observing Muslim societies. In the next chapter we will attempt to show how they are responding to the climate of postmodernism.

Chapter 4

Studying Islam

Although postmodernism might suggest a more relaxed tolerance, or perhaps permit an even more genuine objectivity in studying others than in the past, in our case, paradoxically, this is not so. This is because the media, through their forced entry into scholarly and academic discussion, have joined the post-modernist discourse and have thereby coloured the contemporary perception of Islam. This has encouraged a shallow, impressionistic and often execratory assessment in the West; in turn, it creates a strident radicalization among Muslims. The more sober voices tend to be drowned. It is precisely this lack of distinction between high and low culture, the refined and the popular, that Huyssen has pointed out to us as a characteristic of post-modernism (1986). Both Muslim and non-Muslim scholarship are thus affected. But there are also the first flowers of the post-modernist academic spring: scholarship that is free of past racial and sectarian prejudices and which points to the future (I discuss this in detail in 1991e and 1991f).

Below, we shall attempt to map out the contemporary intellectual landscape of Islamic studies by identifying its prominent features. We suggest two triangles, the one to depict Muslim scholarship, the other non-Muslim scholarship. For Muslims the three points of the triangle are traditionalists, radicals and modernists. For non-Muslims they are traditional orientalists, the new scholars and the media generalists. The triangles will act as a matrix for the emergent postmodernist writing that we will be discussing in this chapter. This taxonomic exercise allows us to simplify a deeply complex situation, further complicated by incompatibility, collision, acrimony, even a shifting of positions, between the points of our triangles. The exercise will help us to understand the study of Islam on the threshold of the twenty-first century, to observe how the postmodernist age affects its perception and to indicate future intellectual directions and political positions. In order to avoid cluttering the text I will minimize as far as possible the use of bibliographic references, which, for many of the scholars involved, would be long and distinguished.

In our discussion in this chapter we will intentionally give disproportionate importance to media figures in comparison to the more substantial scholars and thinkers. The former intrude on us out of all proportion to their merit in their impact both on the external perception of Islam and its inner self. This is so because of the nature of understanding and information in our times. Even the educated Muslim, who may never have heard of scholars like Ismail Faruqi and Fazlur Rahman, would now have strong views on Salman Rushdie, and he may be debating the different methods of implementing the *fatwa* and their relative merits, and the extent to which Kalim Siddiqui deserves support.

MUSLIM SCHOLARSHIP

Fittingly, we commence our discussion with an image from a university town. It is of an ambitious, bearded young man with a glint in his eye leading a vociferous campaign to seize the central mosque. Capturing it, he freezes the funds and denounces the elders as corrupt and unworthy. A counter-attack ejects him from the mosque and he henceforth establishes his own prayer place. Recrimination and counter-recrimination flow between them. Another time, Muslim students threaten a Pakistan student society function with hockey sticks if the organizers go ahead with plans for a Punjabi ethnic folk-dance. Dancing, they announce, even if it is a village harvest celebration, is un-Islamic. What is of interest is that these events took place not in Tehran, Cairo, or Islamabad, but in Cambridge.

The 'BBCD'

Not surprisingly, Pakistani students, those from Pakistan and returning to Pakistan, amazed at these antics in a supposedly civilized Britain, conferred on their British compatriots a devastating title. It reflected the dilemmas of Macaulay's ideas for Asians and it said it all: 'BBCD' – British Born Confused *Desi* ('native'). In turn, Pakistanis were called 'TPs' – typical Pakistanis – by the BBCD. This perception of each other reflected undergraduate honesty – and cruelty.

Pakistanis found the BBCD either too Westernized or too conservative, either inclined to extolling the virtues of their parents' customs or deriding them, oscillating from one point to the other with alarming frequency. It was precisely this oscillation, this imbalance, which produced, at one end of the spectrum, the young enthusiasts who supported the idea of an Islamic order in Britain and, at the other, the first Muslim strippers (the news of the latter, widely circulated in the English press – including the Pakistani paper, *Jang* – in October 1991, caused outrage and anger when it was flashed to Pakistan, the country of the girls' origin. Predictably, the West was the target and blamed for its corrupting influences). The parents of the BBCD, because they still retained links with, and memories of, Pakistan, were often at a loss as to how to deal with their children.

More than learned discourses or sociological tables, the following case throws light on the dilemmas of Muslim students, as well as the clash of cultures and generations that is taking place. A Pakistani father, successfully settled in Britain, rang out of the blue late one night in the winter months of 1990. With a quivering voice, he described his agony and that of his wife on receiving a note from their daughter at university. She had rejected Islam and chosen to adopt Western civilization. The college, no doubt fearing a father's wrath – indeed, the brothers demanded death – refused to disclose her whereabouts. The police would not intervene, and for the parents the girl disappeared from the face of the earth.

The father did not know me personally but had seen me and heard of me and he poured out his heart; he had not talked to anyone else; the shame was too great. Until the letter, his religious background and affiliation had ensured a strict control of her life. I had to convince a total stranger to set aside traditional values of honour and ideas of right and wrong which demanded stern action against apostasy. I counselled patience and compassion. It was easy advice but it was also in the spirit of Islam, for I knew the man's heart was breaking. His voice was that of the graveyard, and in his anger and confusion he was capable of desperate action. With a new-born daughter in the house I was perhaps extra-sensitive to issues of parenthood. It was one of the most poignant and moving conversations of my life.

In the following weeks I had to attempt reconciliation between an apprehensive college, a bewildered girl in hiding and parents alternating between shame and anger; it was a terrible task, one easy to fail. When we met, after secret talks and in secret circumstances, it was plain that the girl's rejection of Islam was a consequence of the themes I have raised in this book. And although I have respected the confidence of all concerned by not indicating names, the purpose of relating the episode is to confirm this aspect of the argument. What came across was the strength of Western scholarship in depicting Islam as flawed (she cited Montgomery Watt, whom we discuss in this chapter); the success of the Western media in conveying totally negative images of Islam (especially relating to women); and the failure of Muslim spokesmen in communicating Islam's relevance to her life. She had simply had enough; she wanted out. With luck and patience the girl returned home later in the year; but how many more were there like her, waiting to break away?

Cambridge has changed – there are fewer gowns, less class snobbishness and more women visible in the colleges. This is change in the right direction. In the 1960s there was literally no place for Friday prayer in Cambridge; now there are at least three. This is also correct but there is a price. Muslim scholars have also changed; and the tensions of the postmodernist age are pulling them apart.

The Muslim triangle of scholarship

If, for Muslims, late-nineteenth century European colonialism was a modern siege, the Western cultural campaign of the late twentieth century is a postmodernist blitzkrieg. There is thus an embattled tone in much of the contemporaneous Muslim academic response to the West. This touches the three points of the Muslim triangle mentioned above.

Our definitions are broad, and some are in need of clarification, and our categorization is crude. Once again we point out the change in the definition of modernism discussed in Chapter 1. The earlier Muslim modernists had believed firmly that it was their religious tradition and culture which defined them in the modern age. The modernists of the present generation would jettison the baggage from the past altogether.

Although I have labelled Fazlur Rahman a traditionalist, many will see him as a modernist. My reasons for doing so rest on the definition of 'modern'. Unlike those I shall define as modernist in the late twentieth century, at no point does Rahman set aside or abjure Islam; indeed, his work appeared to grow more conservative in his later years and the same could be said of earlier modernist scholars like Sir Sayyed and Iqbal.

Yet Rahman appears modern for many Western scholars because he not only engages with their ideas with an open mind but also writes in English and uses Western academic idiom. He eventually lived in the United States but we also know that Rahman was the son of a religious scholar, educated in the vernacular in a traditional school in Pakistan, a lifelong scholar of Arabic who felt deeply for Islam, although he would grapple with 'modernity' to the end (see his last book and its title, *Islam and Modernity*, 1984).

Rahman is too radical for orthodox Muslim scholars, many of whom actively campaigned to drive him out of Pakistan; yet their belief in Islam binds them together. For precisely the same reasons, he is too traditionalist – too willing for dialogue, too balanced in opinion – for the radicals. For modernists he is an orthodox religious scholar in the traditional mould. Such arguments, reflecting different perspectives, could be applied to other scholars in this chapter and negate our attempts at clarification; we will therefore retain our categories.

Traditionalists

For the traditionalists the larger message of Islam, rather than the narrower sectarian or personal squabbles, is of greatest importance. They believe in the universal message of God and in inter-faith dialogue:

> There is also the very important task which lies ahead for Muslims to try to make peace on a theological level, not only a political level, with other religions in the West, to extend a hand, which Islam has always done, to Judaism and Christianity and to other religions.
>
> (Nasr 1990)

The work of the established names, like Ismail Faruqi, Ali Shariati, Hossein Nasr and Ali Ashraf – and, of course, Fazlur Rahman – is to be found here. That of some, like Aziz Ahmad, 'connects' with Western orientalists. In their lives most of these scholars would attempt to live by Islamic principles. They would be decent citizens, good husbands and fathers. Many of them preferred a life of the scholar-activist to the ivory tower of academia, some even rising to prominence in public life like Khurshid Ahmad, Ismail Faruqi, Ali Shariati and Hasan Turabi.

There was another side to the traditionalists. Many in their lives were isolated from, and in their work inaccessible to, the ordinary Muslim. Their interests – Arab philosophy, Sufi mysticism, sectarian polemics – appeared esoteric and further isolated them. At best these scholars were seen by critics as an irrelevance and cut off from reality, at worst as sanctimonious hypocrites and as humourless patriarchs.

An important branch of the traditionalist position, although not encouraged by the more orthodox, is that of Sufism. Sufism is Islam's message of universalism and tolerance. It is therefore appropriate that European Sufis, like Martin Lings and Frithjof Schuon, represent it. Here is one of the most powerful seams of Islamic culture with its widely appealing message. Unfortunately, by its very esoteric nature, Sufism is restricted in its popular appeal to the initiate or the scholar. Its critics claim that the way of the Sufis is no longer a practical one in our world, that Sufism is a form of escapism. Even its admirers believe that its time has gone:

> The wheel now appears to have turned full circle. Sufism has run its course; and in the progress of human thought it is illusory to imagine that there can ever be a return to the point of departure. A new journey lies ahead for humanity to travel.
> (Arberry 1990: 134)

Sufism is also dismissed by younger radical Muslims (like Parvez Manzoor and Ziauddin Sardar). With it they miss one of the most attractive and endearing sides of Islam, one tracing its origins directly to the Prophet. However, rumours about its demise are premature (for example, see the work and writing of a younger generation of Sufi scholars like Sheikh Fadhlalla Haeri, 1989).

Radicals

The radicals have lost patience with and rejected the traditionalists. There is a fine line – often breached – between traditionalists and those we call radicals in their faith and belief. It is in their strategy and style that the difference lies. The strategy is explained by more than political philosophy. Personal character, age and life-style contribute to the difference. Some of the radicals are not scholars of any kind and wish to implement an Islamic order through armed struggle or confrontation. They are usually driven by hatred and contempt for what they call 'the West'; many are in danger of becoming misologists. They tap the anger and resentment among Muslims. In their rhetoric are doses of populism and suggestions of anarchy. These are not establishment figures and are often rejected by it.

Fazlur Rahman defines their position as one of 'postmodernist fundamentalism' or 'neofundamentalism' and underlines their anti-West stance:

> The current postmodernist fundamentalism, in an important way, is novel because its basic élan is anti-Western. . . . The pet issues with the neofundamentalist are the ban on bank interest, the ban on family planning, the status of women (contra the modernist), collection of *zakat*, and so forth – things that will most *distinguish* Muslims from the West. Thus, while the modernist was engaged by the West through attraction, the neorevivalist is equally haunted by the West through repulsion.
> (Rahman 1984: 136)

If the writing of the traditionalists suggests harmony and balance, even a *modus vivendi* with the non-Muslim world, that of the radicals, like Shabbir Akhtar, Parvez Manzoor, Ziauddin Sardar and M.W. Davies, reflects the general Muslim sense of anger at its injustices. Kalim Siddiqui is perhaps the best-known radical, the archetypal energumen, and is dubbed 'Britain's Angry Ayatollah' (Askwith 1990). He demands the establishment of an Islamic order and leads the campaign in the United Kingdom for the death of Salman Rushdie.

The radicals are contemptuous of the modernists, and, in turn, are branded fundamentalists by them. Most Western scholarship, including that of a younger and more sympathetic generation, is rejected by the radicals as soiled by orientalism. But Muslims are not spared either. Akhtar is dismissive of the work of traditionalists – Nasr's is 'obscure'; that of Ashraf's Islamic Academy in Cambridge and the Jamaat's Islamic Foundation in Leicester 'stale' – and also that of the radicals: Kalim Siddiqui's work is 'imbalanced' (Akhtar 1990: 218–19). Sardar and Davies have attacked unfairly, with unholy venom, almost every established Muslim scholar, as not being sufficiently Islamic, for years (Ahmed 1989). For Davies, it is perhaps the zeal of the convert. Siddiqui's critics will be delighted at the libellous accusations they hurl at him, like embezzling Saudi and Iranian funds (Sardar and Davies 1990: 197–8. As in previous books they need better editing; even Siddiqui's name is misspelt in the index; also see Ahmed 1989).

Because of the nature of the world media and its use of stereotypes, figures from this category are often in the news. They fit perfectly the media stereotype of the fundamentalist. A scholarly treatise arguing for goodwill and balance is not news; a menacing speech threatening an Islamic revolution in London is. Kalim Siddiqui's call for a Muslim parliament in the United Kingdom and abusive dismissal of the West as a 'bogland' have made him a media favourite. He fits – indeed looks – the negative media stereotype of Islam in the West.

These Muslims are contemptuous of the so-called Third World writer or leader patronized by the West for its own ends:

> The joker in the pack has been Tariq Ali, super brat of the sixties. One time burner of effigies, leader of demos, hurler of abuse, he has now joined the Establishment. Comfortably ensconced in Channel 4, he patronises, like Rushdie, the people to whom he once belonged. These cultural mutants are the product of a sustained campaign which has lasted for four centuries. First territory, then labour, then the mind have been progressively colonised and exploited. We have 'third world' politicians and technocrats destroying the ecologies of their own countries, in pursuit of dollars and development, as agents of western aid donors. We also have 'third world' writers and intellectuals who defecate upon the inner ecology of their own people as the agents of secular bigots who recognise no moral limits.
>
> (Khalid in Ahsan and Kidwai 1991: 244)

In a comment which, because of its shrewdness, merits full reproduction, a radical Muslim exposes the network around Rushdie and explains how it operates:

> Both 'Is Nothing Sacred?' and 'In Good Faith' have been hailed as the 'greatest pieces of literary polemics ever written'. Indeed, it seems that Rushdie cannot write anything that can be

described by ordinary, human superlatives. This is partly because he is championing an ideology, an ideology which is incapable of questioning its own assumptions, which sees all Muslims as 'fanatics' and 'fundamentalists'. And partly because he has the undying support of a group of friends who occupy key positions in the media. The situation is such that if Rushdie coughed a diseased phlegm on the face of one of his novelist friends, it would be captured on film by Tariq Ali and turned into a documentary, which would be commissioned by Farouk Dhondy and shown in the 'Rear Window' slot of Channel Four; Blake Morrison would reprint it as the lead story in the *Independent on Sunday* which would also contain an instant poll of various luminaries (Harold Pinter, Fay Weldon, Margaret Drabble, Ian McEwan, Arnold Wesker, Penelope Lively, Michael Foot: 'it is the most brilliant piece of political writing I've ever read in my life' (what an impoverished life!, et al.) and Hanif Qureshi would write a lyrical appreciation of it in *The Guardian* as well as make an extensive appearance on 'The Late Show' or 'The South Bank Show' ('The more filthy the better as far as I am concerned, I too have spat a lot of phlegm in my life . . .'), Bill Buford would put it on the cover of *Granta* and *Granta* would also publish the damn thing as a pamphlet.

(Sardar in Ahsan and Kidwai 1991: 299)

(For another biting comment on the 'cronyism' in this group, also see Yasmin Alibhai's article on Rushdie in *New Statesman and Society*, 15 February 1991.)

Here is solid, legitimate argument and deep hurt; but here is also crass vulgarity. Defecation, phlegm, bile – this is Muslim spleen not Islamic scholarship, Muslim temper not Islamic literary expression. And with Kalim Siddiqui's public statements about the promiscuity of Western women we were entering Hanif Kureishi territory. In denouncing their victims through vulgar abuse, these Muslims were themselves becoming like those they attacked; they had left behind the language of traditional Islamic scholarship and were adopting the idiom of the West. They claimed to defend the holy Prophet with their abusive anger. The irony of defending a man who personified decency, patience, kindness and tolerance with vulgarity is lost on them. The traditionalists in our previous category would be repelled by the imagery, however sympathetic they might be to the sentiments that provoked it. They, too, were passionate in defending their position – often despatching their opponents to hell in fiery language. But their language and deportment in the main reflected the Islamic sense of propriety and decency. The perpetually angry Muslims would do well to recall the story of that Islamic paragon, Ali, related in Chapter 2.

The traditional scholars also had Arabic. It was the language of early Islam, of the Prophet and, most important, the Quran. In contrast, the younger radical scholars in the West are in danger of falling between two stools; they are forgetting their own national language (Urdu for Pakistanis) and have not quite mastered English as a first language.

Many of the radicals live in the United Kingdom for economic and political reasons. Holding British passports, wearing English clothes, speaking and writing in English, relying on the Western media for publicity, their loud proclamations of Muslim radicalism appear paradoxical and contradictory. The remoteness from the Muslim countries and societies they wish to represent is a central weakness in their work. They conjure an 'ideal' society, one they cannot order, far removed from the 'actual' one they left behind.

Modernists

The third point in our triangle is covered by a group so diverse in its intellectual range as to threaten its taxonomic validity. The common feature, the recognizable theme, is the general belief that religion as a force, nostrum, or guide is no longer valid in our age. This approximates to our definition of modernism in Chapter 1, except that the present modernists appear to have dropped the past altogether and succumbed to the global civilization dominated by the West.

On one side of the spectrum is the work of those who are self-consciously associated with the Marxist, socialist or secular position like Hamza Alavi, Eqbal Ahmed, Tariq Ali and Salman Rushdie. On the other side are writers like Shahid Burki at the World Bank in Washington and Rana Kabbani in London. Both sides, whether of the left or the right, echo ideas and concepts outside Islam and Islamic tradition; history and customs are not seen as particularly relevant to analysis of Muslim societies.

Some, like Rana Kabbani, have left this point to move closer to the traditionalists. They have been reviled in the press for it.

Rushdie, who once provided the blurb for the front cover of Kabbani's book *Europe's Myths of the Orient* (1986), now refers to her 'perfect Stalinist fervour' (*The Independent*, 4 February 1990). Her sin was the discovery of her Islamic heritage in the aftermath of *The Satanic Verses* controversy and her proud proclamation of it (1989). With her Cambridge academic background and aristocratic family connections in the Middle East, the Islamic fervour was seen as doubly distasteful by her erstwhile supporters. She was letting down the side, rejecting the club. It was clear: you were either with us or damned forever.

Salman Rushdie, Hanif Kureishi and Tariq Ali are examples of the extreme modernist of the late twentieth century, protagonists in the final act of the drama Macaulay initiated. Their position appears to be defined by two interrelated complexes: an inferior one in dealing with the West, and a superior one with the Muslim community. The West, accepting them as authentic spokesmen, was generous and welcomed them; the Muslims, until the explosion around *The Satanic Verses*, had no way of expressing their resentment. Most in this category are nominal Muslims only; some, like Rushdie, are unclear whether they have rejected Islam altogether or not. Their knowledge of Islam is limited and usually derived from a cursory reading of the orientalists. They abhor, as Rushdie wrote in *The Independent*, 4 February 1990, 'the narrow certainties' of Akhtar and Siddiqui. In turn, these Muslim radicals see them as Uncle Toms serving the negative Western stereotype of Islam; and they do the job with pickaxe and hatchet. Rushdie's *The Satanic Verses*, 1988, and the play Ali co-authored, *Iranian Nights*, are examples of the vilification of Islam.

Iranian Nights depicted most of the negative and crude stereotypes of Muslims in the most offensively puerile manner possible. (The Muslim radical above was right. Friends of Rushdie and Ali launched a campaign to propagate the play; Dhondy promptly had it on Channel 4, whatever its artisitic merits.) Mad mullahs, hypocritical fathers and fanatic drug-dealing sons made up the Muslim cast. Tariq Ali, adroit as always, had jumped onto the Rushdie media bandwagon, clutching the coat-tails of the Rushdie affair. The play, however, not for want of trying, failed to provoke Muslims into burning copies of the text and, therefore, died an early natural death. Perhaps Muslims were learning?

The championing of a *cause célèbre* also tends to be selective, a response to the latest fashion in the Western media, to what is considered 'chic' in the sympathy business. Although they are Muslims – however nominal – we hear little from them of the suffering in Kashmir and Palestine. (Rushdie challenged this assertion, which I had made in a review article on 1 December in *The Independent*, by listing the times he had spoken for these groups also in *The Independent*, 4 December 1990. Rushdie's subsequent public statements, especially after declaring himself a Muslim in public in mid-December, emphatically underlined a message of sympathy for Kashmiris and Palestinians; I replied to Rushdie in *The Independent*, 7 December 1990.)

The Marxism or socialism of the modernists is ironic in view of their privileged families, life-style, and education in élite Western universities. Akhtar calls them 'champagne socialists'. Although well-known and established in the West, they have made little impact on the mass of Muslim society. But they are influential among the future élite from Afro-Asia in the prestigious Western universities. Students find them fashionable and, in a cultural sense, 'sexy'. For these students, in comparison, the traditionalist is an old fogy, the radical a wild man.

Marxism among Muslims has singularly failed. This is because Islam carries its own charter of social revolution (see Ahmed 1988). However, there were Muslim Marxists, largely drawn from the tiny Westernized élite. For them freedom often meant free sex, free drinking and a free-wheeling attitude to life characterized by cynicism and opportunism; it was a travesty of the spirit that breathes in the writing of Marx and Engels. After the early passion of youth had evaporated, the Marxists would return tamely to the family fold and their industries and land; their workers and tenants would not have suspected their Marxist past.

After all, even Marx, with his overriding passion for the suffering of the poor, really talked of the *white* poor; his references to Asians are both racially insulting and sociologically incorrect. Like his friend Engels (whose remarks on the Irish cannot be printed today), he appears to have been an unconscious racist.

The Asian Marxists chose to ignore this aspect of Marx. It was either intellectual dishonesty or plain ignorance; after all, it was easy to regurgitate, to repeat stale ideas, to reproduce without effort the ghastly Newspeak emanating from the Information Ministry. And now that Marx has been officially pronounced dead in the Makkah of communism, Moscow, and by the high priests themselves, these Marxists are at a loss. Like drowning rats they paddle in desperation, justifying their old position with feeble arguments, while frantically casting around for a life-belt.

The collapse of communism did not create any anguished emotional or intellectual outpouring, no queues to commit hara-kiri, in this group. The unchecked genocide, the colossal mismanagement, the state repression, the cult of leadership under communist rule were glibly swept under the carpet. The wasted years, the terror of Stalin, of Ceausescu, of Pol Pot, of Mao were as if they had never happened. Many of them simply turned direction, indicated right rather than left, and with indecent capitalist haste proceeded to join in the chorus of criticism against socialism. Tariq, always showing a healthy capitalist streak to exploit an advantage, even produced a satirical play, with the co-author of *Iranian Nights*, Howard Brenton, called *Moscow Gold*, in 1990. The title was apt: Moscow had certainly produced gold for him.

Some of these modernists formed a tight-knit, mutually supportive cabal based on personal friendship (and we have heard a Muslim radical on this above – see page 161–2). Power, privilege and prestige were involved. Lucrative television, film and publishing contracts were given on the basis of what, in other parts of the world, would be called 'cronyism'. These people were now part of the powerful white liberal establishment in the West, the official media spokesmen on Islam and Afro-Asia. But some modernists outside the magic circle, like Yasmin Alibhai, complained that their work created a 'sense of dismay and betrayal' in the majority of Afro-Asians (*New Statesman and Society*, 15 February 1991). They 'were accused of "selling out" and adding to the anguish of an already deprived group'.

There is also a positive side to the activity of the modernists. In the difficult, even culturally and racially hostile milieu of London, these writers have made a considerable impact. They are part of the cultural scene, indeed even setting the agenda for debate in some cases. They have dispelled, once and for all, the notion that South Asians from a Muslim background could not contribute to modern English literature and thought.

Through the media and because of the notice they attracted, their contribution to the language – in polemic, play and literature – is an indisputable fact. Rushdie, in particular, winning literary prizes, became for the West a postmodernist icon, a new literary messiah, even a Hallaj for its Islamic experts (Ruthven

1990: 163; Ian McEwan, *The Late Show*, BBC2, 7 February 1990; Cupitt 1991). The public platform is sometimes used for Muslim causes (as Rushdie pointed out in response to my review in his letter, *The Independent*, 4 December 1990).

Henceforth, after the *fatwa*, anything Rushdie did would be major news. His novel, *Haroun and the Sea of Stories*, a tale inspired by *The Arabian Nights*, was front-page news (1990). Responses to it became a matter of honour, a comment on the author and his plight rather than the book itself. The literary names – Frank Kermode, Edward Said, Anthony Burgess – rushed to review it with unrestrained enthusiasm. There was talk of genius and grace under pressure, of the well of literary brilliance that had not dried in isolation, of the continuing magical realism; there were comparisons with Lewis Carroll and James Barrie. Every artfully concealed allegory was spotted, every nuance highlighted, every pun duly acknowledged. It was not surprising, then, that Rana Kabbani's lonely criticism (*The Independent*, 6 October 1990) was savaged by the literary establishment ('Going soft on Salman' by Mr Punch, *Punch*, 19 October 1990; G. Greenwood in *Literary Review*, December 1990, in reviewing Rushdie 1990). The saga of Rushdie had surpassed anything written in children's books.

Characterizing Muslim scholarship

We sum up our discussion of the Muslim intellectual landscape by pointing out its prominent features. First, the traditionalists continue to dominate the syllabuses at Muslim schools. They also help produce, for all the Muslim railing against the West and English, the best-known Muslim journals in English: *Muslim World Book Review* (Leicester), *Islamic Quarterly* (London), *Muslim Education Quarterly* (Cambridge), *Impact* (London) and *American Journal of Islamic Social Sciences* (United States). Radical sniping notwithstanding, and making allowances for the usual ups and downs of a publication, these are of good quality and often contain worthwhile material.

Second, we observe the prominent role of South Asians in Muslim intellectual activity. Akhtar and Sardar are from this region; so are Rushdie and Siddiqui, one hiding from the *fatwa*, the other demanding its implementation; as, indeed, are some of the main figures mentioned in the Islamic resurgence in Chapter 1. The Anglo-Indian encounter discussed in Chapter 3 is one explanation. Here is a rich subject for anthropological exploration.

Indeed, it was the coming together, for the first time, of the two sections of South Asian Muslims in Britain that caused the Rushdie explosion. Until then they had existed as distinct, watertight groups, with no communication between them. The one group was composed of middle-class professionals and intellectuals, many from Oxbridge, living and working mostly in London. The other group did not consist of literary people. Many were small shop-owners with a farming background in South Asia, who spoke their own language, Punjabi or Bengali, and lived in Bradford or Birmingham. Irony, humour and cynicism had characterized the middle classes; anger, earnestness and bewilderment the working classes. Paradoxically, it was the former that made their name by supposedly representing the latter, as they pontificated about Pakistan and India and issues of Asian poverty in the media. But they succeeded in convincing only the British of their insight. For their own people they had become more English than the English, and represented none but themselves.

Third, elements of class, age, success and immigrant status affect these positions. The traditionalists are older, more established, more secure in their achievements and well recognized. The radicals are generally younger and less well established. The modernists often represent élite families in their own societies. The immigrant status of many of these figures is a remarkable phenomenon of contemporary Islam. Almost all are permanently based in the West. By definition, immigration creates insecurity and neurosis. It is uprooting socially and disturbing psychologically. Some react by rejecting their ancestral links, others by clinging to them all the more ferociously; still others invent ancestral links and ideological constructs that never existed.

Fourth, the type of institutional base or financial backing suggests the intellectual position of our scholars. The Islamic Centre in Oxford and the Islamic Academy in Cambridge are aided by the Saudis; the Iranians back Siddiqui's Muslim Institute. The Saudis, we know, support the status quo, the Iranians support revolutionary change. In a sense, these institutions assume a surrogate position for the larger political confrontation in the Muslim world.

Edward Said made this point recently with telling accuracy for the Arab world:

It's difficult to find an intellectual who is considered to be

merely a scholar, because everyone is associated with some
tendency, some faction, some ideological or political line. In all
Arab countries, academic appointments are political appointments: you have to be cleared.

(Said 1990: 31)

Fifth, *The Satanic Verses* controversy brought together the three
points of our triangle as never before – modernists like Rushdie,
orthodox scholars like Ashraf and radical ones like Siddiqui; it
provided the radicals a *point d'appui* which gave them great media
exposure. It was *The Satanic Verses* affair which galvanized the
scholars and the generalists, the mullahs and the media, allowing
a meeting point and a platform for their views. Into these strong
emotions fed images of a minatory Iran threatening death to a
British citizen, Muslims violating the principles of free speech and
burning books. Centuries of prejudices and principles fused and
exploded.

What the media exposure did was to open a new chapter in
Islamic commentary and study. While a few academic scholars
were invited to appear in the media, others, equally important,
like Khurshid Ahmad and Ali Ashraf, were marginalized and thus
seldom heard. Formerly an unknown, Kalim Siddiqui became the
voice of Muslim radicalism (Askwith 1990).

THE SATANIC VERSES AFFAIR

No contemporary discussion of Muslim scholarship can be
complete without reference to the controversy around *The Satanic
Verses*. We have noted this from the preceding pages. So before
proceeding with an analysis of occidentalism and orientalism I will
pause to reflect on *The Satanic Verses*. I will attempt to show what
it meant to me personally and to the Muslim community in
Britain, which was in the forefront of the campaign against it.

Why did Muslims not like the book? What did I think of it? I was
asked these questions repeatedly in the Western media. The
answers were simple: they were cultural and religious. No Muslim
could condone or be comfortable with the insulting manner in
which the Prophet, his family and some of the holiest names in
early Islam were depicted. The Prophet in particular, for a
Muslim, is the *insan-i-kamil*, the perfect person. There is a formula
central to Islam which every Muslim recognizes: no Prophet, no

Quran; no Quran, no Islam. So how could any Muslim be indifferent to what was perceived as a scurrilous attack on both?

I was brought up in a home and in a culture where mere mention of his name was accompanied by blessings and praise. My father, in spite of his United Nations job and London School of Economics education, would kiss his lips and eyes when the Prophet's name was mentioned as a gesture of reverence. My mother, like millions of Muslims, celebrates the date of his birth annually with devotion and acts of charity. Besides, the manner in which the false controversy around the so-called 'satanic verses' in the Quran was raised appeared calculated and malicious. The arguments of Rushdie and his supporters about literature and creative writing did not provide mitigating circumstances. And they contained an implicit sneer: what do these illiterate Muslim louts know of such fine things?

The Prophet is central to Islam; there can be no doubt about this to a Muslim. Iqbal makes God underline this centrality in one of his most popular poems, *Jawab-e-Shikwa*, 'Reply to the Complaint'. God is replying to the equally popular *Shikwa*, 'Complaint', and concludes thus:

> If you are faithful to Muhammad then I am yours
> What is this universe? To write its destiny the tablet
>   and the pen are yours.

> *Ki Muhammad say wafa tu nay to hum teray hain*
> *Ye jahan cheese hay kia luh o kalam teray hain.*

If people in the West did not comprehend how dearly Muslims revere the Prophet, in their turn Muslims never appreciated the full impact in the West of their death threat to the author and the burning of his book. These actions have deep cultural meaning and resonate in history. They touch the rawest of nerves in the people of the Western world. Many of what they perceive as their grandest achievements and noblest ideas are involved. Ideally these include the principles of freedom of speech, expression and movement; of the abhorrence of censorship; of the respect for debate; of an open and free society (that is why Voltaire was so frequently cited). The Inquisition, the rejection of the established church leading to the Reformation, Nazi and Soviet censorship – these are the signposts on the road which they have travelled. For them the image of burning books is one associated, for all time, with the Nazis in Hitler's Germany. It symbolizes the darkest of the forces of evil, anarchy and terror; it means racial hatred and intellectual desolation.

Innocent of this cultural and historical background, Muslims, by their actions, evoked these images. At one stroke they alienated not only the entire Western intellectual establishment but also the wider populace. I, as a Muslim, understood all this; but, as an anthropologist living in the West, I also knew that most people would neither appreciate nor comprehend the manner in which Muslims had chosen to express their protest.

There was no hope of dialogue. Muslim passions were running high and their spokesmen vied with each other in expressing anger. For them there was the exhilaration and pride of discovering the power to appear in the media, to command attention, to be heard. In this atmosphere, even to hint at dispassionate analysis of the situation was to risk being labelled disloyal to the cause, a traitor to the community. That is why, after almost every media appearance discussing the matter, I would face sharp criticism from the community leaders: there was no need for me to explain matters that were so obvious to non-Muslims; besides, to discuss in a cool manner issues that were so strongly felt was to suggest moderation, a distancing from their position. Yet patience, balance and compassion, the Prophet had repeated again and again, were the greatest of Islamic virtues.

For all the great and genuine gaps of understanding it was also possible to make a dent in the opposing position. With the crisis over the book, the big guns of the British literary and media establishment opened fire to denounce Muslims for burning it and for the *fatwa*. Melvyn Bragg was one such big gun. The Muslim response ensured continued confrontation. There was no dialogue, no serious attempt to explain. Indeed, when I was first asked to Melvyn Bragg's *Start the Week* I was warned by Muslims of his being 'anti-Muslim'. I found that Catherine Bennett's bristling animosity to Muslims was kept in gentle check by Bragg. She probably saw me as representative of the Muslim stereotype: male macho tyrant, beater of wives, master of a dozen women at home, burner of books and assassin of authors.

A year later Melvyn Bragg was one of the main speakers at the launching of my *Resistance and Control in Pakistan* (1991a) at the Royal Society of Arts; he also invited me to another *Start the Week*. On both occasions his famous charm was on full display. He spoke strongly and movingly for the need of the British community to understand Muslims and what they had to offer their host society. Marina Salandy-Brown, his producer, remarked with a twinkle in her eye, 'the credit for this change towards the Muslims goes largely to you.'

Although many Muslims may not have gone as far as wishing to kill the author, the majority found the book highly offensive. Indeed, what came as a surprise to me was not the Muslim response but Rushdie's surprise at it. After all, here was the Western media's so-called authority on Islam wandering into a mine-field and apparently – if he is to be believed – unaware of the response that was bound to come.

Kalim Siddiqui, by linking Rushdie's book to the crusades and condemning it as a conspiracy to defame Islam, has expressed what many Muslims believe to be true:

> The Satanic Verses, he believes, was only the latest product of a conspiracy to denigrate Islam which has existed in the West 'since the crusades'. As the Muslim Manifesto puts it: 'The circumstantial evidence, eg the size of the advance paid to the author, and the media and literary hype that accompanied its publication, leaves us in no doubt that The Satanic Verses is the result of a conspiracy.'

> (Askwith 1990)

Rushdie's is the dangerous combination of undergraduate innocence and undergraduate arrogance: his writing brings together sharp literary insights and a political naïvety that is sometimes breath-taking. Rushdie still appears unaware of the elemental forces he has unleashed, the raw nerves he touched.

So intense is the hatred against him among some Muslims that there was serious talk of a *fatwa* against me as a result of my interview with him for *The Guardian* (1991c). Many questions were raised: granted I only ever saw him once, and that as part of *The Guardian* team, but why did I even speak to him? Why was I duped into giving him a platform to address Muslims? Why didn't I carry out the *fatwa*? Didn't I see that talking to the 'enemy' meant I had become an 'enemy'?

Many people asked me if Rushdie was serious about his re-conversion to Islam. In the interview, I was aware of a tentative spiritual wish to fill what he had called 'that emptied God-chamber' (1991: 377). Confused in his isolation, he needed to be heard by Muslims, to be talked to; he needed compassion and understanding. But the hard-liners would not allow him to explore this, to budge, to shift his position, neither those in his camp, nor those opposed to him. It meant television and radio appearances for them; it gave them a sense of importance, of leading a major battle, of victory at hand. His death-in-life exist-ence seemed to have become essential for their own being.

In good faith I had done my best to bring about a reconciliation, to start a dialogue with the main Muslim spokesmen in the United Kingdom so that they, in turn, could talk to people in Tehran and Riyadh; only this route could have lessened his burden. I would not only be helping someone who had declared himself a Muslim and was in torment but also, by doing so, assist in creating harmony between Muslims and non-Muslims. But events in late January overtook the endeavour. As a result of the Gulf war the Muslim leadership was dispersed and distracted. Unlike the case of the father and daughter discussed above I failed to reconcile the opposing positions. In this case the egos were too great, the issues too complex and the bitterness too deep. So Rushdie stays suspended to eternity in his unreal, invisible world; punished, like some legendary creature in *The Arabian Nights*, every moment of the day, for his writing.

In a widely discussed essay Rushdie asked, 'Is nothing sacred?' and answered 'No' (ibid.: 416). There is iconoclasm, cynicism and despair in his work. With Islam he will, it is to be hoped, gain balance, compassion and peace. If not, there is still something mis-sing in the conversion, something left incomplete.

A few months after his dramatic announcement about accepting Islam he was already back-tracking. 'I remain', he confessed, 'a pretty secular Muslim, still' (to James Wood in *The Guardian*, 21 September 1991). A 'secular Muslim'. What sort of gobbledegook, what kind of literary conceit, is this? What did it mean?

'Secular' and 'Muslim' are by definition incompatible words, as any dictionary will confirm. There can be no Muslim without God – just as there can be no Christianity without Christ, Buddhism without Buddha, Marxism without Marx or, in another context, no Christmas without Santa Claus, American politics without the Constitution and British politics without the Houses of Parliament. Muslims, more cynical than myself about Rushdie's declaration of faith, pointed out with vociferous righteousness that they were correct all along and I was wrong; his conversion was a sham, a shallow stratagem. Once again Rushdie was reflecting and generating confusion; once again he was in need of clarification; once again he appeared to be deliberately provoking religious controversy.

To better understand Rushdie, let us compare him with his main British opponent, Kalim Siddiqui. Thrown into relief thus, both, in the context of the arguments made in this chapter, reflect the BBCD syndrome, although neither was born in Britain: Rushdie at one end of the spectrum, Siddiqui at the other. On the surface there is nothing similar between Rushdie, hiding from the *fatwa*, and Siddiqui, the self-appointed Muslim champion demanding its implementation.

Yet there are interesting similarities underlining the death dance in which Rushdie and Siddiqui are locked. Both are men with gargantuan egos and dreams of grandeur. Both are Indian Muslims who migrated to Pakistan, made an abortive attempt to strike roots in Karachi, arrived in London and began life as immigrants a second time round. Their earlier careers floundered; Rushdie as a copy-writer and Siddiqui as a *Guardian* journalist – although both would later employ with effectiveness the tricks they learned in these professions. Unpleasant memories of 'being English', which both attempted, have left scars; the episode with the kippers in Rugby rankled with Rushdie, the jibes in London roused Siddiqui's fury and he dismissed the West as a 'bogland'. This was the crossroads for both. One parted company with Islam, the other spoke up for it with increasing stridency. Both made their homes and their names in London through the *frisson* and emotion Islam evokes in that city. Both are caught up in the geo-politics of Islam: one accused of support from Israel and the Jews, the other of funding from Iran and Iranians. Neither touches the central features of Islam, its grandeur, nobility and compassion.

Why did the Asians feel betrayed in the Rushdie crisis? Perhaps it was plain social and economic envy; perhaps a lack of understanding on their part. But it was also a feeling of betrayal; and the betrayal was felt twice over: first, as immigrants they felt like unwanted strangers in the land after living here for a full generation; and second, as their own educated élite distanced themselves.

The élite only condescended to raid their community long enough to pick up the material for a short story or play (of Dhondy's

Tandoori Nights variety; there is a smirk and a nudge in the title; but it is not clear whether the author is laughing with the Asians or at them). In these the author spoke to the English in their own idiom. He wished to be recognized by them; projecting the dignity or hurt of the community was not a priority. In these portrayals something sharp was being used, but it was teeth, not intellect.

Even the public image of the élite alienated them from their community. This is typified by Tariq's strained Oxford accent which, after so much practice, still fails to obliterate the primordial Lahore intonations; it amuses rather than impresses the community – but it also sets up barriers.

A Muslim radical sums up the impact of the Rushdie affair on non-Muslims and Muslims; it may be hyperbolical – which is the preferred style of the author – but it contains an element of truth:

> Meanwhile, the ghost of the Rushdie affair will become a new permanent feature of the postmodern scene. Ever present, it will haunt the Western *literati* till the final moments of their panic-stricken, meaningless, barren and lonely lives, while keeping Muslim intellectuals on their toes and on the look out for the next intellectual onslaught.
>
> (Sardar in Ahsan and Kidwai 1991: 290)

The Satanic Verses affair was a major moment in British social history, a time for self-assessment. It centred on the definition of being British. A substantial number of Muslims now live in Britain, but share few values of the majority. Both the majority and the immigrants confronted the question of Britishness from different perspectives. Sides were taken along lines that were almost tribal, some individuals concealing their real judgements in order not to appear disloyal. Perhaps the spate of books should be read in pairs, one from each side as point and counter-point, attack and defence: as examples, there are Akhtar's *Be Careful with Muhammad! The Salman Rushdie Affair* (Akhtar 1989) and Ruthven's *A Satanic Affair: Salman Rushdie and the Rage of Islam* (1990).

British Muslims constantly complain of the humiliating misrepresentation in the media of their family lives after the Rushdie affair (for one of the few contemporary accounts, post-Rushdie, of Muslims in the United Kingdom by a Muslim, see Raza 1991). Muslim women are ridiculed for leading modest lives. For Muslims the examples of double standards are unending: the British refusal to ban Rushdie's book and yet to ban the Pakistani film *International Guerrillas* about him; the blacking out in the media of good, decent Muslim citizens and the high-profile projection of the extremists; while other religious groups are able to maintain their cultural identity through their own schools, Muslims are discouraged from doing so; and so on.

This is not to decry the many British institutions that consciously support an environment for tolerance. Though in Britain Muslims tend to take so much for granted, there is more freedom here – still a notion of fair play – than in any other European country. How long would Siddiqui have lasted with Le Pen, the leader of the National Front, in France? Hanif Kureishi's terrifying vision of inner-city life in England might well change if he lived in Paris or Berlin, already being compared by immigrants to the time of the Nazis.

Let me support this point of tolerance in Britain by a personal example at the height of the Rushdie affair in 1989, when feelings against Muslims ran high. In the spring of that year my college in Cambridge, Selwyn, which has strong links with the established church, initiated me as the first Muslim Fellow of the college. The impressive and moving ceremony is redolent of Christianity – in the church, late in the evening with rows and rows of candles, the entire body of Fellows looking solemn in black gowns in their allotted pews and the Master, presently Sir Alan Cook, alone on the dais, reciting Latin from the Bible. At one point the new Fellow has to repeat the reference to the Trinity – the Father, the Son and the Holy Ghost. For me as a Muslim, believing only in one indivisible God, this would be an insurmountable obstacle. The Cambridge solution was to drop the reference, leaving only the mention of God which would be acceptable to both Christian and Muslim. Similarly, in order to accommodate the Islamic injunction against alcohol, my glass was filled with orange juice every time the port was passed round the High Table after the formal dinner which accompanies the ceremony.

Customs and rituals which were centuries old in a land that cherishes tradition had been waived for a foreign visitor of a different faith. The magnanimity and chivalry of the gestures touched me. Later, the Bishop of Oxford, another Selwyn man, would tell me of the numerous requests he had received from Muslims to address congregations in the mosque during the Rushdie and Gulf crises. The goodwill and consideration suggest that there is always a glimmer of hope, a possibility of redeeming our common humanity, in the midst of the melancholic, larger confrontation.

Muslims living as a minority, whether in Britain or India, must not be seen as sulking strangers: they must participate. They have a contribution to make to society, as academics, as entrepreneurs, as politicians. In turn, the non-Muslim majority will perhaps begin to respond and the movement towards a genuine harmony can begin. The present state of rupture cannot last.

In Britain, the majority of Muslims are law-abiding, low-profile citizens with no intention of returning to their Asian homes, if they have one. By far the majority were born here. They wish to live in dignity and with honour, preserving their cultural and religious heritage. However, some of the radical voices that claim to speak for them are prodding the half-awake monster of European racism (see my 'The next test for British Muslims', in *The Times Literary Supplement*, 1991d). Equally disturbing, within the community, *adl* and *ahsan*, balance and compassion, *ilm* and *sabr*, knowledge and patience, the central features of Islam, emphasized in the holy Quran, are under threat.

THE GROWTH OF OCCIDENTALISM

Over the last decade the passionate reaction among African and Asian scholars against orientalism has created a kind of 'occidentalism' among them. This is as much a rejection of colonialism, with which orientalism is associated, as it is an expression of revolt against the global civilization dominated by the West (see Chapter 3). No survey of the Muslim intellectual landscape would be complete without a comment on this little-discussed phenomenon.

Muslims, it appears, are in the mood to reject. Most Muslim scholars in the West, whether Arab, like Kabbani (1986, 1989), or Pakistani, like Asaf Hussain (1990), are deeply suspicious of Western orientalism. The radicals we identified above would demand the outright rejection of Western scholarship.

For many Muslim scholars working in Africa and Asia, imperfectly grasped bits of Marxist dogma, nationalism and religious chauvinism create incorrect images of the West. For them it is peopled by creatures whose sole purpose is to dominate, subvert and subjugate them. In the vanguard are the self-styled radical scholars. Unfortunately, there are many in whose work paranoia and hysteria pass for thought and analysis. Fulminating against Princeton and Harvard, Cambridge and Oxford, on the basis of anger and emotion and without suggesting concrete alternatives is no answer; it is intellectual bankruptcy.

The distortions, the travesty, are not only incorrect but also a sad reminder of what Muslim scholarship once was. The academic sterility today is made all the more poignant by the achievements and observations in foreign lands of the great Muslim travellers, like Al-Beruni and Ibn Battuta, centuries ago. After all, Muslims are exhorted in the holy Quran to know and marvel at the variety of people created. The holy Prophet urged his followers to go as far as China to acquire knowledge. And let us keep before us the fact that to an Arab in the seventh century, China would have been at the outermost limits of the known universe.

An examination of what contemporary orientals think of the occident would reveal images as distorted and dishonest as in the worst form of orientalism. This occidentalism merits study. It derives almost entirely from movies, television programmes and the VCR. Consider the common stereotype of Western women as promiscuous. This image is confirmed by the reports of contemporary Western women visitors to Muslim countries (Blandford 1978, Dhanjal 1990, Duncan 1989, Heller 1990, Shaw 1989 and C. Lamb 1991).

According to these women most men appear to have little beside seduction or rape on their minds. This may well be exaggerated, but too many ministers, generals and politicians seem to pant and puff around the bedroom in their amorous pursuit of the authoress for the stories to be entirely fictitious. The priapism of these Muslim males may well be explained biologically, but I suspect is to be traced to their notions of Western women. It is this occidentalist stereotype which explains Siddiqui's public comments about Western women as characterized with their legs wide open, waiting for sex on car bonnets. This is the sort of image which would agitate the mind of any Muslim father, not only the one who talked to me of his daughter leaving Islam. This image of women is an insult not only to Western but to all women.

Siddiqui's images and their currency are made possible because of the lack of Muslim scholarship on the West. Muslims have still to produce a body of significant literature on the West, on its society, culture, ideas and politics. This includes Muslims, about 10 million in number, who live permanently in the United States and Europe, and in whose interest it is to study the countries they have made their home. For them, information and understanding of their host population is critical, not necessarily for academic reasons but practical ones; employment, immigration controls, housing and cultural integration are affected. This has led to the contemporary dangerous gaps in communication. As a result, immigrants, especially in Europe, live in intellectual and cultural ghettos. They face serious discrimination based on race and religion. The lives of Muslims, from North Africa in France and Turkey in Germany, are difficult and humiliating. Politicians like Le Pen in France thrive on religious hatred. It is therefore all the more imperative for Muslims to learn about their host countries if they wish to be accepted or respected by them, let alone survive. The study of occidentalism is uncharted territory and in need of exploration by serious Muslim scholars.

NON-MUSLIM OBSERVERS OF ISLAM

Although the field among the non-Muslim commentators of Islam in the global civilization is mapped rather differently from that of Muslim scholars, we can still employ the image of a triangle, in this case formed by the traditional orientalists, a younger generation of scholars of the orient who self-consciously dissociate themselves from orientalism, and the generalists, especially those who appear in the media.

Orientalists

Our understanding of orientalism derives largely from the widely known book of that title by Edward Said (1978). His critique could be summed up thus:

> For the many reasons I have enumerated earlier in this book and in *Orientalism*, knowledge of Islam and of Islamic peoples has generally proceeded not only from dominance and confrontation but also from cultural antipathy. Today Islam is defined negatively as that with which the West is radically at odds, and this tension establishes a framework radically limiting knowledge of Islam.
>
> (Said 1981: 155)

It followed then that

most of what the West knew about the non-Western world it

knew in the framework of colonialism; the European scholar therefore approached his subject from a general position of dominance, and what he said *about* this subject was said with little reference to what anyone but other European scholars had said.

(ibid.)

Said is dismissive of even the most renowned universities 'like Princeton, Harvard, and Chicago' where Islam is taught (1981: 23). Said's Arab passion may have ultimately damaged his own case. The *rite de passage*, the ritual slaying of the elders (Gibb, Grunebaum and Lewis), has been too noisy and too bloody. Nevertheless Said had some honourable exceptions; Clifford Geertz was one (Said 1978: 326).

However powerfully Said argues his case, the work of the older orientalists was marked by many positive features. These included a lifetime's scholarship, a majestic command of languages, a wide vision and breadth of learning and an association with the established universities. In this category are the well-known names of Hamilton Gibb, Bernard Lewis, Arthur Arberry, Montgomery Watt, Louis Massignon. We must not allow their links of various kinds with the colonial powers and a consciousness of the larger encounter between Islam and Christianity to detract from their contribution. While decrying some of their political assumptions, I, for one, applaud the efforts of the translators of favourites like Al-Beruni, Ibn Battuta, Ibn Khaldun, and nearer home to me in South Asia, Babar the founder of the Mughal dynasty.

Besides, to condemn all orientalists as driven by a pathological hatred of Islam is incorrect; some, like Dr Charis Waddy, have expressed warm sympathy in their work (Waddy 1990; her book is, as a mark of her attitude, dedicated to the Sheikh of the al-Azhar in Cairo). Here are the private thoughts of another orientalist while translating the Quran:

This task (of translating) was undertaken, not lightly, and carried to its conclusion at a time of great personal distress, through which it comforted and sustained the writer in a manner for which he will always be grateful. He therefore acknowledges his gratitude to whatever power or Power inspired the man and the Prophet who first recited these scriptures.

(Arberry 1964: xiif)

This is not the voice of an enemy of Islam. Yet none of this comes through on reading Edward Said. Let us take a closer look at orientalism.

A discussion of the most recent work of Montgomery Watt is indicative of traditional orientalist scholarship and thinking (Watt 1988, 1991). He is one of the last living and best-known traditional orientalists. Two interconnected themes, which are notable in Watt's earlier work, dominate. First, the distinction he makes, along with other orientalists, between 'fundamentalist', 'traditionalist' and 'liberal' Muslims. Second, the need for Muslims to re-think some of the central concepts and features of Islam. Both themes should strike a chord and raise a challenge in Muslim society. For Watt an example of innovation (*ijtihad*) is his suggestion that the 'errors' of the holy Quran be identified and it be recognized that it is a collection of 'messages which came to Muhammad from his unconscious (in a Jungian sense)' (1988: 83). The Quran, as we noted earlier, is at the core of Islamic belief, and few Muslims, however liberal, would suggest its re-interpretation. Even Fazlur Rahman, cited by Watt, and, as we saw above, considered modern by some Western scholars, notes: 'The Muslim modernists say exactly the same thing as the so-called Muslim fundamentalists say: that Muslims must go back to the original and definitive sources of Islam and perform *ijtihad* on that basis' (ibid.: 142).

Watt's most important point for Muslims is the need for them to accept that they live in an interconnected global community. For how long can Muslims continue to prevent the encroachment of their world, however unchanging and static, by the advances of modern technology? The final lines of his book end with a prayer for the believer in God, Muslim or non-Muslim (ibid. 1988: chap. 7, epilogue). It is a reaching out for dialogue. The argument for Muslims to address a universal audience surely comes from within the holy Quran, as we have pointed out above. But in the present climate an early response to orientalists like Watt from the contemporary Muslim world cannot be expected.

Watt points out that the historical Western perception of Muslims came under four headings: '1. Islam is false and a deliberate perversion of truth. . . . 2. Islam is a religion which spreads by violence and the sword. . . . 3. Islam is a religion of self-indulgence. . . . 4. Muhammad is the Anti-christ' (Watt 1991: 85–6).

We can still recognize some of this in the popular images of Islam. Among orientalists Islam has always had its friends and critics. 'For long there was the common belief that Muhammad gave to non-Muslims only two choices, the Quran or the Sword, and further that Islam spread through the Sword', explains an Indian writer presenting a familiar argument but one worth repeating (Zakaria 1991: 30). He then cites an English author to disprove this stereotype: 'Sir Thomas Arnold, after much painstaking research, collected facts and figures for his monumental work *The Preaching of Islam*, and proved that Islam was spread, not by "the exploits of that mythical personage – the Muslim warrior with the sword in one hand and the Quran in the other", but by the force of the teachings of the Quran and the character of the Prophet' (ibid.).

Besides Arnold, Islam had other European admirers, including Napoleon and Shaw. Goethe, contemplating Islam, had remarked, 'If this is Islam, then we all live in Islam'. But Islam also had inveterate enemies. Gladstone, the nineteenth-century Prime Minister of Britain, was one:

> However, it was this Book that William Gladstone, the British Prime Minister, held in his hand and declared in the House of Commons: 'So long as there is this book, there will be no peace in the world'. His wrath was on the Ottoman Turks, who were challenging the might of Christian Europe, but he visited it on the Quran which he admitted he had not read. Prejudices do not die; they thrive on hostility and affect the judgement of even the best of persons. Ignorance breeds them.
>
> (Zakaria 1991: 59–60)

In time, the ideas and views of the orientalists have tended to ossify. Their vitality sapped, they have become mimetic, a storehouse of oriental stereotypes and exotica. The university departments and centres, jealously guarding their monopoly as the true interpreters, are the worst culprits. They insist on purity and tradition (see the attacks on the orientalist attitudes of the School of Oriental and African Studies, London, in Said 1978: 214, and Sardar and Davies 1990: 70; the latter accuse the School of 'skullduggery'). These attitudes help explain why the media commentators have had a greater impact than the scholars; the latter have become the bastion of conservative modernity against the demands of postmodernity and change.

Nonetheless orientalism survives in various forms (for its pervasive influence on my discipline, anthropology, see Ahmed 1986a). Even an essentially civilized and humanistic writer can be influenced by orientalist perceptions. An example is provided by Malise Ruthven in his book *A Satanic Affair* (1990): the Arab spokesmen in London appear as bumbling fools, the Bradford ones as sexually repressed fiends. We are continually reminded of the imperfect Muslim grasp of English. Orientalist scholars are cited in order to illustrate the supposed inadequacies of the holy Quran, suggestions of Muslim fanaticism abound. Even the sub-title, *The Rage of Islam*, reinforces the media image.

It has been a valetudinarian period for orientalists, with the crisis quickening. Orientalists, with a few honourable exceptions, had failed to predict and later to make much sense of the political changes occurring in Muslim countries. Iran was a spectacular failure for them. Muslim society, as in Iran, was progressing along a linear, modernizing, secular path, the outward signs of which were discos, cinemas and jeans. Scholars who had spent a lifetime on Persian studies were projecting a secure and long future for the Shah up to the eve of the revolution. After the revolution their previous commitment to, or simply association with, the Shah barred them from the country. Their knowledge was of little avail in dealing with the religious leaders who took over.

In the very premise of orientalism something central and indispensable is absent: it is the notion of a common universal humanity embracing people everywhere irrespective of colour and creed. By denying a common humanity orientalism corrodes the spirit and damages the soul, thus preventing a complete appreciation or knowledge of other people. In this light orientalism is either cultural schizophrenia or a complex form of racism.

The new scholars

Though most of the renowned orientalists are no longer with us, their influence remains, and the ideas of younger writers, as we have pointed out, continue to be shaped by them. Nonetheless there is emerging a new breed of Western scholars of Islam, born in the orientalist tradition yet different in sympathy and style. These form the second point of our triangle.

Such scholars may not be postmodernist in any conscious manner but are certainly post-orientalist. Their work is scholarly and fair; their aim is sympathetic scholarship, they have a need to know and understand; their methodology is impeccable: in the main they allow respondents to speak for themselves. And it is in this that they differ from the traditional orientalist. They allow the native voice, through its literature and scholars, to be heard. When they interject or interpret they do so with sensitivity. There is little evidence of racial or cultural superiority here.

In time their work will still the criticism of those Muslims who reject Western scholarship *in toto*. Unfortunately in their numbers and viewpoint these scholars are still in the minority in their disciplines. They also tend to be dwarfed by the media attention given to those who belong to the category of generalists.

It is appropriate – and a hopeful sign – that the United States, as the acknowledged leader of the global civilization, has produced most of these scholars. Lois Beck, John Esposito, Ross Dunn, Michael Fischer, Barbara Metcalf, Henry Munson, Jr., Theodore Wright, Jr. and William Chittick are examples. In the United Kingdom Hastings Donnan, Michael Gilsenan, Francis Robinson, André Singer and Pnina Werbner are some who represent this trend.

William Chittick's most recent study of the Sufi figure Ibn Arabi is a worthy example of this scholarship (1989). It is nothing short of a magnificent labour – a lifetime's labour at that – of love. His defence of Arabi's themes of humility and love are deep-felt; his identification with his subject moving. His affection for Ibn Arabi and the vitality of the Sufi message challenge the pessimism of those who we heard earlier in this chapter lamenting the decline of Sufism.

Another book worth mentioning in this frame is John Esposito's *Islam: The Straight Path* (1991). It provides a succinct, up-to-date survey of Islam, tracing the emergence and development of Islam and discussing the formation of Islamic belief and practice (law, theology, philosophy and mysticism). For Muslims it is the struggle to define and adhere to their Islamic way of life, that is 'the straight path' of the title.

An apt universal chord is struck by Esposito when he places Muslim problems in a wider context. He points out that like their 'Abrahamic cousins', Jews and Christians, Muslims today are deeply concerned about the secular drift of their societies and its impact on faith and values. His conclusion is worth noting, for it acts as a corrective to the images in the media:

There is indeed an Islamic revolution occurring in many parts of the Muslim world. However, the most significant and pervasive revolution is not that of bombs and hostages, but of clinics and schools. It is dominated by social activists (teachers, doctors, lawyers, dentists) and preachers rather than warriors.

(Esposito 1991: 218)

Esposito draws our attention to the complex interaction of cultures in our own world in his introduction: 'Muslims are very much part of the mosaic of Western societies, no longer foreign visitors but fellow citizens and colleagues.' This needs to be underlined in the context of race relations in Britain, especially in the wake of *The Satanic Verses* affair and the Gulf war. It drives home the point that Muslims in the United States and Europe have every intention of staying and must be taken seriously. This is a reality the majority population must come to terms with in the 1990s; Muslims, too, need to face up to it.

The heat and fury Edward Said generated by arguing that the West can know Islam only in a demeaning and exploitative manner has obscured a central question raised by him: can the West ever hope to understand, objectively and sympathetically, the other, that is, foreign cultures, alien peoples? Clearly, these scholars indicate that this is possible, *pace* Said. Here is scholarship in the highest tradition, and in its humanity it reflects the understanding which academics at their best are capable of achieving.

It is time, then, to move beyond Said's arguments. In an important sense he has led us into an intellectual cul-de-sac. In attempting to transcend the idea of the orientalist system we end up by replacing one system with another. There remains the real danger of simplifying the complex problem of studying the other or the foreign. Said has left us at the end of the trail with what he set out to denounce: stereotypes, images devoid of substance. Orientalism is now an empty cliché, the orient a geographical location only in our imagination.

The generalist and the media person

The third point of the triangle for non-Muslim scholarship reflects the postmodernist era. Like the era, the images of Islam are constantly shifting and they are eclectic, ironic, often unpleasant and hurled at us endlessly. The immediate spectacle is more important than the fact, the image and the impression more than reality. This point in the triangle is covered by a rag-bag of journalists, novelists and media persons, many posing and speaking as instant 'experts'. For most people in this group Islam is an instant media villain, a monstrosity to be reviled and beaten. It is the volume and power of these voices in the media that have drowned the more sober tones of the scholar. Indeed, they raid the orientalist cupboard for alimentation, picking up old prejudices and scatological bits of information. In turn, they use these in the most tendentious and absurd manner.

Muslims, especially the radicals, point to the orientalism evident in even the so-called ethnic media programmes which are supposedly friendly to immigrants. The two sticks that orientalism uses to beat Islam with – its treatment of women and its politics – are constantly and not so subtly to be discerned in action. *Network East*, the BBC TV programme for Asians, is quoted as a perfect example. 'Is it meant for the entire Asian community or only the Indians?' 'It always shows Muslims in a negative light – like Muslim girls as prostitutes or having run away from home; or then Pakistan is about to have another period of martial law.' 'It appears to be run by Muslim-hating BJP people.' 'It is yet another conspiracy – a Hindu–Christian alliance.' These are some of the Muslim responses. This is an exaggeration, but, at the risk of never being invited in the future to *Network East*, I must admit Muslims are certainly conspicuous by their absence in the list of the programme's producers, directors and presenters. The odd Muslim on the programme, usually a female, is scared stiff of being accused of a Muslim bias and is therefore as zealous as the rest of the team to 'expose' the ills of Islam. Although it ran the religious TV series *Mahabharat*, immensely popular in India, for months, it has not encouraged Muslims to project their religion in cultural or intellectual terms for fear of cries of 'fundamentalism'. When they are shown, Muslim programmes concentrate on the social evils in Islam – all adding up to a lurid and dark picture of it. Traditional-minded Pakistanis may not have recognized the links to Macaulay's Minute – the Anglicization in ideas, values and behaviour of Asians – but did talk darkly of the dilemmas of the BBCD. Muslims, therefore, tend not to trust the media.

Yet as I hinted earlier, the Western media can – and does – respond to Muslims if they are prepared to engage with it seriously. Take the Gulf war. The BBC preferred a cricket commentary style of reporting, in the early days at least: 'Our team on this first day of the first innings scored a brilliant 2000 sorties, the other team zero. Well done, boys.' There was never a black or brown face around its main war anchorman, David Dimbleby, to balance the discussion. In contrast ITN, Channel 4, regularly invited many non-British participants, including myself, on to its *Midnight Special* programmes, lasting two hours each time. Nicholas Owen, the presenter, constantly went out of his way not only to include me, a novice, in the cut and thrust of television debating, but provided me with every opportunity to represent the anguish of and anger among the Muslims.

'Now that the *Midnight Special* has come to an end', wrote the producer, 'I feel I ought to write to those guests who have made it such a splendid success. For what it is worth you made three appearances – more than anybody else. You were certainly one of our favourite guests – both for your spirited contribution and your general kindness and goodwill.' One of those guests, Harold Pinter, considered anti-Muslim by Muslims for his consistent public support of Rushdie, wrote: 'Anyway, I was indeed delighted to be on the same platform with you.'

Joining the media persons were numerous academics, including many Islamic experts. They have abandoned their role as neutral observers and become active participants in the political drama portraying Islam in an unfriendly light. They have advised governments, prepared reports and appeared on television. The voices of scholars explaining the gentle aspects of Islamic civilization – Persian paintings, Arabic calligraphy, Sufi mysticism – were drowned by those arguing about geo-political strategy and imperatives. Indeed, some experts argued for the outright invasion of Muslim countries in order to capture their wealth, their oil wells and ports, so as to make them 'safe' for the West. This was J.B. Kelly's position on the Gulf (1980). In Kelly's case the words were prophetic. In 1990 the Western troops landing on the Arabian peninsula appeared to confirm his line of thinking. The war in 1991 was its logical outcome.

The following introductory sentences of an academic book on Islam are calculated to send a chill down the spine of the Western reader:

Sadat was murdered by Muslim extremists in October 1981. His murderers left behind a pamphlet, 'The Neglected Duty', which their lawyers regarded as a valid, Islamic defense of their act of terrorism. This pamphlet was published for the first time in December 1981. For a long time to come, so a certain Jamal al-Banna writes in a book published in March 1984, this pamphlet, called in Arabic *Al-Faridah al-Ghaibah*, will dominate the discussions on fundamentalist and extremist Islam.

(Jansen 1986: xvii)

Having skilfully introduced Islam as, and associated with, 'terrorism', 'fundamentalism' and 'extremism', the author proceeds to explain the significance of Jamal al-Banna:

Jamal al-Banna derives his prestige from writing about these matters partly from his close family relationship to Hasan al-Banna, the founder of the Muslim Brotherhood. The preface and the cover of this book on the creed of Sadat's assassins explicitly mention that he is a son of Abd al-Rahman al-Banna, a brother of Hasan al-Banna.

(ibid.)

Recently the British media have thrown up numerous 'Islamic experts' like Robert Kilroy-Silk, ex-MP, television chat-show presenter and columnist in the *Daily Express*. 'They are backward and evil', wrote Kilroy, about Muslims, 'and if it is being racist to say so . . . then racist I must be – and happy, and proud, to be so' ('Kilroy on Monday: West is best', the *Daily Express*, 25 February 1991. His words on race are similar to those expressed by the porter at the Cambridge college, which we heard on page 116). 'Islam, once a great civilization worthy of being argued with', observed Peregrine Worsthorne, 'has degenerated into a primitive enemy fit only to be sensitively subjugated. But if they want a *jihad*, let them have it' (the *Sunday Telegraph*, 3 February 1991).

'Muslim society looks profoundly repulsive', observed another expert, Conor Cruise O'Brien (who is mentioned in Said's *Orientalism*, 1978):

It looks repulsive because it is repulsive. . . . A Westerner who claims to admire Muslim society, while still adhering to Western values, is either a hypocrite or an ignoramus, or a bit of both. At the heart of the matter is the Muslim family, an abominable institution. . . . Arab and Muslim society is sick, and has been sick for a long time. In the last century the Arab thinker Jamal al-Afghani wrote: 'Every Muslim is sick and his only remedy is in the Koran.' Unfortunately the sickness gets worse the more the remedy is taken.

(*The Times*, 11 May 1989)

This from a man once Professor of Humanities at New York University, former Chief Editor of the *Observer* and a member of the Irish Senate; and he was not alone. Countless others, like the novelist Fay Weldon, a vocal supporter of Rushdie, were equally forthcoming on Islam. The intensity of the prejudice against Islam was surprising if only because of the quarters from which it sprang: diplomats, editors, writers, members of Parliament. Many of these so-called Islamic experts, as we saw earlier, were hailing Rushdie as a Hallaj (Ruthven 1990: 163; Ian McEwan, *The Late Show*, BBC2, 7 February 1990; Cupitt 1991).

Late in 1990, at the height of the Gulf crisis, the tabloids were distorting anything on Islam, even a straightforward academic lecture on the subject. This was illustrated by my talk at the Royal Anthropological Institute in London on 13 September 1990, arranged for Her Royal Highness, the Princess of Wales. The *Sun's* headline averred that the Princess 'takes Islam books home after war lesson', that she 'was swept up in the Gulf crisis' and given 'a lecture on "holy war"' (14 September 1990). The *Daily Express's* headline said: 'I'm not Diana's guru says top academic' (15 September 1990). For the record, I had neither talked of a holy war, nor given a war lesson, nor claimed to be the guru of the Princess, or indeed anyone. The *Sun* had chided me with some petulance: 'newspapers were accused of "distorting" the religion that holds thousands of Britons hostage.' Islam was thus reduced to nothing more than a religion of hostage-takers in the reference to Saddam Hussein's detention of Western visitors in Iraq.

Some Muslims responded in kind, exactly as the media would have wanted them to, without knowing what was in the lecture. The President of the Muslim Youth Movement of Great Britain, based in Bradford, reading in the local papers some garbled account, criticized me for talking to the Princess (in a letter to me dated 16 September). He also strongly attacked my position on those who wished to kill Rushdie (the Muslim Youth Movement had been in the forefront of the campaign). He sarcastically accused me of being a toady of the British, 'a good boy of The British Empire'.

The communication was not as minatory as it sounded – and more than balanced by the many positive Muslim responses. It came from an organization whose very name, Muslim Youth Movement, was a misnomer – its members may have been Muslim, although their grasp of Islam, judging by the letter, was far from complete; its president, if we went by his appearances on TV – advancing waistline matched by a receding hairline – was no picture of youth, and its limited, localized membership hardly constituted a movement.

The central point made here concerns the nature and involvement of the media in our discussion of Islamic scholarship and thinking. What filters through are distorted meanings and prejudices. The arguments are prejudged and passionate. People believe what they wish to believe. Their aim is to score points, not to arrive at the truth.

The Satanic Verses first, then the Gulf war crisis and finally the BCCI, destroyed the dam, flooding out the sober side of scholarship. Reality and illusion, prejudice and fact, scholarship and gutter journalism, world politics and strategic interests came together to colour the contemporary understanding of Islamic scholarship. Neither the traditionalist Muslim scholar nor the sober Western scholar was on television or in the tabloids. Few people had any idea of Ali Ashraf and Hossein Nasr – or John Esposito and Francis Robinson – or what they looked like. It was Kilroy-Silk and Siddiqui who were heard and seen in the media.

Unless the more balanced voices of the scholars are able to be heard, the media battle – and therefore the chance of under-standing between Muslims and non-Muslims – is lost. For, like it or not, what matters in our world are the images and arguments that flood into Western living rooms for hours, daily, through the television. In these Islam is usually depicted as the embodiment of evil and hatred.

It is precisely at this point that the loud, radical Muslim, like Siddiqui, connects with the argument. O'Brien does not have to look far for an example of a Muslim spewing hatred for the West and threatening its stability. He has many Muslims in London who act and behave exactly as he says Muslims do. Who can forget Siddiqui, eyes blazing and beard bristling, on the international television news, pointing a threatening finger at the camera, and promising Islam will get you. This is a caricature, confirming and feeding another caricature.

Confronted with such primeval emotions and stark simplicity we yearn for the learning and sophistication, however hostile, of the traditional orientalist scholars. Surely, Said would admit, Watt is more palatable than Kilroy-Silk, a lesser evil, one even worthy of a riposte?

In concluding this survey of Islamic studies I will end on a note of optimism. This unlikely conclusion, in the face of the arguments so far, derives from the information regarding the new, post-orientalist scholarship. It is supported by the analysis I conducted based on the comments and reviews received by *Discovering Islam* (120 responses from across the world were analysed in *Asian Survey*, 1991e). Placed on one axis was the main constellation of ideas – theological, academic, political – and on the other the cultural-geographical location of the author. Several interesting and unpredictable conclusions emerged. For our purposes it is relevant to point out one. Although orientalist influences remain visible and pervasive, and feed easily into the media allowing simplification and ridicule of Islam, there is evidence of a new scholarship. These are the voices prepared to understand Islam with sympathy, *contra* Said. They confirm the arguments in this chapter.

By reducing Said's serious arguments to caricature, that the West can know the orient only in a negative, exploitative way, friendship across borders is removed from human relationships. Yet we know of the many long-lasting and fruitful friendships between people from the West and Muslims: Thomas W. Arnold and Muhammad Iqbal, Olaf Caroe and Iskander Mirza, E.M. Forster and Ross Masood; or nearer our times, Salim Ali and Dillon Ripley, Ralph Russell and Khurshid-ul-Islam. They were equal friendships, symmetrical in their balance, not divided by 'border, nor breed, nor birth'. Renowned books were dedicated (*A Passage to India*, 1967, to Ross Masood, *The Pathans* 1965, to Iskander Mirza), and odes written for the fraternity, Iqbal's for Arnold, Ripley's for Ali.

Postmodernism, with its emphasis on globalization and plurality, equality and tolerance, will perhaps encourage such friendships. Perhaps the present technology will provide more and better information which will dispel prejudice based on ignorance. Perhaps it will nourish the new breed of scholars. That is one ray of light in an otherwise bleak picture.

Chapter 5

Culture and change

The changing nature of culture in our postmodernist age and what it tells us about society and politics are examined in this chapter. The interconnectedness of our lives will be apparent in the examples I provide. First clothes, then the sermon in the mosque, then humour and finally art and architecture will be consulted for signs of change. The diversity of images will convey to us the socio-political condition of contemporary Muslims, while pointing to the contradictions and dilemmas in society. The role of the media – and media figures – in helping to change society will also be examined. At the end I will discuss the dangers of crossing cultural boundaries through the examples of Madonna and Rushdie.

YOUR JEANS FOR YOU, MY ROBES FOR ME

Jeans, so universally popular in the West, have failed to catch on in Muslim countries (see Ahmed 1990c). This failure provides us with important clues about Muslim society and culture. In the West jeans represent a breakdown, a levelling, of class. They are convenient to wear; they don't need pressing and cleaning; they suggest weight-watching and body care, and, if the ads are to be believed, they bestow an aura of trendy sexuality on the wearer. 'Americanos', the recent hit song by Holly Johnson, described America as 'the land of the free', of 'movies and heroes', the land of 'blue jeans'. Selecting jeans as a popular symbol of America is semiotically significant.

The reasons why jeans have failed in Muslim countries, except among the Westernized young, are wide-ranging. The first is religious. Islam is specific about modesty in men and women. A dress which looks best when 'skin-tight' and is intended to indicate the contours of the torso violates this injunction. Besides, the sitting prayer position, with legs tucked under the body, requires loose garments. Tight jeans would be sheer lumbar agony. Another reason is sociological. People in Africa and Asia, especially in the rural areas, prefer to sit for long periods on carpets, or on floors, usually cross-legged. In jeans this would once again expose the external reproductive apparatus to damage. Dietary habits form yet another reason. Heavy meals are eaten at lunch-time, and this, combined with a need to avoid the heat, induces a stupor or siesta. Loose dress requires no adjustment and the girth of the baggy trousers is conveniently loosened. This regimen will not be found in any of Jane Fonda's fitness plans nor is it recommended for those seeking longevity but it is a pattern established for centuries.

Traditional Muslims are not the only ones to prefer robes and loose clothing. Christian priests and Oxbridge scholars have traditionally worn them. Their spiritual and academic state is enhanced by free-flowing clothes. 'Thought', suggested Umberto Eco, 'abhors tights', in an essay called 'Lumbar Thought' (Eco 1986: 194). 'A garment that squeezes the testicles makes a man think differently', he reflected (ibid.: 193). 'Women during menstruation; people suffering from orchitis, victims of haemorrhoids, urethritis, prostate and similar ailments know to what extent pressures or obstacles in the sacroiliac area influence one's mood and mental agility' (ibid.).

Failing the tie test

There is yet another sartorial test which gives us further insights into Muslim society and politics. This is the tie test. The first chapter pointed out that in the early years after independence from the colonial powers Muslim leaders stood for modernity and progress. They planned huge dams, national airlines and development schemes after the Western fashion. Take the well-known names, each representing his region: Nasser of Egypt, the Shah of Iran, Ayub of Pakistan and Sukarno of Indonesia. Although nationalist, in the manner of the leaders of the post-colonial period, their 'Islamic' position was not emphasized. Nasser advocated Arab socialism, the Shah Persian nationalism, Ayub SEATO and CENTO and Sukarno the Bandung idea.

Whatever their relations with the West, ties formed a

prominent feature of their dress. No official photograph was complete without one. The Shah and Sukarno wore theatrical army costumes, Nasser and Ayub, though military men, preferred conventional Western suits. All wore ties.

A generation later Muslim leaders are failing the tie test. The tie has become a symbol of modernization if not Westernization, of a frame of mind, a set of values, a way of looking at the world, an acknowledgement of non-Islamic tradition and non-Muslim networks. Let us look at the three who represented three major Muslim cultural regions, the Arab world, Iran and South Asia more recently. We do not see photographs of King Faisal, Ayatollah Khomeini or General Zia wearing a tie. Their ministers and senior officials would follow their lead. Their self-presentation was austere, their clothes non-Western. Where some of the earlier leaders spoke European languages with pride, these leaders displayed similar pride in their use of their native language. They not only spoke of a pan-Islamic identity but were dressed for the part; their aim was the re-integration of Muslim society.

What was the significance of the tie? The tie, I was assured several times as a youth forced to wear it at school, was the most dangerously insidious item of Christian cultural imperialism. The tie, my Muslim friends explained, hung like a cross around the neck and drew the wearer towards Christianity. This may have been exaggerated and inaccurate but, on reflection, the tie, with the collars sticking up, did suggest a decapitated cross. It discouraged tie enthusiasts among Muslims and made me aware how people spotted and interpreted symbols in society.

King Hassan of Morocco, tucked away in one corner of the Muslim world, and once noted for his natty European suits, is now to be seen only in traditional robes. The trend is continuing. Oxford-educated Benazir Bhutto, who represents a younger generation, consciously deferred to Muslim sentiment as Prime Minister. Her first trip abroad as Prime Minister was to Makkah, and in public she covered her head and rolled beads in her hand.

However, the tie has not completely vanished from the Muslim wardrobe. King Hussein of Jordan and Saddam Hussein of Iraq are noted for their smart Western suits and ties. Their clothes communicate their political position: one is a Westernized monarch, the other a socialist dictator. Both are reminiscent of the earlier generation of Muslim leaders; under pressure both have waved the Islamic flag.

Gossip – and little more – linked the earlier Muslim leaders with international female names; Ayub Khan was said to have had a soft spot for Christine Keeler in London, Nasser for the Indian actress Vijanthimala in Bombay and Sukarno for too many to name. These were colourful, charismatic figures and it is not too hard to imagine a liaison. Indeed, in the mid-sixties, like many Pakistani students in England, I was agog to follow Miss Keeler's revelations in the tabloids as she helped to bring down the Conservative government. She even mentioned an incident in a swimming pool with Ayub. After the 1970s not even the mildest whiff of sexual scandal is attached to the Muslim leaders; it is difficult even to imagine King Faisal, Ayatollah Khomeini or General Zia beside a swimming pool, let alone in bathing trunks. They had also resisted that archetypal Western beverage, whisky, which had sustained many of the earlier generation of Muslim leaders through their arduous nationalist struggle. For the present generation of leaders their time is best spent in the mosque.

The sermon in the mosque

If the trend is towards greater Islamic identity we may enquire: Which is the most reliable method of understanding Muslim sentiment? For this critical answer let us go not to the corridors of power in Muslim lands or their scholars or, indeed, their media for they are all, to an extent, influenced by the West, whether rejecting or accepting it. Let us instead look at the core of their religious structure, the mosque.

This is a route that is seldom taken and therefore ensures that often even experts get it wrong. Iran in the 1970s is a famous example. Many experts then were predicting a long reign for the Shah on the eve of Ayatollah Khomeini's revolution in spite of the overflowing mosques. The error is compounded by imposing simplistic labels derived from Europe, like 'fundamentalism', on Muslims.

Is there a coherent, unified and recognizable 'Islamic' perspective? And how do we identify its physical form in society? We do so through the little-studied mosques and their networks. And it will be misleading to equate the mosque in Muslim society to the church in the West. The church simply does not carry the political and social clout among Christians that the mosque does among Muslims.

A remarkably coherent perspective on major events, considering the variety of Muslim discourses, cultures and nations, is
thereby created and sustained. The ideas that are generated in this
network cut across national borders; they permeate the bazaar
and the souk, the favela and the lower echelons of government. In
the ambience of the mosque customary values are perpetuated,
strategies for action are laid out and political and social issues of
the day are explored. During the month of fasting it feeds the
poor, during crises it gathers resources and funds for the
distressed and in normal times runs schools and organizes talks.

In mosques from Karachi to Cairo, in the Muslim world, and
Seattle to Cambridge, in the non-Muslim world, I have been
struck by the universality and similarity of themes expressed in
the *khutba*, the sermon delivered on Friday to the congregation.
About half an hour in length, the *khutba* is delivered before the
main prayer. The audience in the mosque is highly receptive and
a mood of quiet harmony usually prevails among it. It consists of
anywhere from fifty to 50,000 people, depending on the size of the
mosque.

The main themes emerging in sermons reflect the apocalyptic
mood among ordinary Muslims. In Muslim countries the national
language is used, in non-Arabic-speaking lands it is often
interspersed with Arabic, and English is often used in mosques in
England and the United States. The great days of Islam, the
nobility of the past, are evoked; Quranic references support the
arguments. The analysis is simplistic, the colours black and white
and the expression hyperbolic. The audience, largely rural and
often illiterate, responds with heart-felt passion. Broad, atavistic,
familiar ideas comfort it in these times of rapid change.

Several clear themes are apparent: there is the eternal and
universal struggle between good and evil. The world is seen as
increasingly dominated by the power of the West, especially the
United States, which represents moral and spiritual decadence.
Sex, drugs and violence are what the West offers and Muslims
must resist them with their piety and moral strength. Stereotypes
and hearsay often pass as truth in the arguments; the VCR and
some of its more vulgar exhibits are taken as exemplifying the
West. The museums, parks and libraries are seldom, if ever,
mentioned. This is the obverse of Said's orientalism; it is a kind of
occidentalism, the growth of which we have already discussed
above.

Specific contemporary Muslim problems form another theme. The loss of Jerusalem and the fate of the Palestinians are at the top of the list. In this case political, racial and religious responses fuse. National issues are also raised. Corrupt rulers, the inequality between the rich and the poor, the malpractice of government are highlighted. They are also linked to the West, which is seen as supporting undesirable rulers to obtain concessions: for oil, a military base or strategic reasons.

Once we appreciate the vast networks of the mosques, their well-established and organized nature, and the content of the sermons, we begin to throw light on some apparently confusing recent phenomena. The Gulf war is one. Many people were confused by the way in which certain governments, like Egypt and Pakistan, supported the Allies while large crowds in these countries demonstrated loudly in favour of Saddam. While many Muslim nations went along with the UN resolutions, most Muslims remained cynical about the use of the UN, pointing out that UN resolutions continue to be ignored by Israel. Similarly, Western commentators are confused regarding the latest developments around Salman Rushdie. They ask, if he has become a Muslim why is he still in hiding? The answers lie to a large extent in the mosque, which has become a barometer for politics among Muslims.

Ayatollah Khomeini's revolution in Iran was perhaps the most dramatic example of the mosque overwhelming the secular palace of the ruler. But in other countries, too, rulers who may tune in to the BBC for the main news are also careful to listen to what is being said in the sermon at home.

Although Imams in charge of mosques are amenable to pressures from government and often accused of being on their payroll, by and large they act as the voice of opposition. Because of this in many cases they have suffered terribly. But no one seen as deviating from the tenets of Islam is spared. Even General Zia-ul-Haq, widely identified with the Islamic position, was often the target for scathing criticism from the mosque; earlier, Zulfiqar Ali Bhutto, Benazir's father, was toppled because of the intensity of the campaign spearheaded by the religious parties. Little wonder that Benazir was cautious about Muslim sentiment (Bhutto 1988). After the Gulf war, even those leaders who are not particularly associated with Islam, like President Mubarak in Cairo or King Hussein in Amman, pay special heed to the sermon.

It is in this context that we are able to understand Muslim support for Saddam Hussein or the continued condemnation of Salman Rushdie. Saddam, although many religious figures suffered at his hands, was seen as someone standing up to the West. Even those who opposed one another united behind him as a symbol, a rallying point. In an emotional meeting in Bradford the Supreme Council of British Muslims unanimously expressed their support for him. In Pakistan, where he was never popular because of his support for India over Kashmir, processions burned effigies of Bush and Major. Maulana Noorani, head of a religious party, announced that 100,000 volunteers were ready to fight for Saddam.

Similarly, Salman Rushdie remains a symbol of the cultural humiliation of the Muslims by the West. In the mosques they remain suspicious of his declaration of faith in Islam. It is no surprise that the main mosque of British Muslims, by Regent's Park, London, remains in the forefront of the campaign to reject him. Indeed, its Imam, because he met Rushdie and accepted his conversion to Islam in December 1990, was ostracized and prevented from delivering the *khutba*. Even after denouncing Rushdie publicly as an apostate in May he was not allowed to deliver the *khutba*. The Imam, a soft-spoken and learned Egyptian scholar, never recovered his former status in the community.

The policy statement published by the Islamic Research Centre, London, on 10 September 1990, and entitled 'Crisis in the Gulf', thus reflects, as it sums up, the themes we are identifying. It points out what it sees as the 'secret master plan' of 'the only super-power, US':

The secret master plan thereafter [after the war] is:
1 Force Iraq to pay war compensation of $100 billion.
2 Disband the Iraqi Army, similar to the German and Japanese Army after World War II.
3 Allow the US forces to stay on Iraqi soil for the next fifty years, again similar to post-war Germany and Japan.
4 Allow Iraq to keep only a police force.
5 Dismantle nuclear reactors, arms and industries, so that Iraq will have to purchase from the West.
6 Depose Saddam and his family after a Nuremburg type trial.
7 Keep several bases in the Saudi Peninsula and US troops to guard the oil fields.

8 Full control of OPEC from Arabs to control both production and world price.

Some of this appeared far-fetched in September, but to many Muslims it was soon appearing plausible. It is worth repeating in full, for it holds wide currency among Muslims. As long as Muslims perceive injustices in the world, the sermon in the mosque will remain vindicated.

Do Muslims laugh?

From matters solemn and serious let us find respite in a parenthesis about Muslim humour. Negative stereotypes of unstable politics and subjugated women among Muslims are common. What is rarely discussed is the Muslim sense of humour. Based on the media images it would seem that Muslims have no sense of humour, that they never laugh. Furthermore, Muslim writers do not appear in any collection of humorous prose. For example there is not a single Muslim writer in *The Oxford Book of Humorous Prose* (Muir 1990). No matter. Muslims must not feel aggrieved. There are no Hindu writers either in the book, although many of them, like V.S. Naipaul and Nirad Chaudhuri, have won international prizes for literature (the early stories of the former would have made a worthy contribution).

Muslims enjoy a joke. Even the mullah, although he carries the image of anger and rage in the West, is often warm and capable of humour in private. The humorous, self-mocking stories of Mullah Nasruddin are part of Persian folklore and literature. Many mullahs whom I know are prepared to repeat 'mullah jokes', so popular in rural society, about themselves.

One of the most original comedians in the Indian cinema is a Muslim who calls himself Johnny Walker. Rangeela in Pakistani cinema is also capable of original and unconventional humour. The people, the anonymous crowds, the bazaar folk, the ordinary citizens, have always exhibited razor-sharp humour with a high degree of political consciousness. This is as true in Cairo as in Islamabad.

The following joke illustrates the postmodernist elements of self-parody and a drawing together of varied references. It was coined and circulated by Pakistanis at the height of the rather sombre and grey era of General Zia. Zia, whose personal reputation was actually impeccable, is the butt, as he represented the programme of Islamization. It is in the vein of jokes about the Pope; the more unlikely, the more humorous. An attractive middle class lady came to see Zia. 'Madame', he said, 'you are wearing an Indian *saree*. This is unpatriotic. Please take it off.' Being a loyal Pakistani she obeyed. Eyeing the bra and panties he then said, 'And what about those Marks and Spencer's things? Do you know they help finance Israel?' When she had removed them, she asked, 'What shall I do now?' Opening his arms, he said, 'Come and embrace Islam.'

The diversity of Muslim society

In our discussion of culture and change I wish, once again, to dispel the notion that there ever was – or is – one unified and monolithic Muslim society. Consider Muslim South Asia and its main language, Urdu; both display synthesis and eclecticism. There are numerous excellent books on this subject, but I shall mention only one as it has the merit of being the most recent: *Urdu and Muslim South Asia: Studies in Honour of Ralph Russell*, edited by Christopher Shackle, 1989.

South Asia, with its rich and colourful tapestry, is as varied in its life-styles as it is in the range of its philosophical ideas. Here Muslim Emperors appear as champions of Hinduism ('Vaishnavism flourished under his rule'; ibid.: 32); here Pathans, traditionally renowned as warriors of Islam, write poems in praise of Hindu gods ('Such a figure is the sixteenth-century Hindi poet Raskhan, identified by tradition as a Pathan named Sayyid Ibrahim and renowned for his elegant and impassioned verses in praise of Krishna', ibid.: 29); here are Sufi mystics of Jewish origin, like Sarmad, embroiled in the imperial contest of succession (ibid.: 123); homosexuality is glorified: Raskhan in love with a Delhi lad, Sarmad with a Hindu boy; here foreign romances are Indianized (like the Persian romances of Amir Hamza); here are stories which appear to go on and on, unending like the forty-six volumes of *Dastan-e-Amir Hamza*; stories that are steeped in what postmodernists call magical realism.

Moreover, the explosion of colour and exotic imagery, which mutually influences different cultures, is not confined to South Asia. In concluding a masterly essay Victor Kiernan points this out for us:

More broadly, the contradictions and dilemmas that beset the dominant class of middle and Western Asia, throughout its long term of life, made up in a sense a paradigm of the human condition, of a human race perpetually homeless and journeying. A testimony of this is the spell that the best of its poetry laid on a Europe disoriented by sudden and bewildering change, when it came to be known there; on Vambery making his ecstatic discovery of it in early life in a corner of Hungary, or Goethe at Weimar imitating Hafiz, or Fitzgerald translating Umar Khayyam in a Suffolk village.

(ibid.: 17)

Regula Qureshi in her discussion of *qawali* defines it as a 'Sufi assembly held for achieving mystical experience' (1989: 176; also see Qureshi 1986). But the *qawali* is now a widely popular cultural form. An example was provided at the Iqbal Day function in Cambridge in November 1989, which, as the Iqbal Fellow, I helped to organize (also see the last section of Chapter 6). My friend Haji Sabri Qawal, with his group, the Sabri Brothers, performed in the Peterhouse auditorium. They were in Cambridge for the first time and we were privileged to hear them singing Iqbal's most popular poems, including the *Shikwa* and *Jawab-e-Shikwa*. *Qawali* in Cambridge to a mixed and enthusiastic audience, which included the Pakistani High Commissioner and luminaries like Ernest Gellner and Sir Andrew Huxley, supports Kiernan's thesis. What the dons of Peterhouse, reputed to be the oldest Cambridge college, thought of the Sabri brethren is not recorded.

ISLAMIC ART AND ARCHITECTURE

The story goes that Aurangzeb, the Mughal Emperor, once asked a lamenting crowd on its way to the graveyard, whom they were burying. With a flash of wit, which confirms my point in the previous section of a Muslim sense of humour, they answered, 'Music'. Not to be outdone, the Emperor replied, 'Bury it deep so it does not rise again'. Aurangzeb was expressing the orthodox disapproval of any form of human activity which detracts from the worship of God. However, there is also a strong tradition among Muslims of expressing spiritual fervour through popular music. The *qawali*, as we noted above, is one form. Perhaps it is the postmodernist era that will release the arts in Islam.

Because postmodernism means access to the media, to information and to the rich artistic inheritance of Islam, it can provide a legitimate platform for an Islamic renaissance. Through television, for the first time, the *qawali* has vast audiences in South Asia; indeed in the West, too, *qawali* is publicly performed in the United States and the United Kingdom. Through exhibitions and in the media, Arab calligraphy, Persian paintings and Mughal architecture dazzle the viewer while creating a sense of pride in their legacy among Muslims.

The legacy of Islamic art

The tradition which consciously bonds spirituality with art is a continuing one among Muslims (Burckhardt 1976, Mandel 1979, Nasr 1987). *Contemporary Art from the Islamic World* (Ali 1989) displays the impressive work of about 200 major artists. There are more than thirty government and private museums in Egypt alone, and its Museum of Modern Art is in the lead. Whether in Amman, Cairo or Karachi, art acts as a 'bridge that will carry the flow of inspiration, trends, styles and ideas between Islamic and Western cultures' (ibid.: xii). Islamic, Mughal, Arabic and Western modern themes jostle and juxtapose; the pull of the Quran and the village on the one hand, the modern voices of nationalism and politics on the other are all reflected in this book.

However, there is little adventure or postmodernist expression in evidence. This is not surprising. There have been periods in many Muslim countries when art was actively discouraged. At the best of times, patrons are difficult to find and even more difficult to hold. The expression of art in Muslim society is, therefore, doubly to be appreciated in the sterile landscape. Little wonder that Iqbal, surveying Muslim achievements, chided Muslims in *Jawab-e-Shikwa*, when comparing them to their glorious ancestors, with the contemptuous refrain, 'What are you?'

Contemporary Muslim artistic talents have found the most unlikely expressions. Although there is no Muslim postmodern cinema – centralization, censorship and long periods of martial law severely discourage innovation – this does not mean that Muslims are devoid of cinematic talent. The Indian cinema is one example. The Muslim contribution to the Indian cinema, which has the largest cinema industry in the world, is substantial. From among the Muslims come some of the most glittering names of the Indian cinema based in Bombay: Dilip Kumar (né Yusuf Khan), the most popular tragic actor of the Indian screen; the actresses Madhubala and Meena Kumari; the singers Rafi and Talat; the directors Mehboob and Naushad; and Ludhianvi and Badayuni, both poets. Today, Shabana Azmi and Naseer-ud-din Shah are among the most talented and popular stars of India. This is evident in other fields of art, too. Hussain Khan is one of India's most celebrated painters, and Indian classical music has been traditionally dominated by Muslims. Let us not forget, either, that Naguib Mahfouz won the Nobel Prize for Literature in Cairo.

Postmodernist Muslim architecture

Jencks precisely identified the moment of the death of modern architecture as 3.32 p.m., on 15 July 1972 in St Louis, Missouri, when the infamous Pruitt-Igoe scheme was given its *coup de grâce* by dynamite (Clarke 1990: 18). Without being as precise about the actual moment, we can trace the birth of postmodern architecture in Muslim society. It has made its first tentative appearance from an unexpected quarter and in an unexpected place. Not surprisingly, it comes via Harvard and Prince Karim, the Aga Khan, who studied there.

In the West the title of the Aga Khan is synonymous with fabulous riches, exotic oriental mystery (see my interview in *The Guardian*, 1991g). What seldom comes to light is the serious work performed in the last decade by the present holder of the title, to relate Islamic ideas to contemporary life. For him Islamic architecture is a symbol of the best in Islamic history and thought, and through it he is expressing a philosophy. The grandeur, symmetry and nobility of Islamic architecture help create a sense of pride and identity among Muslims. From the newly constructed Serena Hotel in Quetta, Pakistan, to the Serena in Zanzibar, housed in a restored building, he encourages synthesis between past and present.

The Aga Khan's projects are spread from Indonesia to Morocco, but the ideas are generated from the Aga Khan Programme for Architecture at MIT-Harvard and the Trust in Geneva. The Great Mosque of Niono, Mali, which won the Aga Khan Award for Vernacular Architecture, and the Haj Terminal at Jeddah Airport, which won the Appropriate Building Systems Award, in 1983, provide interesting and contrasting examples from two different continents.

Here is irony. For the Aga Khan is the head, the hereditary Imam, of one of the most close-knit and traditional sects among the Muslims, the Ismailis. More irony, as this soft-spoken, unassuming, even shy person, is bringing about a quiet but far-reaching economic and social revolution in the lives of his followers. Final irony: his work now brings together Ismailis and non-Ismailis as never before in history, and it thus provides a lead to mainstream Muslims many of whom consider the sect to be unorthodox, even heretical.

My interview was conducted in Granada, where the Aga Khan and the King of Spain inaugurated the medieval Zafra House on 5 June (1991g). Restored by the Aga Khan, the house will henceforth be the Centre of Historical Studies in Granada. Its arches, calligraphy, courtyard and fountain tell us of an age of Islamic artistic glory. This is especially ironic as Spain prepares to commemorate the 500th anniversary of the fall of Granada and the final expulsion of the Muslims in 1492.

The postmodernist example in architecture I wish to refer to is the Serena in Quetta, which opened in 1988. The brown mud walls and starkly simple architecture of the low buildings reflect the tribal society of Baluchistan living in fortified villages, but none of the modern luxuries are missing inside the rooms. Baluchi tribal designs and the latest concealed lighting, palm fronds and marble: this is kitsch, but in the deserts and mountains of Baluchistan marvellously refreshing and different. There is a hint of self-parody, even of irony. However, not all clients of the Serena are satisfied. Many Baluchis complained to me that they missed the modern Western architecture. Mud walls and towers reminded them too much of homes from which they wished to escape for a while.

However, modernism is far from dead among the Muslims. In the mid-1960s President Ayub Khan inaugurated the most luxurious, most modern hotel of Pakistan, the Inter-Continental in Karachi. Its exterior architecture and interior decorations were typical of the period. The hotel could have been duplicated from any metropolis in the world – London or Tokyo. The present generation of the best hotels in Karachi – the Avari Towers, Sheraton, Holiday Inn – are in the same tradition: large, expensive, anonymous blocks. The Lahore and Islamabad hotels have followed meekly, form following form. Even small hotels in remote areas ape the trend, as best they can.

The Aga Khan was breaking with two architectural traditions; first with the historical architecture found in the old Muslim cities, and, second, the modern architecture of more recent cities. Cairo and Lahore, centuries old, with their perfectly symmetrical mosques, their gardens and buildings, although many are run down, are examples of the first. For the second tradition he was challenging, one example comes immediately to mind. It is Islam's Brasilia, Islamabad, the capital of Pakistan, built on a deserted plateau in the 1960s. It was to be Ayub Khan's monument to modernism. The same architect, the guru of modernism, Le Corbusier, who had flirted with Mussolini, worked with the generals in both cases (for an authoritative account of Le Corbusier's modernism, see Benton 1991).

Looking back at Brasilia, modern architecture appears an intellectual disaster, a moral sham:

> I had forgotten what a vision of hell Brasilia was: the illegitimate offspring of an intellectual love affair between an architect and a dictator. Everyone must have cheated on the contracts, because what had once been intimidatingly new was now shabby and peeling. I was in Metropolis, locked in the past's vision of the future.
>
> (Hilton 1991: 371)

In spite of its name, the city of Islam, the architecture of Islamabad does not even hint at the grandeur of the Islamic vision or the nobility of its ideas. Islamabad was constructed, the popular saying goes, as a graveyard, where bureaucrats might be peacefully buried before their death.

Islamabad is not unlike its bureaucrats: lifeless, anonymous and dull. Its streets are planned in straight lines, its buildings and houses look anonymous. The central buildings could have been dropped here from any other capital city of the world without loss of identity. Like modern architecture everywhere in the world, form followed function in Islamabad: fluorescent lighting, central air-conditioning, stripped-down massive buildings. These include the President's secretariat, the National Assembly and the Foreign Office. Some, like the President's secretariat, have been under construction for years and cost billions of rupees. These buildings are designed according to standard international specifications, without concession to Pakistan's climate. The air-conditioning system breaks down easily, and the windows, not meant to be opened, have to be forced open to allow in fresh air and no one remembered to supply any heating, essential in Islamabad's cold winters.

Even the high point of Islamabad architecture, the Faisal Mosque complex, is isolated both from classic Islamic tradition and the immediate natural environment. The Turkish architect who designed it preferred triangles and jagged edges to the soft curves and domes of the Islamic tradition. To British writers the 'four 90-metre – (300-foot) – high concrete minarets look like rockets on launching pads' (Shaw 1989: 213), 'The minarets remind one irresistibly of space rockets' (Dhanjal 1990: 184). It is an imposing building but fails to inspire. The hype is familiar: it is the largest in the world, most modern, and so on. I must have been to at least half-a-dozen mosques claiming these honours. Largest or not, traditional or modern, it is now the landmark of Islamabad.

A major illustration of modern architecture thoughtlessly and disturbingly imposed on Muslim tradition comes from the core of the Islamic world, the *haram sharif* in Makkah; another example is the Victory Arch in Baghdad representing Saddam's arms holding swords (see Samir al-Khalil 1991). In December 1989, I performed the *umrah*, the religious visit to Makkah, staying at the Pakistan House, by the *haram sharif*. The pilgrim, escaping the noise and motion of the world, was surrounded by both in Makkah. Outside the immediate premises of the *haram sharif* there was little peace from the noise, bustle and dust. The gigantic tractors, earth-movers and drills worked round the clock, keeping us awake at night. Clouds of dust hung in the air like smog. Sites were being cleared for high-rise buildings. The solid mountain of rock in the heart of Makkah was being drilled for tunnels to provide fast-lane roads. One of these tunnels would cause the death of over a thousand pilgrims a few months later, eliciting the widely misconstrued remark from King Fahd that it was their fate to die.

The untiring activity is centred on the construction of a city-within-a-city, a maze of palaces, adjacent to the *haram sharif*. It looms offensively over the holiest shrine of Islam, like a vulgar parvenu hotel or office block, and is visible from the courtyard. In its modern, anonymous severity there is not the slightest concession to cultural surroundings or postmodernist ideas on Islamic architecture. Airless, windowless and faceless, there is an air of mystery and secrecy about it. The occupants will be of royal

Saudi blood, they say, but who knows? The Old Man of the Mountain could live up there and we would not know. The idea of its proximity is to allow the occupants to slip into and out of the *haram sharif* unnoticed through special passages. Even at their holiest shrine, it seems that some Muslims are able to challenge the essential egalitarianism and simplicity of Islam.

Modern Islamic architecture reflects more than the failure of energy and originality. It is also a failure in history. At one stroke the heritage of the Mughals in India, the Arabs in Spain, is deleted. In need of money, patronage and stability, the architect reflects the tastes and opinions of the leaders of Muslim society.

Muslim architecture, when not inspired by tradition, tends to be an expression of individual tastes, the patron's ideas. Let me provide two examples. To an Islamic zealot, the Wali of Swat fell unconsciously into an interesting architectural trap. His little palace in Saidu Sharif – which has hosted, among other dignitaries, the British Queen and the Duke of Edinburgh in 1961 – boasted marble pillars and designs of a distinctly Greek character. The Wali had moved a long way from the mud hut of his ascetic and saintly ancestor, the Akhund of Swat (immortalized by Edward Lear in his famous *Nonsense Rhymes*, 'Who or why, or which or what is the Akond of Swat?'). But the Wali was not being adventurous. Swat was one of the sites of Alexander's Indian excursion and is known for its Greek remains.

The other example is the mosque I built in the Commissioner's House in Sibi, Baluchistan. It was the first built in this locality since the creation of Pakistan. I hoped it would match the British colonial architecture of the house, set in 25 acres and one of the grandest of its kind in Baluchistan, while conveying the simplicity of Islam. The point was not lost on a writer who visited me while researching a book on Pakistan: 'He showed me the mosque he had built at the end of the alley: plain white, a front with three columned arches, and arched wooden doors behind, answering the arches on the veranda of his colonial bungalow' (Duncan 1989: 136).

Mosque versus mall

Beside innovations in mosque or hotel construction there is another architectural development with wide-ranging implications for Muslim society. It is the American concept of the shopping mall. The mall has arrived in Muslim cities and flourishes even in Saudi Arabia, the land of the holiest shrines of Islam. How Muslims reconcile the mall to the mosque is a question which raises as many theological issues as it does sociological ones.

In the present postmodernist era the mall for the Americans is the contemporary equivalent of the mosque. It acts as a social focus, and people go to it faithfully, daily, for renewal and companionship. The mall represents an explosion of consumerist images which appeal to the senses. It is the consumerist pleasure-dome and its seductive charms are available round the clock. Every item appeals to the here and now. The state-of-the-art mall is the wonder of the consumerist culture.

The postmodern couple lives in a continuous present of instant gratification, of rapidly changing moods, as they respond to what is on display in the shopping mall:

> So Nick and Deborah go to a movie, *Salaam Bombay*, and agonise about third-world poverty for about 30 seconds. They buy new outfits and go dancing at a champagne and oyster bar. They get smashed on margueritas in a Mexican restaurant.
>
> (Moore 1991: 28; see also Heller 1991)

The mall is the 'total experience', a metaphor for the hyperreality of postmodern life:

> The mall as the cool, organ-less, dead zone beloved by theorists of hyper-reality may be a 'total environment' where shopping is no longer shopping but a 'total leisure experience' [Moore 1991: 28]. 'Whatever can happen in your life can happen in a mall', says film-maker Paul Mazursky. Which is just as well, as he has set his latest film almost entirely within one of these cathedrals of consumerism, and called it *Scenes from a Mall*.
>
> (ibid.: 27)

The mall is also fun, a carnival, there is irony in its juxtaposition of the serious and the comic; people visit it to relax. Traditional modern architecture intimidated, it strove to impress; man was quite secondary to it.

In contrast, the mosque brings the believer away from the maelstrom of daily life, suspending it. Calmness and peace characterize it. The believer is encouraged to think of the timelessness of God and the perishability of life on earth. However, like the mall, the mosque has seen a remarkable growth in its numbers in recent years. American air-conditioners and Japanese sound systems indicate the influences of modern technology.

The mall and the mosque, one a paradise of colour and fun, the other a paradigm of piety, suggest alternative life-styles, opposing philosophies. Future generations of Muslims will have to make their adjustment and express their choices. It is an issue not yet highlighted by those discussing Islamic architecture (see, for examples, Ateshin 1990; Saqqaf 1987; and the ongoing project of the Institute of Oriental Culture, University of Tokyo, under the heading *Urbanism in Islam*). Postmodernist expressions of art and architecture will, therefore, be a mixed blessing, liberating while also raising disturbing questions of a fundamental nature.

THE CHANGING NATURE OF WESTERN SOCIETY

Culture and change in Muslim society cannot be studied without a comment on the West. Until well after the Second World War two dominant ideas tended to push Muslim countries into the two blocs formed around them: capitalist and communist. Certain deep-rooted themes, which were repellent to Africans and Asians, remained visible in the otherwise attractive Western capitalist model: Western xenophobia and racial arrogance (which we discussed in Chapter 3). A consequence of this was the Western disdain for traditional, a euphemism for backward, societies in Africa and Asia.

It was in the 1960s that certain significant changes manifested themselves in Western society – the one lying at the heart of the global civilization. These posed a challenge from within. In time they would dramatically influence the course of events in the communist states. The dissolution of the world order and its philosophy in the 1980s would be the culmination of these changes.

In the 1960s, a post-war generation, young and restless, was coming of age. It rejected the rigid class and social structures which had held for a century, being set in place in the Victorian age. It attacked authority in every form, whether the church or the household head. There was a lot of anger in the air and John Osborne's 'Angry Young Man' came to represent his generation. One of the most evocative slogans of the 1960s was *père pue* – father stinks. A new idiom, a new weapon was discovered. This was satire in the media.

Programmes like *That Was The Week That Was* and journals like *Private Eye* in Britain, bursting with undergraduate Oxbridge vitality, helped revolutionize political satire. From the United States came the philosophy of flower power, deeply bearded eastern gurus, usually from India, easy sex, the growth of popular rock culture associated with drugs and the early, unnatural deaths of the icons. Culture became increasingly iconoclastic, sex and violence increasingly explicit (the three Lawrences – T.E., D.H. and Durrell – were essential reading for the undergraduate who wished to show how non-conformist and up-to-date he was). The exuberance was matched by a sense of rootlessness and anguish; dementia praecox was apparent. It was the American military involvement in Vietnam that brought to the fore the crisis in Western society and posed the most dramatic challenge to its notions of the self.

The real danger of a nuclear holocaust and the explosion in communication technology, especially television, brought the people of the world closer than ever. Humanity could witness history being made – as in the Cuban missile crisis – and, through television, feel a sense of participation in its enactment. This process involved people across the world in debates that would normally be left for leaders to worry about. The period culminated two decades later, almost inevitably, in the consolidation and triumph of Western consumerism. The collapse of communism sent the former communist states scurrying to join the consumerist order.

These changes in the non-Muslim world naturally affected people in Muslim countries. The self-doubt, the crisis of confidence, the dramatic changes in non-Muslim society did not inspire confidence among Muslims. The Muslim world thus moved during the same period along quite a different trajectory, marching to a different tune, as we saw in Chapter 1. Starting from a point where many Muslim leaders consciously talked of 'Western models' – whether inspired by Westminster or Sandhurst – they were, by the 1970s, groping towards a more authentic Islamic past. A reversion to cultural tradition, a revival of religious ideology, a pride in traditional custom and culture followed. Never far from all this was the explicit rejection of the West and what it stood for.

The world as television box, humanity as performers

Carlyle once remarked that the three greatest elements of Western society were gunpowder, printing and the Protestant religion. In our age he would add a fourth, the audio-visual media. We have identified postmodernism as the era of the media; to comprehend postmodernism it is necessary to understand the media (as we see in the next chapter). By definition, television is probably the most important instrument of the modern electronic media. Like the cinema two generations ago, it is the central medium of our times. It constitutes a radical break with the past. As two experts point out:

> The written word (and particularly the printed word) works through and so promotes consistency, narrative development from cause to effect, universality and abstraction, clarity, and a single tone of voice. Television, on the other hand, is ephemeral, episodic, specific, concrete and dramatic in mode. Its meanings are arrived at by contrasts and by the juxtaposition of seemingly contradictory signs and its 'logic' is oral and visual.
>
> (Fiske and Hartley 1988: 15)

(For the impact of television on society also see Balio 1991; Buxton 1990; R. Collins 1991; Dahlgren and Sparks 1991 and Seiter *et al.* 1991.)

Huge audiences in the Western world habitually watch television for several hours daily; many others would like to do so if they had access to sets or the time. The television set is the focus of domestic life, around which the family organizes its movements. Although there is some evidence that even children watch television critically, it can be nonetheless addictive (Hodge and Tripp 1986, Seiter *et al.* 1991, Thompson 1990). It can create zombies, their eyes glazed, who come alive sporadically between shows and exhibit withdrawal symptoms if they stop watching. One of the most popular British television programmes is called *Telly Addicts*. It shows us how wide the knowledge of TV has become among ordinary folk. In Spielberg's *Poltergeist* the television set actually swallows a child belonging to a typical, middle-class, suburban American family. We can interpret the story metaphorically; the set has become a demon.

Some television programmes have come to symbolize the

1980s; *Spitting Image* is one. Its political comment is sophisticated, the sex explicit, violence brutal, satire savage, pace rapid, lampooning of the élite merciless, and eclecticism dazzling. The caricature is itself a caricature of the age.

Reality and illusion melt into one another in *Spitting Image*. Seeing Mrs Thatcher on *Spitting Image* and seeing her, a few minutes later, on the television news, creates a sense of imbalance. Which is the real Mrs Thatcher? The media not only distorts but can create its own characters, obliterating the original. My young son, on seeing Mrs Thatcher or the Foreign Secretary, Douglas Hurd, on the television news would shout to me in my study, 'Papa, come, *Spitting Image* has started.' Like many others he was no longer able to distinguish reality from illusion, caricature from the original.

Nevertheless, many find this kind of humour unpleasant. Indeed, it often crosses the bounds of decency, to demolish the victim. Mrs Thatcher is shown on *Spitting Image* masturbating Reagan, the Queen is constantly picking her nose. Prince Charles is shown as a taxi-driver giving unwanted advice to his passengers on every conceivable topic starting with the words, 'And another thing'. In one of the few public responses to *Spitting Image* by a victim, Mrs Major, the wife of the Prime Minister, said it was 'cruel and unfunny' (*Cambridge Weekly News*, 7 March 1991). 'I get particularly annoyed', she further confessed, 'about the way they show some of the Royal Family.'

It was the royal marriage of Prince Charles and Lady Diana Spencer in 1981 which both introduced and established the mega-media event. It was watched by virtually the entire world. The glamour, romance, pageant and colour made for a perfect media spectacle. Henceforth, increasingly major media events would be repeated on this scale, whether drawing attention to the plight of the starving Africans or celebrating the release of Mandela in 1990.

Such things have much more for us than mere entertainment value. For example, in the 1990 World Cup nations appeared to be locked in surrogate battles; we saw attack, counter-attack, battle plans and victory celebrations, tears and ecstasy. And although we saw crude jingoism and racism we also saw chivalry and gallantry. In spite of the gloom of the pessimists, some positive values still survive into our times.

A new kind of royalty derives from the media. Few politicians, members of the clergy, or indeed royalty possess the mystique that surrounds media stars. Television royalty, like Dan Rather in the United States and Terry Wogan in Britain, represent the highest aristocracy of our age in influence, life-style and popularity.

Television does not have to be condemned as simply a medium for anarchy and disintegration. It has made great use of its powers in raising money for charity, broadcasting programmes on education, informing us of world events and about important people while entertaining us. It was the media that brought to our notice the plight of the homeless, living in cardboard boxes in London, that of starving Ethiopians and, in 1991, the savaging of the Kurds in northern Iraq. The human drama on their television sets compelled people to respond by raising money and putting pressure on their governments.

Politics and television

As Shakespeare says, everyone is performing: the world is indeed a stage, in our times a television box. And now that television has invaded the Mother of Parliaments in London, the nation of shopkeepers is now a nation of television stars (Napoleon would have reassessed the British thus). MPs are kept busy presenting their best profiles, covering their bald patches and brushing off their dandruff. Their clothes and gestures clearly indicate professional media coaching. Once again, the media dictate to and dominate people who are in the demon's thrall.

The television debate between Kennedy and Nixon in the early 1960s was the turning point for both politics and the media. The debate made clear the importance of a winning smile, a firm jaw-line, a thick mop of hair and a twinkle in the eye. Nixon's perspiration and '5 o'clock shadow' (the emerging bristles on his chin) made him look nervous and sinister. Viewers were not interested in ideas or promises or language, or at least not interested just in these. The images triumphed. Kennedy won the elections, and American politics were never to be the same again. The triumph of Reagan, the actor, in the 1980s was as logical as inevitable. The medium was indeed now the only message.

An attractive mask can now successfully conceal the *arrivisme* of a *blagueur*; form not substance matters. In the words of Mrs Thatcher, 'A picture is worth a thousand words of print.' But not only Anglo-American politicians were discovering the media.

President de Gaulle openly used French television, saying, 'I have two political weapons, television and television.' In 1991 the major political parties of Britain, the Conservatives and Labour, bowed to the inevitable and hired two top film directors to project them: John Schlesinger and Hugh Hudson, respectively.

One cannot help thinking how disastrous the wonderfully human and sensitive Mr Lincoln, with his thick eyebrows and beard, his lugubrious face, his black clothes and stove-pipe top hat, would be on our television. It is easy to imagine a media person interjecting with exasperation as Lincoln launches into his celebrated address at Gettysburg, 'Abe baby! What sort of a shit opening is this? This speech is gonna end up in the garbage can of history.'

'"Fourscore and seven years ago"', he intones sarcastically, '"our fathers brought forth on this continent a new nation conceived in liberty and dedicated to the proposition that all men are created equal." The sentence is too long. The attention span of an audience is less than one minute. Here's how I've arranged it.' At a gesture from the media man four black entertainers jump onto the stage and croon, 'It's liberty time, baby. We're gonna be on the freedom express', they chant. 'And while I have your attention', says the media man, now in his stride, and eyeing Lincoln's face, 'get rid of that funny beard'. He had no doubt heard that Lincoln's generals were calling him 'a well-meaning baboon' and 'the original gorilla'. 'And what sort of a name is Abraham? Too oriental. Let's think up an honest to God American name for you.' 'Choo, choo, choo, freedom bound', chants the black quartet. At this point, Mr Lincoln looks heavenwards, praying for an early end to the deceitful, insensitive and stupid world the media man represents.

DANGEROUS CROSSINGS

In the introductory chapter we cited the examples of Rushdie and Madonna in order to discover how the controversy around them helps us understand postmodernist life better; in this section we return to them (also see Ahmed 1990d). Newton's third law of motion was not understood by the British Board of Film Classification when it initially banned *International Guerrillas*, the Pakistani film about Salman Rushdie in 1990. Every action, Newton had concluded, has an equal and opposite reaction. The film, which has little artistic or intellectual merit, suddenly became international news by crossing cultural boundaries.

Overnight, Shahzad Gul, the Pakistani producer, and Muhammad Fayyaz, the United Kingdom distributer, were learning the truth of Warhol's prediction that, in our era, everyone will be famous for fifteen minutes. They were quoted in the international media and were in demand for interviews. Gul explained the motivation behind his film: 'We wanted to hit Salman Rushdie badly. We think he's a man who is ruthless and cruel and mad' (Ahmed 1990d). Such was the public hatred for Rushdie in Pakistan that Afzal, who plays Rushdie, has been abused and molested in public. Afzal atoned by visiting the holy places at Makkah. Fayyaz complained that while he was appealing against the Board's ban on the film, pirates were already selling it for £100 per copy.

Journalists have described the film as 'a bizarre marriage of Islamic fundamentalism, commerce and pop cinema' (ibid.). Only the merest nod to facts is made. The film is pure Pakistani fantasy. The movie star Rushdie, in fact, looks nothing like Rushdie. To start with, he has a thick crop of hair on his head. He spends most of his time slashing Muslims to death. An international conspiracy to insult Islam backs him. Israeli bodyguards protect him. He can duplicate himself. Four Rushdies sit side by side, enjoying themselves in a discothèque in one scene. This allows the heroes to do violence to him several times without shortening the plot. At the movie's climax, even the bravest Pakistanis fail to kill Rushdie. Only divine intercession, in the form of bolts of lightning, finishes the job. 'We are entitled to interpret a story as we wish. Besides it's fiction', says Gul (ibid.), echoing Rushdie himself defending his novel. The fate of the film in the United Kingdom provides another fact-is-stranger-than-fiction twist to the Rushdie drama.

The film has been the biggest box-office hit in Pakistan in recent years, almost single-handedly reviving a moribund industry, which repeated bouts of martial law and a sterile intellectual climate have not helped. In Pakistani films the action is fast and furious, the heroes loud and tough and the villains bellowing and menacing. The film must not be taken as a sample of South Asian Muslim cinematic talent; we have already noted in the preceding chapter that some of the most glittering names in Indian cinema, the largest industry in the world, are Muslims.

This part of the story of the film is understandable. What is not is the action of the Board. It drew justifiable Muslim ululations of

British double standards. That the British refused to ban Rushdie's book and yet disallowed the film was seen as contradictory. For the British it was a neat case of being hoist with your own petard; the ban ensured the widest possible publicity to the film.

'A material girl in a material world'

For the Pope, the very name of Madonna was an affront and her performances an insult to Catholic sensibilities. For orthodox Christians the Madonna controversy had arrived hard on the heels of that surrounding Martin Scorsese's film *The Last Temptation of Christ*. Scorsese, one of America's most renowned and respected directors, had overturned the traditional images of Christ. Doubt, *blague*, ambiguity, cowardice, rage and lust now marked his behaviour; in short, he was the hero of the 1980s. Judas knocking Jesus about and abusing him, calling him 'coward', were just some of the controversial images. The predictable Christian anger centred on the picture of Jesus the stud in place of Jesus the saviour. Nonetheless, it was still an attempt to explore the story with serious intellectual purpose. What was galling for Christians about Madonna was her deliberate use of parody focused on religious themes, her almost conscious intention to provoke controversy.

Although her iconoclasm is not restricted to the church – she has deliberately used the American flag in a way which has infuriated many patriotic Americans – it is her conscious representation of the church which is calculated to rouse its fury. Included are the virgin/whore dichotomy, the cross, priests' robes, interracial sex and masturbation in church with a Christ-like figure. Shaken by the anger of the church, Pepsi Cola withdrew its $5 million advert featuring Madonna. The Vatican has also succeeded in having her shows cancelled in Rome. But her message appears to be more relevant than that of the church for her followers, as the students of Cambridge made clear while commenting on 'The immaculate collection' in *Varsity*:

And it came to pass in the dark night of the 1980s, when swinging kiddies could no longer claim drugs and rock'n'roll as their birthright, and sex (number one of the unholy trinity) became dangerous, that *lo*, in the west, was born a star. And the people saw that she was good, that she delighted in a spot of rumpy-pumpy, and in her they were well pleased. And upon the earth she was known unto all generations as Madonna. . . . Listen and note that Madonna, like her less illustrious son, was made to walk on water.

(Smith 1990)

Supremely in command of the media, Madonna exploited this to her advantage with gusto and irony. Her performances at Wembley Stadium, in London, in Barcelona and in Tokyo could have been designed with the Vatican in mind. During 'Like a virgin' she pantomimed sexual ecstasy and, for the song which particularly incurred Papal wrath, 'Like a prayer', would have the entire stadium clapping, arms aloft. 'Papa don't preach', the song about teenage pregnancy and rebellion, reprised the renegade Catholic theme with crosses suspended overhead, aglow in neon. 'You want to fuck us?' she asks on stage of a group of young men in one number. Her latest video on US television, 'Justify my love', and her film, *Truth or Dare: In Bed with Madonna* (in which she fellates a bottle of fizzy water and is seen in action in bed with gay dancers), ensure that the controversy will continue.

Alongside the hedonist philosophy, the unabashed materialism, are signs of culture and tradition. The church, the crucifix, the father figure are never far away; every performance is preceded by a prayer. 'I'm spiritual', 'religious', she told an unusually awed Wogan on his show (22 July 1991 – the 1,000th edition).

'Yes', she says, when asked about the prayer meetings before each show on the tour, 'I am religious. They were sincere, at least as far as I was concerned. . . . It's not that I'm trying to build a bridge between sex and religion. It's just that the Catholic Church insists on separating the two and they always have, and it's bullshit.'

(Malcolm 1991)

Madonna is a child of the postmodernist age, a cliché, a mask, the supreme product of the consumerist culture. Her life and performances are expensively choreographed theatre. Her wit, her style, her gestures, her sexual references speak directly to her large following across the world. Madonna, pop philosopher of postmodernist culture, hit it on the head when she intoned in her monotonously squeaky voice: 'I'm a material girl in a material world.'

Marilyn Monroe was controlled and eventually destroyed by the media; Madonna controls and is expressed through the media. What Warren Beatty confirmed was true: she could not live off camera (*In Bed with Madonna*). She is in total command: 'I call the shots', she said in a BBC *Omnibus* TV programme shown in Britain (on 7 December 1990). But the level of interchange is not inspiring; it rarely soars above the waist. 'Typical reporter's question: "How big is Warren Beatty's dick?" Answer: "I haven't measured it. Why don't you ask him?" ' (Malcolm 1991). When pressed for a statement on her philosophy of life she replied: 'Pussy rules the world.' For her this was not metaphor, not figure of speech, not metonymy; it was meant literally, as philosophy.

She is now the subject of intense study. Learned academics have written Ph.D. theses about her; fiery feminist intellectuals have deconstructed her image for their followers. Post-feminists, less critical of her recently, feel she reasserts the role of the sexual realm, the control of female sexuality.

Casting about for the New Woman, they have selected Madonna as the model for the 1990s:

> There are signs of hope. There is a new and even younger generation whose icon is singer/performer Madonna; she stands hand on crotch, preaching to her sisters: masturbate. Madonna is no male masturbatory fantasy – though she is that too – but rather she embodies sexual woman/working woman and yes, I think you could put mother in there too. I can see Madonna with a baby in her arms, and the hand still on her crotch.
>
> ('Sexual fantasy in the nineties', by Nancy Friday in *Weekend Guardian*, 12–13 October 1991)

An academic gushes: 'Playing with the outlaw personae of prostitute and dominatrix, Madonna has made a major contribution to the history of women. She has rejoined and healed the split halves of woman: Mary, the Blessed Virgin and Holy Mother, and Mary Magdalene, the harlot' (Paglia 1991). And goes on gushing: 'But Madonna's most enduring cultural contribution may be that she has introduced ravishing visual beauty and a lush Mediterranean sensuality into parched, pinched, word-drunk Anglo-Saxon feminism' (ibid.). For her, even *The Economist*, which characteristically sounds like a 'superior' Oxford don (not surprising considering the composition of its writers), drops its guard and plunges into unabashed postmodernist jargon: 'Perhaps more important, it ignores one of the most intriguing questions posed by postmodernism about authenticity and celebrity: what matters more, seeming real or really seeming?' (27 July – 2 August 1991: 90).

Madonna's stature as a super-celebrity continues to grow, in spite of the church's disapproval. She stole the show at the 1991 Cannes Film Festival. As a besotted art critic wrote after interviewing her: 'You could feel her presence – at a distance of 20 miles . . . the only real star in town' (Robert Sandall, 'Let's get metaphysical', in *The Sunday Times*, 19 May 1991).

But she may be spoiling things; she is beginning to take herself seriously; she talks of running for President. And why not? Ronald Reagan blazed the trail for Hollywood stars. But underneath the titanic media figure, the deafening fizz and pop, the pervasive glitz and glamour, there appears to be nothing at the centre; just a dull, empty and cold void – a fact that even Wogan, with his characteristically gentle probing, discovered so quickly on his programme.

The provocative irreverence, explicit sexuality, garish appeal to the senses, celebration of materialism and the emptiness underneath it all add up to a figure as far as it is possible to get from the Muslim ideal. That she has fans, admittedly small in number, in Cairo and Karachi, adds to Muslim disdain, as it underlines the need to guard cultural boundaries. Orthodox Muslims, then, would express the same revulsion as the Pope against the public persona of Madonna; for them she would be the embodiment of the postmodern age of the Western media, its demonic siren queen (public protests were mounted in Pakistan in 1991 to express disapproval of the rumour that Madonna was to visit the country).

Crossing cultural borders

The British Board of Film Classification was not alone in discovering the perils of crossing cultural boundaries. Our other two cases provide interesting parallels. Two perfectly respectable people had reacted to what they saw as provocation in the context of their own cultures. Ayatollah Khomeini had condemned Rushdie because his book was considered blasphemous; the Pope condemned Madonna for her provocative songs. As head of his respective religious structure each did what was expected of him by his followers. Any Muslim cleric would have reacted to the book in the same manner as the Ayatollah; any Catholic priest would have found Madonna's songs distasteful.

That both Rushdie and Madonna belonged – or once belonged – to their respective religions made matters worse for them; their ex-co-religionists were convinced of a cold-blooded exploitation of their 'insider' knowledge, which added to their fury. On the other hand, those defending the author and the singer rested their arguments on the right of freedom of speech and artistic expression; the volume of the derision in their voices indicated deeply felt conviction.

What neither the Ayatollah nor the Pope could have anticipated was that their protests would produce the opposite effect of what they intended. Rushdie's book, the sales of which had begun to falter, became a best-seller, and the demand for Madonna's records soared. The media attention was a publicity agent's dream. The condemnation was attracting the primary and golden rule – one identified by Wilde himself – of the media: say anything as long as you get the spelling of the name right. However, for Rushdie personally, the *fatwa* has become a nightmare as he spends his life waiting for the assassin's move.

Clearly, in the cases of Rushdie and Madonna numerous overlapping national, intellectual and cultural boundaries are being crossed. Tradition, respect for the sacred, the willingness to sacrifice in the cause of religion characterize present Iranian society. The opposite holds true for literary Britain. Satire is an essential part of English comment, the more biting the better. Among Muslims, where humour is not so savage and personal, jokes are easily misunderstood. English satire is not reserved exclusively for Muslims; the English are habitually satirical about the Scots, the Irish, the Germans (as we were shown in the controversial Nicholas Ridley interview to *The Spectator* in 1990, which caused him to resign his Cabinet post), and, most of all, themselves. English humour would cease to exist without jokes about the royal family (the distasteful jokes about Prince Charles's ears run on and on), mothers-in-law, politicians and the weather.

The word of the Ayatollah is law in Iran and honoured by Shias all over the world. Had Rushdie been in Iran at the time of the *fatwa*, his fate would have been sealed. Yet by announcing the *fatwa* against a citizen of a non-Muslim country the Ayatollah crossed into a different arena with different rules and laws. The crossing for British Muslims was difficult to define, more ambiguous by nature, and induced a culture-warp. Most Muslims were deeply offended by many passages in the book, but not all of them wished to see the author killed (my own position is clearly stated in *The Independent*, 7 December 1990). It was precisely this exquisite ambiguity which fed into the media: radio and television news, comic and chat shows – the essential ingredients of popular culture – revelled in the Rushdie affair.

Early in 1991 another controversy, which may well end in another death threat against an author and media figure who had also crossed boundaries, developed in South America. It was against Gabriel García Márquez, the master of magical realism and author of widely read novels like *One Hundred Years of Solitude* (1978). In his latest work, *The General in his Labyrinth* (1991), he has offended South American admirers of Simón Bolívar who are protesting against the treatment of their hero (this was the theme of a *Rear Window*, Channel 4 documentary, shown on 14 May 1991). Latins regard Bolívar as a legendary warrior and political visionary who sought to unite the region from Panama to Peru in the single nation of 'Gran Colombia'. They cannot tolerate his depiction as a spiritually and physically frail human being riven by wavering doubts and passionate instincts.

In this chapter I have shown how instant communications crossing cultural boundaries can create devastating misunderstandings between different peoples. Such crossings are unpredictable and dangerous. Dante's warning, 'Abandon all hope, you who enter', applies to the entrant. The media distorts and corrupts. It does so with exuberant neutrality, being no respecter of persons. But it does have its likes and dislikes, and 'establishment' figures, whether Ayatollah or Pope, generally fall in the latter category. The discussion of cultural crossings brings into relief the dangers of dealing with the media and helps explain normative attitudes to its images. In the next chapter we will attempt to define and understand the nature of the media.

Chapter 6

The evil demon: the media as master

Throughout the book my arguments have maintained that the media constitute a central feature of postmodernism and even define the dominant global civilization of our time. The pervasiveness of postmodernism – its hope, ambiguities and challenge – is not possible to understand without an understanding of the media; it is appropriate, then, that we return to a discussion of the media in our concluding chapter.

Considering the open-ended, on-going and ambiguous nature of the subject we cannot, therefore, at the end of the book, attempt a firm and coherent summary; we can only point in some initial directions. Our arguments are thus tentative and propaedeutical, indicating further and essential areas of research. In this connection we have raised a range of central questions while identifying certain principles that govern contemporary society. I will first attempt to explore the nature and the temperament of the Western media – the evil demon in the title of the chapter. I will then make some observations about their impact on family life; a direct causal relationship between the media and strains in the family is thus suggested. It is partly this which repels Muslims who lay such great value on the family; the Muslim reaction will then be discussed. Finally, some broad concluding thoughts are indicated.

Early on in the book we touched on the three great encounters between Islam and the West. We are now in the midst of the third encounter. Many, both Muslim and non-Muslim, see this as the final clash, given the nature of globalization that has taken place. Logically, only one can dominate unless in the West there is toleration of plural systems – but that will be our concluding argument and we will come to it later.

Nothing in history has threatened Muslims like the Western media; neither gunpowder in the Middle Ages, which Muslims like Babar used with skill on the fields of Panipat thus winning India for his Mughal dynasty, nor trains and the telephone, which helped colonize them in the last century, nor even planes which they mastered for their national airlines earlier this century. The Western media are ever present and ubiquitous; never resting and never allowing respite. They probe and attack ceaselessly, showing no mercy for weakness or frailty.

The powerful media offensive is compounded for Muslims: they appear not to have the capacity to defend themselves. Worse; they appear unable even to comprehend the nature and objectives of the onslaught. The empty bluster of the leaders and the narrow-minded whining of the scholars makes them appear pitiful, like pygmies arguing among themselves while the powerful giant of an enemy is at the gate. It is the ordinary Muslim – invariably more trustworthy than the leader and the scholar where Muslim instinct and common sense are concerned – who senses the immensity of the danger. He is conscious of the potential scale of the battle and the forces arranged against him; his tension is made worse because he has so little faith in his own leaders.

It must have been something like this in 1258 when the Mongols were gathering outside Baghdad to shatter forever the greatest Arab empire in history. But while the Abbasids remained in ruins, other, equally significant structures with glorious edifices were created: the Fatimids in Egypt, the Umayyads in Spain, and, later, the Saffavids in Iran, the Mughals in India. This time it will be a final – a total – decision; there will be no coming back. The demon is a jealous and spiteful creature. Therefore in this concluding chapter we try to delineate some of the characteristic features of the media; it will help set the larger arguments in the book in context. It will also help us better understand the response of Islam to the postmodern age.

UNDERSTANDING THE DEMON

Whereas modernists sought not only to understand but also to change the world, postmodernists appear more modest in their aims: they wish to de-construct it in order to understand it. That is proving difficult enough.

A long time ago, in the 1960s, when the world, compared to the prospects we face today, appeared a fresher, less dangerous and certainly more innocent place, the eponymous ancestor of the media sages had sounded the warning about 'electric technology', and 'our central nervous system' (McLuhan 1964: 3). The only message, he warned us, was the medium; in our age the medium is the master, a demon master.

For in their power over us, their capacity to subvert reality, to simplify issues dangerously and influence events the media are like an omnipotent, omnipresent moody demon of our times; the cause and effect of the *Zeitgeist* of the postmodernist age (*The Evil Demon of Images* was Baudrillard's title, 1988a). The media can easily create a caricature of the image that is desired. Like the embrace of any demon lover, the embrace of the media can be fraught with danger:

> It is precisely when it appears most truthful, most faithful and most in conformity to reality that the image is most diabolical – and our technical images, whether they be from photography, cinema or television, are in the overwhelming majority much more 'figurative', 'realist', than all the images from past cultures.
>
> (ibid.: 13–14)

The nature of this demon and the dangers it generates are still not fully understood; we therefore bring notice to it by deliberately using the word in all the headings in this chapter. The assumptive power of the demon will be greater and the scope for friction between different peoples higher, as the world continues to shrink into the global technological village through the 1990s. Future leaders would do well to have on their teams semioticians and hermeneutical experts to decode the danger signs in their dealings with the media and advise them when crossing sensitive and dangerous cultural boundaries.

In grappling with the electronic media, which form such a central feature of the dominant global civilization, we are assuming a firm locus, a defined position, an identifiable object. But let us not simplify a complex phenomenon, let us not nail down too vigorously matters which are still elusive. As Eco asks:

Where is the mass medium? Is it the newspaper advertisement, is it the television broadcast, is it the polo shirt? Here we have not one but two, three perhaps more mass media, acting through different channels. The media have multiplied, but some of them act as media of media, or in other words media squared.

(1987: 149)

Let us try to peer a bit more closely at the nature and the temperament of the media. A tentative probing will reveal for us some of the characteristics which lie at its heart. We learn of its inherent ambiguity, contradictions and unpredictability; but the exercise may help us comprehend better the nature of the demon.

One: The media have no loyalty or memory of friendship. Perhaps one of the most important characteristics of the media is the lack of loyalty; hence the feeling of ambiguity they arouse. We know the mass media mean power, assertion of cultural superiority and extension of political philosophy. They are a critically important weapon in the arsenal of any country. We also know that never before in history has a super-power been so baffled by the manipulation of its own weapons by the enemy as the United States was in the Gulf crisis in 1990–91. This is because the media are like a double-edged sword.

President Bush, seizing the media initiative, quite consciously projected his golf-cart style of leadership in late 1990:

The result was that the news was often interchangeable with what information specialists call 'horizontal propaganda'. Horizontal propaganda isn't lies; it isn't even necessarily an organised effort. It is merely part of the process by which any culture perpetuates its ideals and beliefs. In the press, the process tended to suggest that our institutions were sound, and our leaders capable. There is certainly nothing sinister about such a process; a culture that failed to perpetuate its precepts wouldn't survive.

(Freund 1990: 19)

Within days, however, the media had shifted their attention to the hostages in Baghdad. Bush was left to react to announcements from Saddam. He was discovering the double-edged nature of his weapon. 'What distinguishes modern pop news from its pre-decessors is that it is no longer willing to be part of a continuing effort in organised persuasion; it has become adversarial' (ibid.).

As *The Spectator* noted:

> CNN, by its own frank admission, recognizes no legitimate restraints on what it should or should not broadcast. Back in the early days of the crisis George Bush was furious that his unconvincing efforts to portray Saddam Hussein as a latter-day Hitler were undercut by live coverage of the Iraqi leader's amicable meetings with Western hostages.
>
> (S. Robinson 1991)

Although Muslims complain that the Western media dislike them, Dan Rather's interview allowed Saddam prime-time access in America. Instead of confirming the picture created by those who dismissed Saddam as a cowering, neurotic Hitler in his bunker days Rather appeared chastened in his public response: 'Every signal he sent out, including his body language, said that he is not feeling cornered, and indeed that he thinks George Bush is the one cornered. He is not a person I'd want to fight' (*The Sunday Times*, 2 September 1990).

Without loyalties, the Western media have allowed some powerful messages from Muslims to be heard and seen. Those Muslims who dismiss all Western media as biased must ponder the international impact of television programmes like *The Promised Land*, *Malika's Hotel* and *Terror* in projecting the Palestinian cause with sympathy (see Chapter 2).

The villains of yesterday can become today's heroes. The American film *The Wind and the Lion* was based on the true story of a Berber tribesman in Morocco who took American hostages. Sean Connery played the Berber, Candice Bergen the American. Teddy Roosevelt, suitably sabre rattling in Washington, was almost a secondary character. Yesterday, Saddam was the Arab moderate *par excellence* in the West, today he is a Hitler.

Deng was hailed as the leader who would lead China into the modern world, then he was reviled as a savage butcher, after the killings in Tiananmen Square in 1989. Friends of the Americans like the Shah of Iran or Marcos suddenly become *personae non grata* in the United States; Mrs Aquino, the former rebel, suddenly a saviour. Rushdie is presently the symbol of the oppressed writer in the West, a villain among Muslims, but his declaration of faith in Islam in December 1990 and his subsequent behaviour may well affect these perceptions in the future. As Tracey Ullman, herself a victim of the inconsistent affections of the media, once remarked, 'The media build you up one minute, only for the pleasure of pulling you down, the next.'

Two: The media are colour-conscious and overtly racist. The Western media are dominated by WASPs (White Anglo-Saxon Protestants) – or the recently discovered IWPs (Insensitive White Persons); their ideas continue to be shaped by the DWM (Dead White Male, see Chapter 2). Media heroes must be white, or if brown, tanned white. Blue eyes and blond hair are favoured. The villain is usually an Asian. The black is still a stereotype: the bad one is a mugger and anarchist, the acceptable one a pop-singer or athlete. In the future, Spike Lee's generation of black directors, after the anger subsides, will no doubt correct this (discussed in *Home Boys in Hollywood*, BBC2, 5 October 1991).

Only three decades ago, McLuhan had alerted us to the fact that blacks in Africa could not comprehend or follow Western media like the cinema, 'chanting and shouting during films' and moving their eyes with the images (1964: 287). *The Cosby Show* reverses the white stereotypes and is therefore mould-breaking.

Let me insert a parenthesis here as a tribute to the black population of America. Contemplate the scale of their tragedy: descendants of slaves, 24 million of whom were estimated to have been forcibly transported in 'floating coffins' across the Atlantic, 9 million of whom were exterminated in the crossing, almost 50 per cent are still born in poverty, and a larger percentage still face discrimination at all levels. Debased, enslaved, dehumanized and demonized – what is surprising is not the anger among them but the dignity, humour and energy. *The Cosby Show* is therefore significant. It portrays for us a healed and integrated black family; it is telling us implicitly that the ghosts of the past are exorcised; of the need to get on with life. This may be Hollywood but it is also a tribute to the human spirit.

The regnant media heroes, the top role-models, help us to understand this point. If we compile a list of the world's ten best-known figures on the basis of media representation it would probably be something like this: one of the British royals (possibly the Queen Mother or the Princess of Wales), one of the American astronauts, Gorbachev, Elizabeth Taylor, Elvis Presley, James Dean, Reagan, Roosevelt, Marilyn Monroe and one of the Johns (take your pick, Kennedy, Wayne or Lennon).

This is of course an arbitrary list; it is also a postmodernist list. There is little moral or spiritual substance in these lives; their essence is capricious and capriccioso (many are *spericolato*). Sainthood is bestowed because of their media projection. Some are, of course, extraordinary figures who have changed the course of history, like Gorbachev. We notice the preponderance of media figures, also of white Americans.

We also notice that not a single Muslim features on this list. In this list of super-celebrities, the only Muslim with any hope of inclusion is Benazir Bhutto. But the reasons for this – a pretty face and feminine glamour – may neither please her nor the main body of Muslims. On the other hand, a similar list of the most disliked figures based in the Western media would be thick with Muslim names. London tabloids, like the *Sun*, drew up just such a list during the Gulf crisis in August 1990. Not surprisingly, Saddam Hussein had rocketed to the top of the 'ten most terrible tyrants'. Also, not surprisingly, Ayatollah Khomeini and Colonel Gaddafi figured highly.

Billy Joel's 'We didn't start the fire' presents a potted history of the major world events and personalities of our generation. The names confirm the arguments in this book: Monroe, Elvis, Dean, the Beatles, Kennedy. The only two Muslims on the list are Nasser and Khomeini, both employed as anti-West symbols. The name 'Palestine' is used and rhymes with 'Terror on the airline'. Again, in Park's *Cultural Icons: Figures Who Made the Twentieth Century What It Is* (1991), Saddam Hussein represents the Muslims. This is a travesty. The arguments here are confirmed by the figures who appear in the *1000 Makers of the Twentieth Century* announced by *The Sunday Times* on 22 September 1991. Once again Saddam represented the Muslims. Once again the overwhelming majority were first American and then British.

Christianity is related to this position in some interesting ways. It inspires the WASP perception of the world. Take the malignity and power of the devil, who is a central figure in numerous films (for example, *The Exorcist*, *The Omen*, and their sequels and spin-offs). The cross, the key symbol of Christianity, is brandished to keep the devil at bay. Non-Christians by definition cannot do so and are therefore doomed. There is also the question of colour. Traditional images of the devil depict him as a dark figure; protests by black activists and their supporters changed his colour to dark red.

Popular television programmes like *Bangkok Hilton* or *Amongst Barbarians* portray Asian societies as irrational and volatile. The life of one white person – whether a murderer or drug addict – legally held in an Asian prison is news. A thousand Asian deaths in Bangladesh or China is no news. Even in the extensive reporting of the refugees detained in Iraq during the Gulf crisis the media were selective. We were flooded with images of Europeans and Americans; the Egyptians and South Asians were forgotten. They were raped and looted by the Iraqis but their story was of little interest to the world media; they simply did not exist. To her credit, only Kate Adie attempted to show this side of the war.

Tending towards xenophobia, racism surfaces easily in the Western media. We see this in different degrees in the quality papers and the tabloids. We have already pointed out that recent films, like *Black Rain*, contain racist innuendoes difficult to imagine a decade ago. This is also true of the material of comedians and journalists.

Muslims ask: now that the Western media have helped conquer communism, who will be their next opponent? It is not difficult to guess: Islam. Islam continues to be marginalized or degraded; in a hundred hours of television Islam may get ten minutes of projection, which will be Muslims burning books or forming threatening mobs. Muslims are rarely, if ever, invited to appear on the popular chat shows like *Wogan* and *The Clive James Show*.

We noted the one-dimensional picture of Saddam and, by extension, of all Arabs, created during the Gulf crisis. It therefore dehumanized Arab civilization, reducing it to a nonsense. Arabs were shown as either playboys squandering money in European casinos, or bully-boys terrorizing smaller neighbours. For the American GI on the Arabian peninsula there was little difference between the Arabs he was defending and those he was to attack. Both were 'desert niggers'; and he had contributed a racist neologism. When the GI on television said 'I'm here to kick ass', it was difficult to predict which posterior – friend or foe – was destined to receive the imprint of his undoubtedly large boot.

Beards convey age, authority and dignity in traditional Muslim society. They are often a badge of wisdom and learning. In Muslim countries beards are sometimes required of public figures: '*Bearded justice*. A beard is essential for an Islamic judge even if it means a long wait to find suitable candidates, the new Prime Minister of Pakistan-ruled Kashmir, Sardar Abdul Qayyum, said yesterday' (*The Guardian*, 9 August 1991).

But as we have pointed out the media disapprove of whiskers:

remember the votes lost due to Nixon's evening shadow? Therefore bearded Muslim mullahs and Jewish rabbis are not favoured in the Western media. Beardless rabbis, on the other hand, are a different matter. Lionel Blue's television essays, *In Search of Holy England*, for Channel 4 in 1990, portrayed a charming, thoughtful and beardless rabbi (for an even more charming, thoughtful and beardless rabbi we refer to Julia Neuberger). The media have imposed a virtual veto on beards. We cannot imagine a pop-singer or a Western politician in possession of a beard, hoping for favourable coverage in the media.

Nevertheless the Western media can be understood, even won over by those who believe in the Semitic tradition. Although we saw above the failure in communication between the Pope and the media we have also pointed out Christians, like the Evangelists in the United States, who have used the media with vigour and success. The Jews, the archetypal Semites, also provide us with an interesting case in this regard.

Unlike Muslims, the Jews have become the greatest masters of the media. Take their role in Hollywood. *An Empire of Their Own: How the Jews Invented Hollywood* explains how Jews, arriving from Europe, often in poverty and not even speaking English fluently, invented the values, myths and archetypes that enabled them to appropriate the American imagination (Gabler 1991; also see Gledhill 1991 and Kent 1991). In turn, this appropriation helped to shape and define the culture and consciousness of America. Many of the greatest American stars – Gregory Peck, Elizabeth Taylor, Kirk Douglas, Burt Lancaster, Paul Newman – the list is unending – are Jewish. They helped provide Hollywood with its notions of beauty and glamour. Indeed, the nearest thing to an ancient Greek statue of male perfection is the young Paul Newman.

The media have also allowed Jews to emphasize, preserve and broadcast one of the most barbaric episodes in human history, the Holocaust in Germany. Baudrillard makes a cynical postmodernist comment on the event and the television special, *Holocaust*, that it inspired:

> The Jews are no longer forced to pass through the gas chambers and crematorium ovens, but through the sound track and picture strip, the cathodic screen and microprocessor. The amnesia, the oblivion, thereby finally attains an aesthetic dimension – consummated in retrospective and retrogressive

fashion, raised here to mass dimensions. Television as the event's true 'final solution'. . . . The *Holocaust* [the television special] is, *first of all* (and exclusively) a *televised* event (one must not forget McLuhan's basic rule).

(Baudrillard 1990: 160–1)

Three: The media are self-perpetuating and fiercely incestuous. Popular stories and films, which reinforce the sense of a unique cultural heritage, are kept alive by constant revivals. Generations have grown up watching old films like *Casablanca*. Pre- and post-film discussions on television further reinforce the sense of a common culture. As a consequence, actors like Humphrey Bogart remain in vogue. He was as much a cult figure in the 1980s as he was a generation ago. The icons are thus deified. Safe from being dethroned by any scandal or criticism, they are far removed from the bile of critics. Besides, their constant appearance in the media makes criticism irrelevant. Clones all over the world are encouraged to flourish. Manila Madonnas and Bombay Brandos copy the Western originals with unrestrained gusto.

The media reinforce their own ideas, values and opinions through their highly incestuous character. So a successful film for a star will be followed by chat shows on television, interviews in the dailies and glossies and appearances in advertisements. Music from the film – a soundtrack perhaps capturing nostalgia (of the 1960s in the late 1980s) – will further market the product; it is what the industry terms 'synergy'. Scandals in the tabloids for the star will follow; more publicity will result. No boundaries exist between one medium and another. The media thus incessantly nourish their favourites. So, Jason Donovan from Australia would appear on the best-known chat shows like *Dame Edna* and *Wogan* in London. He would also appear in pantomime and in the tabloids. This not only applies to singers. Sports stars, like Ian Botham, or Oxford professors, like Norman Stone, are now media celebrities and on the same media network.

The main sources of Western culture – from Homer to Shakespeare – are simplified and popularized through television and films. This allows the widest possible exposure to them. They are mentioned in serious films, in comic strips and in comedy shows and referred to in news programmes and political commentary. Thus, each generation interprets these authors according to its own light and perpetuates the cultural legacy.

Consider the one-liners, popularized through repetition in the media. They are now sanctified and immortalized through their inclusion in *The Oxford Dictionary of Modern Quotations* (Augarde 1991); included are 'Play it again, Sam' (actual words: 'If she can stand it, I can. Play it!' in *Casablanca* 1942; ibid.: 77); 'Beam me up, Scotty' (actual words: 'Beam us up, Mr Scott', ibid.: 182); 'What's up, Doc?' (ibid.: 15); and 'Go ahead, make my day' (Clint Eastwood in *Dirty Harry*, 1971, ibid.: 79). The sources are Westerns, cartoons, science fiction and Second World War romance. These sentences are made immortal through the media, a cultural gift to the entire world. They are quoted, parodied, copied and are constantly in print. From presidents to common folk, people prefer not to quote Shakespeare or Goethe but Clint Eastwood, Bugs Bunny or Humphrey Bogart. In the Gulf crisis, President Bush did not refer to Shakespeare, Agincourt and letting slip the dogs of war; he dared Saddam to make his day.

During the challenge from Michael Heseltine to Mrs Thatcher for the position of Prime Minister, the ITV News, London, ran a major programme on 14 November 1990 (which was to win a BAFTA Award in March 1991). It showed him walking in slow motion to the song from *High Noon*, 'Do not forsake me, oh my darling'. These shots were interspersed with scenes of Gary Cooper preparing for the showdown. Towards the end of the Gulf war when Bush issued an ultimatum to Saddam, which would expire at midday on 23 February 1991, many American and British newspapers that morning carried the headline 'High Noon'. Both the narcissistic nature of the media and their capacity to blur reality and illusion are thus illustrated.

Museums and cultural centres also help preserve for all time to come popular media images and figures; the heritage industry thrives in the postmodernist era (Harvey 1989a: 62; also Ahmed 1991i, Corner and Harvey 1991). The Museum of Modern Art in New York, the Tate in London, the Prado in Madrid, the Louvre in Paris – these are the temples and cultural centres of post-modernism. Some, like the Museum of the Moving Image in London, are state-of-the-art temples which draw unending visitors. The numbers who visit them testify to their huge success; their appeal is further enhanced by the media. The process began a generation ago; we saw Dr No stealing a famous painting which, of course, James Bond recognized and recovered; the pop song 'Mona Lisa' by Nat 'King' Cole helped to ensure that the painting became part of everyday idiom and a symbol of romance and mystery to those not interested in high culture. The lives of the painters – Van Gogh and Picasso – have become the subject of popular films and books.

The exhibitions learn and borrow from department-store windows. There is challenge and excitement when pictures are hung anew. The visible patronage of the arts by royalty and presidents enhances their prestige. Paintings are like public investments and big business; their sales are the stuff of headlines. The merchandising section has the shopping mall and theme park in mind: postcards, books, ceramics, souvenirs; here culture and consumerism fuse and not always is the result kitsch.

The democratic process has ensured that millions are now involved in looking at and learning about art; it is no longer the preserve of the high-brow connoisseur. This has also underlined the implicit understanding that here is a shared legacy of the West, one which the common person can identify with and appreciate with pride irrespective of (Western) national borders. So when a Van Gogh painting was sold to a Japanese, the media publicity was as much about the enormous sum paid – the national budget of an African country – as the jingoistic response to losing a cultural treasure.

Four: The mass media have conquered death. We need to understand this sociologically rather than eschatologically to appreciate the phenomenon. A star's death does not affect a career in the media. Shuffling off the mortal coil is seen as a sensible professional ploy. Elvis is a case in point. When Elvis died it was said he had made his best career move.

'Elvis Presley', began an article in *Punch*, 'has had a busy and rather trying time since his death' (Cook 1991: 43). The article was right. Elvis appears regularly on television and radio. Books and articles continue to be written about him (see, in 1991, Childress). His home, Graceland, continues to attract record crowds. Its name inspired the title of a well-known music album, sung by Paul Simon, in the 1980s. Fan clubs celebrate events from his life all over the world. 'Elvis: the legend lives on', proclaimed the collection called 'Elvis lives!', organized by the Reader's Digest Association to promote his records (advertised in, for example, *The Guardian*, 2–3 February 1991). In 1990 a perfume was launched, named after him. People on chat shows claim to have seen him or talked to him (as on *The Clive James Show*). Oprah

Winfrey had an entire show on Elvis impersonators (in 1991). Even the crack British troops, the Desert Rats in the Saudi desert in 1990, resuscitated him by coining a military term: Elvis. It referred to a soldier not prepared in the case of a gas attack by Saddam Hussein, in which case he would be Elvis – or history. Listening to Elvis's 'Are you lonesome tonight?' even helped Boris Yeltsin survive and overcome the coup in August 1991, as we saw earlier.

Jonathan Ross's death anniversary offering, *Viva Elvis* (Channel 4, 12 August 1991), showed us the cult of Elvis through the Elvis impersonators in the United States. Among the thousands, we were introduced to the Mexican Elvis, the black Elvis, a 4-year-old Elvis, and even a female Elvis. The Elvis worshippers displayed memorabilia which included toilet paper, a toe-nail and even a surgically removed wart.

This was grotesque and nausea-inducing, but it illustrates the status of Elvis as an icon of contemporary American culture; of the refusal to let him go gracefully. The only person who appears to have been affected by the death of Elvis, is Elvis himself. For the rest of us he is alive and available at the touch of a button.

This is equally true for the other media icons like Marilyn Monroe, John Kennedy and John Lennon. In 1991 Nat 'King' Cole made the Top Thirty with 'Unforgettable', a song he first recorded in 1951; the technological miracle is not the re-release but the duet provided by his daughter Natalie. Father and daughter sang together, twenty-five years after Nat died of cancer. Death had indeed been overcome.

There is a distinctly ghoulish side to the media. They appear to be almost as obsessed with death as with life. Hollywood, the media capital of the world, illustrates this for us. Two generations ago Aldous Huxley and Evelyn Waugh had satirized the obsession with death. Nowadays Graveline Tours, for $30, will expose tourists to a hundred years of death, sin, and scandals. For three hours, tourists ride in a long, black hearse for a visit to the dark side. The tour includes the home where Marilyn Monroe committed suicide and the hotel where John Belushi overdosed on cocaine and heroin. The customer receives a cornucopia of morbid trivia, songs and satire with 'genuine' death certificates. An example of the humour: 'Cathy Smith [who served the heroin/cocaine cocktail] went to jail, Belushi to Massachusetts cemetery.' The tour is an example of the postmodernist attitude to death.

Five: The media are genuinely democratic and represent the 'common' person. The democratic principle at the heart of the media reflects the origin of the media in the Western democracies. They do not respect rank or authority; nor royalty. By its very nature, royalty can be either revered or reviled: but it can rarely be both at the same time. The media make it difficult to maintain the illusion of reverential seriousness essential to the survival of royal mystique. Of the most satirically irreverent humour we may note the puppets of *Spitting Image*, the wit of *Blackadder*, and the obsessive trivialities of the tabloids.

During the Gulf crisis we saw English schoolboy or housewife, American professor or soldier, Saudi soldier or Kuwaiti prince on television; each had a story to tell and an opportunity to tell it. Anyone can be on the news if he or she is at the right place at the right time. Through the media anyone can be momentarily famous; it is the Warhol principle. Hostages, students or housewives – any of these may be propelled into world fame, at any moment.

Also, through the media each one of us is able to indulge any fantasy. Public Access television in the United States allows every kind of sexual and violent act into the home. The nightmares and fantasies are as old as human society, but now every individual has the means to order their own personal nightmares and perversions at the most convenient time.

Six: The media have made facts stranger than fiction and therefore more desirable to see and hear. The television news is presented in a way which rivals all but the best fiction and drama. Often running into an hour, with dramatic music, well-known newscasters with star status, with archival film and on-stream reporting from the most remote corners of the world, the news is riveting. The media can convert ordinary, everyday situations into spectacle.

Where there is high drama – as in the Rushdie affair, Iraq's invasion of Kuwait, Mrs Thatcher's resignation, the Gulf war, the arrest of Gorbachev and the collapse of the Communist Party in Moscow – audiences reportedly preferred the news to popular plays and songs. Fact was proving far more interesting than fiction. The reason is plain: the viewer must be titillated and entertained or he will press the button and switch the channel.

The global perspective, the desire to be informed in an amusing manner, affected the entire way the Gulf crisis was reported:

The American Cable Network News has changed the whole art of war coverage. The network has become essential to following the crisis, linking up capital cities and adversaries, and acting as a sort of alternative forum to the United Nations. It now reaches all over the world, and claims eager subscribers in Washington, Moscow and Baghdad.

(S. Robinson 1991: 12)

For the duration of the Gulf war in early 1991 ITN, Channel 4, ran, as mentioned above, a popular news programme called *Midnight Special* from midnight to 2 a.m. The panel, which usually comprised half-a-dozen academics and political analysts, discussed the news as it came in from all over the world. The 'entertainment' value remained high. The reporting was up-to-the-minute and slick, the panellists were themselves celebrities; Harold Pinter was one of them. The programme was singled out by the Sunday papers for the best 'seriously sceptical commentary' (as John Naughton of the *Observer* noted in his TV review of 3 March 1991).

This is all very well when such momentous events are taking place but what of prosaic, everyday subjects? What of the one considered by many schoolchildren as the most boring – that is, nature? As all Wodehouse devotees know, anyone interested in nature – like Gussie Fink-Nottle who kept newts – was considered soft in the head. The main character of what is probably Wodehouse's funniest scene, one he himself selected as such, was Gussie Fink-Nottle in *Right Ho, Jeeves* (1934). But programmes like David Attenborough's twelve-part wildlife spectacular, *The Trials of Life*, for BBC TV, prove this common assumption wrong. Attenborough's series were not only visually superb but also contained absorbing drama. They overshadowed in popularity even the adventures of slasher heroes like Freddy Krueger; although some would say David packs in as much sex and violence as Freddy.

Seven: The media are coldly neutral to moral positions and spiritual messages. They can flash images of Christmas abundance in America one second and starving Ethiopians the next. This, therefore, creates problems. Those few seconds do not and indeed cannot depict the complexity of American or African society. It raises the question: how do we relate these images to each other and what is our position in relationship to them?

The television ads are an example of the juxtaposition of diverse images. The perfect bodies, like Greek statues, sitting by swimming pools, leaning against cars or drinking cola are a visual pleasure. The humour is often original and witty. There is so much money, energy and planning invested in those few minutes. The image is the message, the form the final word. We are mesmerized, but the moral and political implications are easily forgotten. From Africa or Asia – where people still starve to death in thousands – the extravagance of the advertisements suggests callousness towards the less fortunate. The demon image repels as it fascinates.

The media adore violence, they exhibit shootings and killings with relish. Red blood and yellow fire make effective pictures. In a flash, violence, from villages in South Asia or towns in Eastern Europe, is projected into our sitting room. The most unlikely events create violent images. The imposition of the poll-tax in 1989 in the United Kingdom or the World Cup in Italy in 1990 triggered violence and generated these images, which triggered more violence.

On the other hand, media influences can also play a positive role. A generation ago smoking cigarettes was considered glamorous and sexy. The tough guy was rarely without a cigarette between his lips. Clark Gable and Humphrey Bogart smoked incessantly. Across the world, actors who looked to Hollywood, imitated them. One of India's most famous actors, Raj Kapoor, was never seen without a cigarette dangling between his lips; it was his trademark. Fans who scanned the jackets of the Beatles' records for symbols would have noted not only the bare feet of Paul but also the cigarette in his hand on the *Abbey Road* jacket. The campaign against smoking has not eliminated it altogether from the screen – the young hero of the cult film *Sex, Lies and Videotape* is a chain-smoker, so are the hero and heroine of David Lynch's *Wild at Heart*. But the Western concern for health, exercise and ecology, emphasized in the media, discourages the smoking of cigarettes generally and, in turn, affects fashion all over the world.

Eight: The media are strong on high technology but remain weak on cultural anthropology. The Gulf war is a case in point. While high technology gave us a minute-by-minute account of what was happening in the Gulf in military terms – numbers of air sorties, manner of troop, ship and tank movements – the commentary displayed vast gaps in interpreting the cultural and social significance of those events. Saddam's use of children in his now notorious television interviews in 1990 illustrates the point. Both Arab culture and Western civilization interpreted them in fundamentally opposed ways which were locked within the context of their own cultures. This further widened the gap between them.

Saddam was consciously addressing two different audiences. For the West the implicit message, frightening and sinister, said: if we are attacked, your hostages will be harmed. Asking 5-year-old Stuart Lockwood about corn-flakes and milk appeared harmless enough but the tousling of his hair back-fired in the West: 'The obscene pictures of Saddam stroking children repeat to the smallest detail the body language in the picture 50 years ago of Hitler being nice to children and animals', wrote a German writer (Enzensberger 1991). But the image of Hitler would be lost upon non-Western viewers.

Space is jealously preserved and physical contact between people not encouraged in Stuart's culture. There may well have also been a subconscious connection with the stories of child molestation which circulate in the media. It is not usual for men to touch boys in the West. The result was a general outcry of revulsion. This did not prevent the further tasteless using of young Stuart by Jesse Jackson on their arrival in London, when he carried him down from the plane straight into the television cameras.

The other audience was Saddam's own people. In his culture an elder, or figure of authority, often displays affection to children by patting the child or tousling the hair. It is socially approved and appreciated. In his own terms, Saddam was going out of his way to signal friendliness and kindliness in his encounter with the Western children.

Hospitality, generosity and bravery are the three great heroic Arab virtues celebrated in folklore and literature. The Arab media projected Saddam as possessing all three in the crisis: by his lavish care – in the light of Arab standards – of the hostages; by allowing first women and children, then, everyone, home; and by standing up to the overwhelming forces of the West.

Even the personal slanging match between the main players reflected the cultural context. When one Sunday morning in September 1990, Mrs Thatcher called Saddam a 'loser' on British television, within hours Baghdad retaliated. Mrs Thatcher was an old 'hag'. In Thatcher's vocabulary, and the consumerist society she presided over, a 'loser' is the biggest blemish, the worst insult;

in a certain rough section of Arab society, the harridan is a figure of derision.

To the West – and many others – Saddam was a tyrant and a coward. But when he shifted between his eight bunkers in and around Baghdad he was not only hiding from Western assassins. There were many in his own country who were eager to see him go. Invading and occupying a smaller neighbour was bad enough; holding foreign civilians – some in transit – was unforgivable. The invasion was neither Islamic nor Arabic, whatever tags of patriotism were subsequently attached to it. We know from the wise doctor that 'patriotism is the last refuge of a scoundrel'.

It is also true that many Arabs were disgusted at the thought of their corrupt governments and pleasure-loving élite being propped up by Western powers. With the arrival of the first American soldiers, the regimes that they wished to protect were at their most vulnerable. With the shooting they stood in danger of starting a sequence of events which would ensure their disappearance; precisely what the intervention was supposed to prevent. Saddam had shrewdly tapped Islam, Arab nationalism and the Palestinian question. To see all Arabs who support the West as 'good guys' and those with Saddam as 'bad guys' is both insulting to Arabs and dangerous over-simplification; but that is the choice the media provided.

As it is, many Muslims across the world felt that although Saddam's invasion was an evil, the presence of non-Muslim troops was a much bigger evil. This is an important point and it needs understanding. Although an entire desert separated foreign troops from the holy shrines on the Arabian peninsula, a few drunken soldiers, rowdily determined to visit the sacred shrines, where non-Muslims are not allowed, would have sent shock-waves throughout the Muslim world. The course and nature of Middle East politics could have been completely altered.

We noted how in 1258 the Mongols, then the super-power of their age, attacked and destroyed Baghdad. The city had been, for centuries, the flourishing capital of Islam's most powerful empire. But the rot had set in long before the Mongols arrived. The caliph's prayers went unanswered; Baghdad would never recover and the map of the Middle East was changed for ever. That was a long time ago. In 1991 Baghdad was again pounded incessantly in what was, to date, the most ferocious air strike in history; the cultural and social map of the Middle East would change again dramatically. For a start, the greatest upheavals in recent history were experienced by groups like the Kurds in northern Iraq, and the Shias in southern Iraq. The media pundits had talked non-stop of the great Western military victory, but had failed to warn us of the disruption that this would create.

And in the rubble, after it is all over, we ask: what of the Palestinians, those Saddam stood up for? The Gulf war has left them more vulnerable than at any time in their history:

> The victors in the Gulf War can now proceed with the policy articulated in February 1989 by Yitzhak Rabin of the Israeli Labour Party, then Defence Minister, when he told Peace Now leaders of his satisfaction with the United States–PLO dialogue: 'meaningless discussions to divert attention while Israel suppresses the *intifada* by force'. Rabin promised: 'the Palestinians will be broken', reiterating the prediction of Israeli Arabists forty years earlier: 'They will be crushed, turned into human dust and the waste of society, and join the most impoverished classes in the Arab countries'.
>
> (Shiblak 1991: 132)

Finally, the media in our world play a key role in international affairs and they will do so increasingly. The media experts are selecting and sending out the message they would like us to receive. 'Of course, the picture does not appear to be so fluid as we watch: there are "preferred" meanings inherent in every message' (Fiske and Hartley 1988: 18). Although this is a task complicated by the double-edged nature of the media, as we have pointed out above, governments continue to manoeuvre for a position of advantage.

'Media imperialism', Giddens calls this, pointing out the pre-eminent position of the United States (1989). He also warns us that 'Third World countries are held to be especially vulnerable, because they lack resources with which to maintain their own cultural independence' (ibid.: 555).

Reality, as the last lines of Fiske and Hartley's study sum up, is constructed for us by the media experts: 'Semiotics is beginning to reveal to us the extent to which our universe is "man-made", and we have argued in this chapter, as in the rest of the book, that "reality" on television is a human construction' (1988: 193–4; *The Truth about Lies: The Tube is Reality*, a Channel 4 programme, shown in the United Kingdom on 22 April 1991, reinforces this argument: 'we'll tell you any shit you want to hear', says the television boss in it).

The nub of this point was perfectly illustrated during the Gulf crisis of 1990–91. Pictures of President Bush playing golf and boating during the Gulf crisis were contrasted with those of President Saddam patting British children on Iraqi television in Baghdad. The focus had shifted from the realm of military strategists and political analysts to that of media experts and communications analysts. Bush attempted, quite consciously, to project confidence in his golf-cart style of crisis leadership; he did not wish to hear the word 'wimp' again. He did not wish to look like President Carter during the Iranian hostage crisis: 'besieged' in, and 'a prisoner' of, the White House. Earlier John Kennedy during the Cuban missile crisis had allowed photographers to record White House activities; Kennedy and his staff seemed to have kept their jackets on and ties up during the ordeal and wanted to be seen that way. Style and leadership are deeply intertwined. The style a people demands from its leaders reflects what that culture thinks of itself. The immediate result of the Gulf victory was to make Bush the most popular President in history; he was no longer a wimp but a veritable Achilles.

It is the American mass media that have achieved what American political might could not: the attainment for America of world domination. Hollywood had succeeded where the Pentagon had failed; the link between the two is established in the fact that films and defence equipment are the two largest export-earners for the United States. J.R. Ewing has triumphed in a way John Dulles could not even dream. The world watches with hypnotic fascination the episodes of American soap: across the world people ask 'Who shot JR?' in *Dallas* or 'Who killed Laura Palmer?' in *Twin Peaks*. The American dream is seen as irresistible.

The demise of communism and the disintegration of its monolithic state structures are considered widely as the Western media's greatest victory. With their incessant propaganda, their capacity to satirize and ridicule, the Western media made deep inroads into the communist world. Communism was doomed years before Gorbachev arrived on the scene.

We have here a proposition, a thesis, in need of investigation: the more traditional a religious culture in our age of the media the greater the pressures upon it, the more grave the predicament; so the least pressure on Christianity, the greatest on Islam. However, all traditional religions whether Buddhist, Hindu, Muslim or Christian encourage piety, contemplation and mysticism. In contrast, the full-scale onslaught of the media is an obscene cry for noise, materialism, for consumerism and *blague*. The seductive ads, the glamorous stars, and the riot of colour flood into the living room, drowning thoughts of piety and austerity. Then it robs human beings of that most delicate of crowns, dignity. In the knock-about irreverence and turbulence of the postmodern wit there is no dignity allowed to anyone.

The relatively harmless example of music provides us with a contrast between the popular televised musical shows and traditional carol singing and hymns in church. The former is a riot of colour, shock, noise, movement and blinding lights, the latter is soothing and peaceful. The purity of the past can no longer be guaranteed. It is thus understandable why Muslims reject post-modernism as 'nihilism' and 'anarchy' (see Chapter 1).

For the Western media, civilizations 'out there' – and not only Muslims – tend to be shown in stereotypes. Hinduism and Buddhism are holy priests, half-naked and meditating, to be dismissed in the popular media as exotic relics of the past. Some individuals from these civilizations do succeed in the West but only by mimicking it (as we saw in Chapters 3 and 4).

What I wish to emphasize is the concept of media as power, as assertion of cultural superiority, as extension of political argu-ments, indeed, as main player. Through the media the opposing position can not only be triumphed over but also, by denying it access, it can cease to exist altogether. Media is thus one of the most important weapons in the arsenal of any country. This is the paramount lesson of our times. It is a lesson the experts from McLuhan to Comolli and Narboni have been pointing out to us for some time. The media are also responsible to a large degree for change in another direction. The very symmetry, composition, stability and style of the family are changing. The links may not be satisfactorily established, but what is clear is the extent of change and disintegration taking place.

THE DEMON AND THE DISINTEGRATION OF THE FAMILY

In this section I shall bombard you with a collage of common images from the media; I crave your patience. Anyone living in the West would be familiar with these images. Most of them are disturbing and point to an unsatisfactory state of affairs. They suggest advanced decay in society. However, it would be unfair to treat this as representative of the West. I am not indulging in a spot of occidentalism, anti-West rhetoric and sentiment. The positive aspects of the West – and there are many – have already been pointed out in Chapter 3 (pages 98–102). In the same chapter we observed the 'exploding' nature of Western civilization in influencing the rest of the world in culture and in politics. But while triumphant on the world stage the basic unit of human organization, the family, is in grave danger. In this section we will attempt to illustrate the impact of the media on the disintegration of family life.

One of the main quarrels Muslims have with contemporary Western culture concerns the disintegration of the Western family. This is because in Islam the family is a key social unit, each member being valued and playing a special role. Integrity, unity and stability are the ideal. Muslims see the pressures of the consumerist culture of the West – the promiscuity, the drugs, the high expectations – as taking their toll of Western marriages with about half falling apart. They fear that these pressures are now being brought to bear on Muslim homes, although there are few systematic studies of these developments. They fear *din*, religion, is in danger of being totally submerged under *dunya*, the world; this is cataclysmic to the Muslim concept of a just and balanced order.

Why do Muslim parents blanch at the modern Western media? Because of the universality, power and pervasiveness of their images; because of their malignity and hostility towards Islam; because these images can so easily invade the privacy of the Muslim house and because in Muslim homes in the West they help create what Pakistanis were calling the BBCD (the British Born Confused *Desi*). The images on television that come non-stop at the viewer are of couples performing sex (and 'perform' is the right verb, as they puff and pant through the compulsory sex scene with the excitement of an aerobics class in most films), men inflicting terrible pain, limbs and guts dismembered, *disjecta membra* everywhere. The video cassettes that accompany the pop songs produce ever more bizarre images (in 'Black or White' we see Michael Jackson's transmogrification into a panther). They blot out other images, whether the *gravitas* of the serious documentaries or the false conviviality of the chat shows. Tabloids continue to debase women with their nude photos and stories as in the infamous page 3 of the *Sun*. And the VCR, and what can be seen on it freely, is a trap-door to the darkest, most depraved images humans can possibly conjure up – anything and everything is available; even a Marquis de Sade would be satisfied at what he can find there – and let us keep before us the fact that de Sade is a European phenomenon; there is no equivalent to him in Muslim literature or culture.

In the West authority structures, under attack for the last two generations, now crumble. Take Britain. The father at home, the Bobby in the street, the teacher at school and the monarchy and politicians in public life are the subject of constant media ridicule. In particular, men are singled out. To be a male in authority is to be a suspect. The media – led by feminist writers – reverse Freud: the penis is the source of all evil, to be publicly and ritually denounced. Postmodern man is riven with doubt and still looking for a role – which varies in its extremes from the gentle, caring New Man to the cannibal with a palate for female flesh.

People in authority were the special target of the brainless Marxist intellectual brigade of the last generation; they were to be removed. Who was to replace them? In the ideal Utopia, the classless proletariat. The reality in the communist states was that of the 'beloved' Great Leader with his 'benevolent' centralized state and 'reforming' secret service. In the West, stories of political corruption in public life, incest at home, ritual satanic abuse at schools (see Tate's *Children for the Devil: Ritual Abuse and Satanic Crime*, 1991, and cover story 'Is the Devil back?' *Sunday Times Magazine*, 29 September 1991) have finally ended whatever little respect remained for authority. In the place of the old structures is a vacuum. Nothing has formed and at this juncture it is difficult to see what can take their place.

The American dream

Miss Saigon portrays on stage the American dream in its songs and values; it also depicts the Asian response to it. The only significant motive driving the characters in the play is their desire to migrate to the United States, to be able to participate in that dream. Only one man resists, and he is the dour, humourless, unattractive stereotype of the communist leader. The dream is plainly less concerned with the ideals of freedom and principles of democracy than with the exciting things the dollar can buy. Cars and sex are singled out. We cry for Miss Saigon and her terrible life, but also feel sorry for her limited vision of life. Not only Muslim occidentalists – those who think of the United States as the Great Satan – should warn her that she may be trading one kind of hell for another.

In Chapter 3 we noted the achievements of Western civilization and its irresistible cultural advance on the world stage. It is significant that the first advance contingent of American culture in the USSR was in the form of the McDonald's hamburger shop in Moscow. Russian prostitutes, acknowledging the world hegemony of the Stars and Stripes, soon demanded dollars for their services. The Marxist Utopia crumbled like a paper bag before the onslaught of the American dream – like the Iraqi army before the Allied troops.

McDonald's, Disneyland and the mall are the core of this society – embodying its here-and-now philosophy, its concept of life (and I do not need to cite Muslim critics of the West, or occidentalists, but Western writers like Baudrillard 1988b, Davies 1991, Hoggart 1990, Holt 1990, 1991, Jameson 1991, Pfaff 1991, Raban 1990, Ruthven 1989, and Taylor 1991). The 1991 film, *Scenes from a Mall*, starring Woody Allen, established that the mall was indeed the arena in which life could be fully lived and experienced; the mall had become a substitute for reality. It is a 'total environment', where shopping is no longer shopping but a 'total leisure experience'.

'Santa Barbara is a paradise; Disneyland is a paradise; the US is a paradise', intones Baudrillard with postmodernist wit (1988b: 98). Consumerism is the ontological basis of society; the phrase, 'I shop, therefore I am', is the philosophic summation of this existence. The visions of the Semitic prophets or the Marxists do not disturb the pursuit of instant, physical pleasure.

'I want it all and I want it now'

Presiding over the 1980s in Britain Mrs Thatcher called her society 'the enterprise culture'. Individualism, consumerism and materialism defined the philosophy of this culture. In a profound cultural and political sense she wished to attach British society to that of the Americans, whom she so admired. The philosophy of the age was summed up in the title of the 1989 Queen song, 'I want it all and I want it now'.

But the lies, the hypocrisy and moral bankruptcy have taken their toll. The 1980s is already being labelled as 'the decade of lies', and the spokesmen of society, politicians and journalists, are singled out as the worst culprits (Lott 1990). Higher pay and higher standards of living do not lead to greater happiness. The divorce rates, the drug abuse, the suicides, the revelations of paedophile rings and satanic rituals, the child prostitution and the poverty – the cardboard villages, so visible in the bigger cities – discredit this vision. The statistics pile up, becoming larger every time they are compiled, overwhelming us with their seeming inexorability. Take one of the most disturbing: over one year a million teenagers attempt suicide in the United States. Perhaps the controversial American series *Twin Peaks* was not as bizarre and as unreal as many thought. Underneath the surrealism of the soap-*noir* we were given an authentic glimpse of a slice of American suburban life. Murder and mayhem, perversion and paranoia lay beneath the tranquil beauty of the landscape and seemingly orderly lives.

In the West the random violence and unprovoked killing of celebrities confirm an undercurrent of irrationality. The strain of anarchy and the nihilism – an extreme reaction against the authoritarian and stifling pre-Second World War European social structures – are now a cause of general concern.

The morbid obsession with longevity, looking young, and physical fitness are guaranteed to create neurosis. The cult of youth is now part of the media ideology: looking young and trim, aerobics, plastic surgery, facial creams – an entire culture is based on it; to be old is unpardonable, the unforgivable sin, it is the negation of the youth culture and all the hype which surrounds it. 'Granny-dumping', the latest trend in America, is a logical step. It is when grandparents, too sick and old to fend for themselves, are unceremoniously left on the doorsteps of a strange institution or hospital as the offspring speed away into the night.

Women as victims

The elevation of sex into the single most important human activity – the tabloids work their stories around boobs, bums and bonking – suggests cultural bankruptcy; it also illustrates the position of women. The pressure on women in this society is especially horrific. 'Killers on the Campus', was a typical story carried in the quality press: 'Slasher movies bring in big bucks at the box office.' But the savage reality of serial killing can fill entire communities with terror. 'Alan Davis was charged with the murder this month of two girl students at the University of Florida, the scene last August of five similar slayings' (Harris 1991; 'Killing of women soars towards 10-year record', announced a story title in *The Sunday Times*, 29 September 1991).

Rape, mutilation and abuse – these seem to be the destiny of the postmodern female. The hatred and prejudice against women are apparent even in the heart of the most civilized spots in the Western universe. This is Oxford in the 1990s:

> Women stare blankly in the face of shouted insults, and lie in bed while the sozzled rugby team beat past their door. . . . In Oxford, it is all there, waiting to be read. In the toilets beneath the arching, domed reading room of the Radcliffe Camera, the wall is scarred with the graffiti of bigotry – homophobia, anti-Semitism, racism, sexism, and scrawled drawings of elephantine dicks. It is stuff that falls in between a seedy pub and Raymond's Revue Bar, but here the clientele is quite sober.
>
> (Blackburn 1991: 13)

Not only is the female the direct object of most films exploiting sex and violence, she must live up to the images depicted by the models in the media. For women the age of the media is a tyrannical and seductive trap, the painful beauty trap (for an anguished cry of the younger generation, see Wolf 1990). Her facial features must be elegant yet attractive, her body hard, slim and sexually alluring, her clothes fashionable. Women cannot have bad breath, body odour, pimples, secretion. Neurosis, anorexia and tension in the ordinary woman are ensured. So while an average woman must look like Brooke Shields, it scarcely seems to matter that Brooke Shields may want to look like an average woman.

Western women have been released from bondage at home; a new promise, a new freedom is assured, but the freedom has also brought new – and sometimes terrifying – consequences. Loneliness is just one. They are now the open target of men's wildest fantasies and most violent plans. In these they are to be sadistically raped, strangled, chopped up, and – especially in recent years – eaten in little bits and pieces. They face the serial killer as much as the sexual pervert. The stifling horror of boredom in the home may well appear attractive in comparison. All of this confirms the impression that there is an inherent tendency in Western society to view women as hate objects, one which is glibly projected onto Western media images of women in Islam.

Disintegrating lives: the family as metaphor for society

Marriage in this society is seen as a straightforward battle between the spouses. But from the simple story of domestic clash between husband and wife in films like *Kramer vs. Kramer* the recent trend in films like *Sleeping with the Enemy*, *The War of the Roses*, *A Kiss before Dying*, *Over her Dead Body* and *C'est la Vie* suggests more sinister undertones. The spouse is the enemy, the family the core of all the problems.

To some American female writers the family is indeed the core of corruption and in need of abolition:

> The primary arena for this dominance is, of course, the family, which Alison Jaggar, a professor at the University of Cincinnati and the head of the American Philosophical Association's Committee on the Status of Women in Philosophy, sees as 'a cornerstone of women's oppression'. The family, in Jaggar's view, 'enforces heterosexuality' and 'imposes the prevailing masculine and feminine character structures on the next generation'. . . . Jaggar, for one, would like to abolish the family altogether and create a society where, with the aid of technology, 'one woman could inseminate another . . . men . . . could lactate . . . and fertilized ova could be transferred into women's or men's bodies.' All that is preventing this, according to the gender feminists, is 'phallocentricity' and 'androcentricity', the view that society is organized around the male and his sexual organs. The feminists, ablaze with revolutionary rhetoric, have set out to overthrow this system. 'What we feminists are doing,' the philosopher Barbara Minnich has said, 'is comparable to Copernicus shattering our geocentricity, Darwin shattering our specimen-centricity. We are shattering androcentricity, and the change is as fundamental, as dangerous, as exciting.'
>
> (Taylor 1991: 7)

'An American family at war', the title of an analytical piece, sums up the problems of family life:

> The excesses of the 'Me' generation, of what Christopher Lasch labelled, 'The culture of narcissism', and what in Texas I found they disapprovingly called the process of 'Californiasation' inflicted terrible damage in the way they have led to expectations in couples – that each should have all needs gratified all the time, without considering the partner, and no

longer expecting to undergo the personal effort, struggle and compromise taken for granted in the past.

(Skynner 1990)

The Oprah Winfrey Show on American television is a window into society. On it ordinary folk discuss everyday matters, revealing just how extraordinary the ordinary has become. Child rapists confess they wish to repeat their crimes; husbands reveal their only ambition is wives with bigger breasts; others speak of the perennial American obsession with looking better by losing weight. It is a society obsessed with the material, the trivial and the immediate: the consumerist society *par excellence*.

That was America. However, the picture appears to be as bleak on this side of the Atlantic. 'The evolution of the family in Britain', noted a report called 'Family ties unravel', 'has become a process of involution, a poisonous, corrosive decline' (Ciriello 1990).

The long-cherished Christian values of meekness, humility and kindness, those directly traced to Jesus Christ – Scorsese's film notwithstanding – are undergoing fundamental changes. They are under full frontal attack:

The same point about the unbalanced emphasis on the individual was made by John quoting book titles such as *Eat to Win* and *Zen Gives You the Competitive Edge*, and remarks by American coaches promoting such extreme competitiveness that winning becomes all-important and sportsmanship is increasingly devalued: 'Winning is not everything, it's the only thing' . . . 'Nice guys finish last' . . . 'Show me a good loser and I'll show you a player I'm going to trade' . . . 'Defeat is worse than death, because you have to live with defeat.'

(ibid.)

'The meek', the Bible had promised, 'shall inherit the earth'. But the world today belongs to the predator, the aggressor, the conqueror. To be humble and meek is to be damned, to be a 'wimp'. We are told, 'If you've got it, flaunt it', to be aggressive, loud and predatory, because 'it's a jungle out there'. The philosophy of this culture was summed up in this pithy motto of body-language: 'limp handshake, limp dick'. Indeed, everyday vocabulary, never far from the genitalia and the anus, was invested with cloacal imagery: 'idiot' became 'ass-hole'; 'get lost' became 'piss off', 'sod off', 'bugger off'; the former exclamation of shock, 'Jesus', became 'fuck' or 'shit'. The wimp is a despised object of impotence and ridicule.

George Bush almost lost the American presidential election the first time round because he was accused of being a wimp. The Wimp Factor became an important element in American politics; it partly explains Bush's unnecessarily over-tough posture through the Gulf crisis and war. The large-scale killings, around 200,000 Iraqis, after the Iraqi army had collapsed and begun heading for home was part of the same response.

The very games children play reinforce the apocalyptic message, the images of anarchy, of the age. Here are some typical instructions that accompany the electronic games advertised in *Club Nintendo* (Vol. 3, Issue 2, 1991, United Kingdom). The first game is called 'Rescue: The Embassy Mission'. Instructions read as follows:

> Mission Briefing: Strictly Confidential. (For your eyes only!) Terrorists have been holding hostages in the embassy for over 24 hours now. Peaceful negotiations have failed to get results. Assemble your finest group of men, and send them in to rescue the hostages. Be careful – these terrorists may be crazy, but they're not stupid. Good luck.
>
> (page 4)

The feature called 'Bad Dudes' visualizes the collapse of society:

> The President is missing! The USA of the future is not a pretty sight. Gang warfare is rife, and some of the crime organizations have expanded so rapidly that they now have enough muscle to threaten a whole country. It's not safe to walk the streets during the day, let alone at night.
>
> (page 6)

'Double Dragon', the most popular game, explains its philosophy thus:

> Jimmy and Billy Lee grew up on cold, tough streets; Learnt the ways of the Martial Arts to protect themselves from the vicious street gangs – so Jimmy and Billy can kick, punch and headbutt their way out of trouble, and are inseparable – But it's mean out there on the street.
>
> (back cover)

Even the dreaded and terrible Nazis are back through the marvel of video games. We are informed that the cult of the Nazis is once again thriving in certain quarters:

Video Nazis: Video games in which players become concentration camp managers are being imported into France from Germany. They are made for home videos and feature graphics of Hitler, swastikas and gassed prisoners. There are thought to be about 140 games, and titles include Aryan Test. They contravene French laws forbidding the propagation of hatred, but police haven't been able to track down the makers.

(The Guardian, 4 July 1991)

Little wonder that the messiahs and heroes of this promised consumerist paradise were troubling more conservative parents. Some were being prosecuted in court for driving followers to satanic ritual and even suicide – as in the case against Judas Priest, one of Britain's most successful heavy metal bands. The philosophy in the Queen song pushes towards immediate gratification for sex and violence.

The following responses from ordinary, everyday people recounting their experiences in the cinema provide disturbing insights:

I worked in a Soho building which also housed a porn cinema. The manager told me of the things they found under the seats after shows, ranging from sticky handkerchiefs to old punters who had collapsed with heart attacks and the bruised and bloody corpse of a rabbit which had obviously been fucked to death. But, as he said, it was a very attractive rabbit, probably 'asking for it'.

(Breakwell and Hammond in *New Statesman and Society,*
7 September 1990: 25)

In this extract, the youngsters are after blood:

Man, they knew what to expect, they knew the formula inside out. If someone turns into a wolf, the wolf is going to brutally dismember, and then devour, a young girl. And there will be blood. Still, virgin blood or not, the boys knew one other thing, too: if the girl was walking somewhere by herself where the wolf was free to get at her, then clearly she was asking for it and had gotten no more than she deserved. 'Kill her ass!' the boys were shouting out to the screen. 'Screw her buns off!' 'Eat her titties!' 'Destroy the mother!' By then, at least, nearly all of them had sat down, eager for the blood to start pouring on the screen.

(ibid.: 26)

So terrifying had the images become that in a celebrated case the established and hardened publishers, Simon & Schuster, cancelled their contract to publish *American Psycho* by Bret Easton Ellis as they found it too shocking. With the attendant publicity it was guaranteed to become a bestseller when published by Picador in 1991. The novel's hero is a successful Wall Street yuppie. He is also a crazed sex killer. Descriptions of fellatio with a severed head, slicing out women's vaginas, attaching jump leads to their breasts and skinning them alive are provided in graphic detail. Predictably, a feminist novel about a female serial killer has appeared hot on Ellis's heels: *Dirty Weekend* by Zahavi (1991).

Ellis explained his novel thus: 'It's really about the 1980s greed generation and how no one looked beyond what kind of suit someone wore, how much money they earned and where they ate their meals. That's how a man like this can keep doing what he does without getting caught. It's about a very superficial society that doesn't look beyond the thin sheen on top' (Kmetyk 1991). So Ellis has intellectual pretensions. His is a postmodernist revolt against the decade of the yuppies. Interspersed in the passages of obscene violence are philosophic nuggets like 'God is dead', 'Justice is dead' and 'history is sinking'.

One of the most popular serious films released in 1991 was *The Silence of the Lambs*, based on the novel with the same title by Thomas Harris, 1988. Dr Hannibal Lecter, played by Anthony Hopkins, earns the title Hannibal the Cannibal because, like Ellis's hero, he is partial to eating humans. He is particularly fond of the liver, eaten with 'fava beans and a nice Chianti'. Unlike Ellis's hero he exhibits a sly line in postmodernist culinary humour: 'I'm having a good friend for dinner.'

This was fiction. But not fiction was the notorious Steinberg case – also in New York – in which Joel Steinberg was accused of torturing his lover and two children, one of whom died (Johnson 1991). The televised trial, where the woman gave evidence against Steinberg, rocked America. Reality and fiction had merged. The statistics for murder are reaching record levels. 'The lethal is, as ever, on the omnipresent news. So far this year, more than 23,000 people have been murdered in America, the highest number ever' (Pilger 1991b).

The milieu of violence helps explain the responses to the biggest international crisis since the Second World War, the Gulf war of 1991. It is too early to predict its full psychological impact, but some advance evidence reveals the connection between a social milieu saturated with the idiom of violence and an equally blood-thirsty response to the enemy. Consider this poem written by an 11-year old English girl, at a primary school in Gateshead, commenting on the war (Moncur 1991). Impressed by the poem, the Territorial Army felt it merited publication and it appeared in the *Gateshead Post* (7 February 1991):

> Saddam Hussein is the man we hate
> We'll get him just you wait!
> He's trying to take over, get him out
> 'He doesn't belong there,' we'll all shout
> We'll take his head and mash it up
> Until it fits into an egg cup
> Take off his arms, take off his legs
> Bend them back until he begs
> Take his head, take his heart
> Rip the stupid man apart
> Poke out his eyes, chew off his nose
> Kick him in the head, pull off his toes . . .

Another report noted that 'Hopping Mad Hulk Hogan, a 6ft 8in TV wrestling star, is "tired of watching the twinklies running our government molly-coddle the Thief of Baghdad". Hogan is planning to run for the White House in 1992 and, once elected, will head for Iraq "to rip off Saddam's turban – while his head is still in it"' (Walker 1991). Not surprisingly, one of the most popular media stars is Arnold Schwarzenegger. As we will see below, he has the biceps to rip off people's heads from their torsos.

Role-models and heroes

New Kids on the Block, currently one of the most popular groups in the United States, has members in it who were infants when Elvis Presley died. But the King has left a legacy of drugs and self-indulgence. It is a path that the New Kids confess to following. On *Wogan*, in April 1990, the lead singer, whose main feature was a pelvic thrust of heroic proportions copied from the King himself when he was still slim enough to be called Elvis the Pelvis, confessed to taking drugs. The tradition which led to early death was established by the rock'n'roll icons: Elvis, Monroe, Joplin, Hendrix, Morrison. The role-model, to use the hyphenated categories so beloved of social scientists, offers dazzling glamour but little else; it leads to a dead end.

The post-war heroes were angry and inarticulate. We recall the mumbling of Marlon Brando, James Dean and the young Elvis Presley. The heroes of our age lace anger with irony and humour. Harrison Ford and Madonna are examples. Even beneath the grim exterior of Arnold Schwarzenegger, and through his guttural Austrian intonations, a sly wit is perceptible. The humour, physical violence, the fast-moving action, the no-expense-spared sets, the futuristic projection, have made Schwarzenegger, in spite of his obvious limitations, the highest-paid show business figure. He is reputed currently to gross an average of $35 million per annum. He is the symbol of the American dream: the white immigrant who made good.

In the cinema another shift is perceptible. The attitude to the central characters, the traditional triangle of hero, heroine and villain, has changed dramatically. Once, after the Second World War, the hero conveyed hope and optimism. There was a sense of right triumphing over wrong, of good prevailing over evil. The big budget musicals, the Westerns and the biblical extravaganzas confirmed this philosophy. In these, noble heroes spoke of honour and courage. The religiously inspired films, like *Samson and Delilah*, *The Robe* and *The Ten Commandments*, and the Westerns, like *High Noon* and *Shane*, gave way to a new generation of films. Their titles made explicit the themes of foreboding and fear which preoccupied them: *Towering Inferno*, *Earthquake* and *Airport*. In turn, these were followed by a wave of films showing explicit sex and violence. The gentler Disneyland fantasy films were replaced by violent ones depicting witchcraft, exorcism and poltergeists, the new demons. Horror now dominated. But some films implied a human need to reach out and touch those not like us. The biggest box-office hit ever has been *ET*; Spielberg implies that perhaps the best place to locate the values of humanity is in space, not on earth. Presumably the audience thinks so too. In another, more recent Spielberg-produced film, *Batteries Not Included*, aliens come to the rescue of an old New York couple when all else fails to take on the ultimate urban villain, the property developer.

The heroes have changed beyond recognition. Once they possessed comforting Anglophone names specially devised for them by Hollywood – Rock Hudson, Dean Martin, Cary Grant. Now they flaunt Teutonic names like Arnold Schwarzenegger and

Rutger Hauer. The regular, perfectly formed, clean-looking heroes – Paul Newman, Robert Redford – now have competition. The newer heroes have cold eyes, massive chests and jutting jaws; they are part-machine, part-man, as in *Terminator 1* and *2*, *Blade Runner*, *Total Recall*, *Megaville*, *Edward Scissorhands*, *Salute of the Jugger*, *Hitcher*, *The Rocketeer* and the *Robo Cop* films. Some, like Freddy Krueger, the slasher hero, the Prince of Dreams, of *Nightmare on Elm Street* fame, are repellent nightmare figures. The heroine, in spite of the high feminist consciousness in the West, fades away, almost irrelevant to the plot. In *Blade Runner* she is a replicant, in *Black Rain* she stays at home. The villain is also changed. In his sadism and acts of violence he is little different from the hero. In *Blade Runner* the hero rapes the robot heroine.

With these heroes we are not sure where the machine ends and the human begins. It is a disturbed vision. But its roots are old, older than the Six Million Dollar Man or the man of steel, Superman, older even than Mary Shelley's Frankenstein. The most expensive and publicized film in this genre is *Terminator 2 – Judgement Day*; in it we complete the full cycle; the half-man, half-machine hero is Homeric in his bravery, nobility and savagery: an Achilles rampant.

There is much to be said for the Greek formula which points to man as a rational being. Man is an animal; add logic and rationality and he becomes a rational animal. But the evidence we have presented so far suggests that rationality is wearing thin in society. Divorce, domestic violence and incest show that the family as a social institution is in danger of collapse. Murder, and other crimes of violence, especially random violence, indicate that society itself has almost collapsed. These mean an altered formula: rational animal minus rational equals animal. Here we arrive at the reasons for the popularity of Rambo.

In *Tough Guys*, Burt Lancaster and Kirk Douglas, the redoubtable heroes who had together so successfully taken on the bad guys in *Gunfight at the OK Corral* a generation ago, appear old-fashioned and out-of-touch. The world has changed during their long period in jail. Like Rip Van Winkle they awake to a different world. They yearn for a lost world of simple divisions, of black and white characters, of straightforward villains. Another message is also clear for the global civilization emerging in our times. Compassion and care for the less privileged, the aged, the underclass, the criminals, must not be forgotten in the postmodernist age.

MUSLIMS AND THE DEMON

Muslims have won the Nobel Prize. As a civilization they have produced philosophers like Ghazzali, mystics like Rumi, scholars like Ibn Khaldun, poets like Ghalib, and buildings like the Taj Mahal. However, in the modern world, Muslims have singularly failed to appreciate the irresistible power and all-pervasive influence of the Western media. This is surprising, as, in spite of the controlled nature of the media, Muslim countries like Egypt and Pakistan produce some of the highest-quality television productions and acting.

Because of the power and aggressiveness of the Western media and its anti-Islamic posture, Muslims appear to have lost the capacity to represent themselves, even to express what they see and know as the reality of their lives. Indeed, Muslim reality, for the world, has become the images on television, the countless hostile words in the papers, the cruel humour in the universal jokes. Muslims in the media have no voice, no platform, so they cannot object or explain. Muslim expressions of cultural identity are dismissed as fanaticism, Muslim demands for legitimate rights seen as fundamentalism. In this media game Muslims – weak and impotent, it appears – cannot win. Their frustration thus finds expression in anger and in violence. Here we note the paradox of Muslims expressing their Muslimness in an essentially un-Islamic manner (as we saw in Chapter 4).

Although we must be careful not to support blanket statements – there is no blindness to Muslim talent: Imran Khan is as popular with the media in London as Lahore – the Western media are definitely seen as hostile. Whatever the reasons, whether atavistic and rooted in history, whether media people simply don't like them, whether Muslims do not picture well in the media, or whether they themselves reject the media because they are depicted badly – there is considerable evidence to support this assertion. Two features of Islam, traditionally highlighted by orientalists, are, in particular, projected in the media for criticism. These are political instability and the status of women. Media images easily promote these stereotypes: crowd scenes of a yelling mob burning a foreign flag and attacking an embassy, or a woman with her head covered, defending her right to be modest.

Many of the prejudices in the West reserved for the established church of Christianity and the antipathy to minority religions, like

Judaism, are now transferred to Islam. Many incorrect assumptions are made. The belief that Islam is dominated by mad priests and that Islam hates women are two of them. As we have pointed out, both are wrong. Islam has no priesthood, as the Prophet's saying, 'there is no monkery in Islam', testifies. Islam's attitude to women in the ideal, as also pointed out, has been the most enlightened of any religious system in history.

If the power of the Western media dictated the 1980s social agenda – feminism, homosexuality, Aids – we are, in the 1990s, already discussing post-feminism, post-homosexuality and post-Aids. Many of the issues which Islam has never conceded, such as the use of alcohol and drugs, are now being widely re-accepted in the West. Above all, the media tend to threaten the stability of the family, which is at the core of the Muslim social structure. Divorce, the challenge to parents, the marginalization of older people, the regular shifting of the home and other related issues – such as alcoholism – weaken the family. Muslims are deeply concerned by these developments.

The legitimate question being raised by them is: why should they be dragged along the path of social experimentation which they know to be diverging from their own vision of society? Why should they disrupt their domestic situation for temporary values, however overpowering? These are valid questions.

Muslim strategy

The Muslim response to postmodernism is the same as it was a century ago: retreat accompanied by passionate expressions of faith and anger. From the Sanusi in North Africa, to the Mahdi in Sudan, to the Akhund in Swat, Muslims appeared to challenge the European imperialist and, under fire, disappeared back into the fastness of their deserts and mountains (Ahmed 1976). In the mountains and deserts was escape from the colonial European; there lay the strength of tradition, the integrity of custom; and the promise of renewal. For the European, the Muslim, in the fastness of his mountains and deserts, had secured a place out of his reach, free from his rules and administrators; the Muslim reverted to the past as if the present did not exist.

But there is one significant difference today. Whereas a century ago Muslims could retreat so as to maintain the integrity of their lives, their areas are now penetrated; technological advances have made escape impossible; the satellite in the sky can follow any camel across any Arabian desert, the laser-guided missile can land in any home in any remote Afghan mountain valley; and the VCR is available in the desert tent as well as the mountain village.

The Muslim tribesman has always possessed a shrewd eye for strategy – more so than his compatriot in the city. He was quick to identify the media as a source of potential disruption to traditional life. Consequently, until a few years ago, a radio, as a symbol of modernity, was ritually shot to pieces in Tirah, deep in the inaccessible Tribal Areas of Pakistan. The rejection was a clear message for the young with ideas of change in their minds. Today, however, the media cannot be stopped; they can penetrate the most remote home and no place could be more remote than Makran, in the Baluchistan Province of Pakistan.

Makran is one of the most isolated and inaccessible parts of the Muslim world. It is a vast, sparsely populated area and still without electricity and therefore television. No highways or railways connect it to the rest of the country. There are only a few miles of black-top road in the main town. The rest are dirt tracks that shift with the sands. Little has changed in Makran since Alexander, returning from his Indus adventure, got lost there.

Even Islam is twisted according to local tradition and clouded in ignorance: the Zikris, an autochthonic sect, possess their own Makkah, Arafat, *haj*, Kaaba and prophet (Ahmed 1986b). Their physical isolation allows them to escape the wrath of the orthodox in Pakistan. Yet the latest foreign films – including blue ones – are freely available. This is through the miracle of diesel-powered generators and the VCR, which are among the first possessions of those who can afford them. These were commonly owned in the most distant villages which I visited as Commissioner of Makran in 1985. What impact contemporary values are making on these societies which are centuries old has not yet been studied. We are left with conjecture, with stories of tension and clash in society. In Makran, traditional values are coeval with the most up-to-date ones; Alexander's age runs parallel to the post-McLuhan era.

Similarly penetrated is the secure, comfortable and timeless Muslim middle class urban life as depicted so well by Naguib Mahfouz, for instance, in *Palace Walk*, 1990 (unfortunately, only the first two volumes of his *The Cairo Trilogy*, *Palace Walk* and *Palace of Desires*, have been translated into English). His story is set in Cairo, but it could be Marrakesh in the extreme west of the

Muslim world, or Kuala Lumpur in the extreme east. The frequent references in conversation to the Quran, the underlying class and colour prejudices, the simmering sexual and political tensions are authentic. But this cocooned, privileged timelessness is now shattered; it is irretrievably lost with the invasion of the Western media. By the late 1980s, television (CNN, the BBC), the Western media's storm-troopers, were preparing to broadcast directly, via satellite, to the Muslim world. Neither Cairo, nor Marrakesh nor Kuala Lumpur are inviolate.

A characteristic feature in this phase of Muslim history is the connection of apparently unconnected institutions. This linking encourages conspiracy theories among Muslims, that there is a global design to do them harm. It can lead to the rapid unravelling of seemingly solid structures It is the media that allows this interlink and interface. When the BCCI bank, headed and owned by Muslims (Arab money, Pakistani know-how), collapsed in 1991 it triggered a chain reaction of disintegration that included the *South* magazine and the Urdu Markaz/Centre in London, which were partly funded by it. Newspaper and television reports in the West hastened the end. Culture and finance, politics and money were interconnected; a collapse in one rapidly affected the other.

Yet another feature in this phase of Muslim history is the emergence of the media star. With the exception of certain courtesans, status and fame used to be almost exclusively the preserve of the political leader or the feudal lord. A singer or film star was once sneered at in high society as someone of lowly origin, little better than a prostitute. It is one reason why, a generation ago, some of the great Muslim stars in India, some of whom we met in the previous chapter, took Hindu names: it disguised their Muslimness.

Huge sums of money are now paid in Muslim countries to entertainers, whose names are made famous through appearances in different media. Top artists can earn sums which, by local standards, are quite unprecedented. The *qawali* singers, the Sabri Brothers, and entertainers, like Anwar Maqsud and Moin Akhtar, earn up to £1,000 an evening in Pakistan, about a year's salary for a skilled worker. These vast sums mean many things. They mean a change in attitude to 'canned' entertainment and live entertainers. They indicate the multiplier effect of fame; there is status attached to the big names. They mean greater involvement in cultural life for average citizens and, in turn, their greater influence upon it. Finally, they mean the dawning of the age of the media in Muslim society. Muslims need to face up to the fact that there is no escape now, no retreat, no hiding place, from the demon.

The postmodernist age in the 1990s hammers at the doors of Muslim *ijtihad*; Muslims ignore the din at their peril. Before they creak open the doors, however, they must know the power and nature of the age and for that they must understand those who represent it. These include figures they do not admire, like the singer Madonna and the writer Rushdie. More important, Muslims must understand why these figures represent the age. The onslaught comes when Muslims are at their weakest: corrupt rulers, incompetent administrators and feeble thinkers mark their societies. For all the rhetoric and symbolic form, the spirit of Islam is often palpably missing from their endeavours, while, more than ever, *ijtihad* is urgently needed where women, education and politics are involved. The old methods and the old certainties will not hold the forces swirling and eddying around Muslim societies; there can be no edulcoration of Muslim society without a comprehension of the non-Muslim age we live in.

Another Muslim ponders on *ijtihad*. The fate of the Muslims in Spain makes the Aga Khan thoughtful (see Ahmed 1991g). He talks of the loss of vigour, the drying-up of initiative, the emphasis on empty dogma as causes of the Muslim downfall. The Aga Khan sees parallels in our times:

> Those who wish to introduce the concept that you can only practise your faith as it was practised hundreds of years ago to me, are introducing a time dimension which is not a part of our faith. Therefore what we have to be doing, I think, is to be asking as Muslims how do we apply the ethics of our faith today? This is a matter for Muslims to think about and it is a very delicate issue whether it is in science, in medicine, in economics.

> (ibid.)

CONCLUSION: TAMING THE DEMON

Stephen Hawking sums up his views on the secrets of the universe in the last lines of his book, *A Brief History of Time*, thus:

> However, if we do discover a complete theory, it should in time be understandable in broad principle by everyone, not just a

few scientists. Then we shall all, philosophers, scientists, and just ordinary people, be able to take part in the discussion of the question of why it is that we and the universe exist. If we find the answer to that, it would be the ultimate triumph of human reason – for then we would know the mind of God.

(1988: 175)

Even for a scientist it is not possible to squeeze God out of existence. Einstein had already hinted at this: 'Science without religion is lame, religion without science is blind.' That is why I find Hawking's book on the universe full of spiritual content, dense with hints of a divine presence; that is perhaps why it remained so long on the bestseller list. He wasn't a scientist expelling God from the universe, he was a searcher pointing to clues that God was to be found somewhere underneath the scientific formulae and jargon. Hawking breaches the thin line between science and religion and illustrates for us the various paths that lead to God.

We attribute many things to poor Marx. His idea of God being dead is one. But the idea of God dead, or of never having existed at all, is not a recent one. From the start of history human beings have been plagued by such doubts; 'Who am I?' 'Does my life have meaning?' 'Is there a higher – divine – Being up there in the skies?' 'If so, how can I know for sure?' Indeed even the prophets from time to time sought to reaffirm their faith, to purify their ideas, to seek clarification; they retreated alone to caves, wandered in deserts, fasted or kept long silences, hoping that this would assist in the discovery of answers.

Neither silence nor escape, we saw above, is an easy task in our times. What the postmodernist age offers us by its very definition is the potential, the possibility, the vision of harmony through understanding. In theory, in posture, even by the logic of its provenance, postmodernism suggests tolerance and *laissez-faire*. To each his own thing. This is not so in practice. In their shrill intolerance of opposing voices, some of those labelled postmodernist authors sound suspiciously like other more conventional authors of earlier times. We saw how lines were crossed in the Rushdie affair at many points, stereotypes negated and paradoxes created. Many staunch Christian priests were vocally supportive of Muslims, while many liberal intellectuals sounded like Inquisition priests in their shrill and blanket condemnations. In the one case, a millennium of hostility to Muslims was set aside; in the other, a century of the liberal philosophy.

In their emphasis on ethnicity, many postmodernist political movements generate racial violence which is as barbaric as any we know of from primeval tribal warfare. Ethnicity is the unprimed and potentially most explosive reality of human society, as we see in the disintegrating communist states. Its links with post-modernism are still to be discovered clearly. Muslims and Marxists slit the throats of fellow Muslims and fellow Marxists; ethnicity in these cases overrides larger ideological loyalties. Our age is littered with notorious examples.

In the coming time there will be major battles in many theatres of war. One will be between the forces of openness, rationality, equilibrium and balance on the one hand, and malevolence and prejudice on the other. One side will stand for tolerance, under-standing and harmony, the other will preach hatred, intolerance and disharmony; and in that line-up it is not altogether clear who stands where. Strange and unexpected allies will form, reflecting interesting points of contact and blurring into meaninglessness the historical binary opposition: Islam and the West, the orient and the occident, North and South. For example, during the Gulf war in 1991 possibly the most sensitive and consistent anti-war writing came from Edward Pearce, Victoria Brittain, John Pilger and Martin Woollacott. In spite of their obvious loathing for military dictators they pointed out the devastating consequences of that kind of war for the ordinary Iraqi.

Muslim and Jew, believer and atheist, will come face to face with opponents sharing the same ideology but with a different approach to it. The preparation for that battle is already beginning to take place. An important shot was fired by a unique conference held in Oslo to discuss 'The Anatomy of Hate' in the summer of 1990. The names of the participants read like a roll-call of the most inspiring figures of the late twentieth century, including Nelson Mandela and Vaclav Havel (see Bunting 1990). But it was also noted that Muslims were conspicuous by their absence; once again Muslims seemed to be out of step with the world.

This was not so in another event – equally unique and equally illustrative of the nature of our age, although different in style and content from the one in Oslo – which took place in London in

September 1991. It was the charity dinner organized by Imran Khan for the first cancer hospital in Pakistan. Assembled were 600 guests, including international celebrities like Mick Jagger, Jerry Hall and Vinod Khanna, the Indian film star who had flown in for the evening from Bombay. Dinner ended with a *qawali* sung by Nusrat Fateh Ali and his group, fresh from their triumph on British TV. As I had a vantage point at the High Table, I was able to observe the impact of the *qawali* on the guests.

Nusrat and his group, sitting cross-legged, made themselves comfortable on the dais opposite the High Table. Like all *qawalis* it began with the *hamd* in praise of God. Many of the Muslims were soon in ecstasy at the power of the *hamd. Allah hu, Allah hu, Allah hu* – Oh God, Oh God, Oh God – chanted Nusrat's group, finding an echo in the spellbound audience. I watched Mick Jagger. Seated at the High Table, opposite the *qawali* group, he was shaking his head and shoulders in rhythm. And I thought: to hear the *hamd* in London before such a large and enthusiastic audience and to see Mick Jagger among them shaking to *Allah hu* was only possible in our age. Here was contradiction, here was juxta-position and here was hope. Somewhere in the midst of the emotions and ideas flowing about in the hall diverse points were meeting in harmony. Truly, as Nusrat sang, God is great.

In any case rigid boundaries are no longer easy to maintain. A person can, and does, possess overlapping identities; in our age this allows the possibility of enrichment and pleasure. A person can be a devout Muslim and a loyal citizen of Britain. Multiple identities mean eclecticism, which requires tolerance of others. Without some conscious attempt to comprehend the logic of this formula, we reduce it to a meaningless shibboleth.

The 'catastrophe' theory, which links every event, however insignificant, to a chain that includes all of us everywhere in the world, no longer appears far-fetched. A leaf falling in India is heard in Canada, a fridge switched on in China causes dismay in Britain. Until a few years ago the United States could occupy Vietnam, the USSR march into Hungary, the Israelis crush the Palestinians and little could be done about it by the rest of the world; indeed little was known. Only the secret services talked darkly of covert operations and politicians used elegant but empty phrases. But with the Iraqi invasion of Kuwait and the war which followed, the world was suddenly faced with the prospect of a major world conflict involving in some degree virtually every major power and, above all, involving us all in some way. All the worst aspects of modern war – chemical weapons, nuclear strikes, hostage killing – loomed before us.

The world is so shrunk, so interlinked and so claustrophobic that the Iraqi action once and for all dispelled the euphoria that resulted in the West after the collapse of communism and the prospects of world peace. From now on one man with a bomb in his briefcase and a wild dream can hold the world to ransom; his ignorance of the number and kinds of boundaries violated will not matter. Ours is, therefore, not a simple world.

There will be, increasingly, little elbow room, limited space, on our planet; this is because of the nature of the postmodernist era. The West, through the dominant global civilization, will continue to expand its boundaries to encompass the world; traditional civilizations will resist in some areas, accommodate to change in others. In the main, only one, Islam, will stand firm in its path. Islam, therefore, appears to be set on a collision course with the West.

On the surface it is more than a clash of cultures, more than a confrontation of races: it is a straight fight between two approaches to the world, two opposed philosophies. And under the great complexity of the structures involved – the layers of history, the mosaic of cultures – we can simplify in order to discover the major positions. One is based in secular materialism, the other in faith; one has rejected belief altogether, the other has placed it at the centre of its world-view. It is, therefore, not simply between Islam and the West – although many Muslims and non-Muslims who are brought up to believe in this simplistic formula will be surprised at this conclusion.

On the threshold of the twenty-first century the confrontation between Islam and the West poses terrible internal dilemmas for both. The test for Muslims is how to preserve the essence of the Quranic message, of *adl* and *ahsan*, *ilm* and *sabr*, without it being reduced to an ancient and empty chant in our times; how to participate in the global civilization without their identity being obliterated. It is an apocalyptic test; the most severe examination. Muslims stand at the crossroads. If they take one route they can harness their vitality and commitment in order to fulfil their destiny on the world stage, if the other, they can dissipate their energy through internecine strife and petty bickering: harmony and hope versus disunity and disorder.

The challenge for those in the West is how to expand the Western idealistic notions of justice, equality, freedom and liberty beyond their borders to include all humanity and without appearing like nineteenth-century imperialists; to reach out to those not of their civilization in friendship and sincerity. In both cases a mutual understanding and working relationship are essential.

The logic of the argument demands that the West uses its great power – which includes the media – to assist in solving the long-festering problems that plague Muslim society. We have identified those of the Palestinians and Kashmiris as of the greatest urgency. There is the need to push unwilling rulers, who subsist on Western arms and aid, towards conceding democracy and a fairer distribution of wealth, of ensuring the rights and dignity of women and children, the less privileged and those in the minority. These problems are interwoven, binding Muslims and non-Muslims together. There can be no just and viable world order – let alone a New World Order – if these wrongs are not redressed.

It is crucial, therefore, that the potential points of conflict are identified if continued confrontation is to be avoided. This is not only necessary but also possible. Into the predicament that postmodernism plunges us there is also promise. This conclusion may appear illogically optimistic in the light of the gloomy arguments above, but it is understandable in the context of the Islamic vision, which is rooted firmly in history and belief. It has much to offer a world saturated with disintegration, cynicism and loss of faith. However, this will only be possible if there is a universal tolerance of others among Muslims and non-Muslims alike, an appreciation of their uniqueness and a willingness to understand them. It will only be possible if this sentiment becomes both personal philosophy and national foreign policy, if it is placed on top of the agenda in preparation for the next millennium. This, too, is in the largesse of postmodernism.

References

Abu-Rabi, Ibrahim M. (1990) Review article 'Beyond the postmodern mind', in *The American Journal of Islamic Social Sciences*, 7 (2), Sept: 235–256.

Aburiche, Said (1991) *Cry Palestine: Inside the West Bank*, London: Bloomsbury.

Adorno, Theodor and Max Horkheimer (1979) *Dialectic of Enlightenment*, translated by John Cumming, London: Verso.

Ahmad, Khurshid (ed.) (1981) *Studies in Islamic Economics*, King Abdul Aziz University, Jeddah and The Islamic Foundation, Leicester, UK.

Ahmed, Akbar S. (1976) *Millennium and Charisma among Pathans*, London: Routledge and Kegan Paul.

—— (1986a) *Toward Islamic Anthropology: Definition, Dogma and Directions*, Washington, DC: International Institute of Islamic Thought.

—— (1986b) 'Islam and society in South Asia', in *Purusartha*, École des hautes études en sciences sociales, no. 9, Paris.

—— (1988) *Discovering Islam: Making Sense of Muslim History and Society*, London: Routledge.

—— (1989) 'Islamic scholarship: crisis of confidence – a review article', in *Muslim Education Quarterly*, Cambridge, vol. 7, no. 1, Autumn issue.

—— (1990a) 'South Asia: roots of decline', in *Economic and Political Weekly*, Bombay, 13 Jan.

—— (1990b) 'The Muslims of India', Paper for International Conference on India, Oxford University, 30 May – 1 June.

—— (1990c) 'Jeans for you, robes for me', in *The Guardian*, 5 July.

—— (1990d) 'Exorcising the demon image', in *The Guardian*, 28 July.

—— (1990e) 'A new religion for a savage civilization', in *The Guardian*, 21 Aug; also BBC Radio 4, 'Southern voices: green arrogance', broadcast on 20 Dec.

—— (1991a) *Resistance and Control in Pakistan*, London: Routledge.

—— (1991b) 'Bombay films: the cinema as metaphor for Indian society and politics', *Modern Asian Studies*, Cambridge, 25 (2).

—— (1991c) 'Salman Rushdie: a new chapter (first interview with a Muslim writer)', in *The Guardian*, 17 Jan.

—— (1991d) 'The next test for British Muslims', in *The Times Literary Supplement*, 15 Feb.

—— (1991e) 'Postmodernist perceptions of Islam: observing the observer', in *Asian Survey*, University of California Press, 21 (3), March.

—— (1991f) 'Islam: the roots of misperception', 40th Anniversary Special Issue, in *History Today*, London, April.

—— (1991g) 'The quiet revolutionary', in *The Guardian*, 8 Aug.

—— (1991h) 'Spain's Islamic legacy', in *History Today*, London, Oct.

—— (1991i) 'Understanding people: the exhibition as teacher', in *Anthropology Today*, 7 (5), Oct.

Ahsan, M.M. and A.R. Kidwai (eds) (1991) *Sacrilege versus Civility: Muslim Perspectives on* The Satanic Verses *Affair*, Leicester: The Islamic Foundation.

Akbar, M.J. (1985) *India: The Siege Within*, New Delhi: Penguin.

—— (1988) *Riot after Riot: Reports on Caste and Communal Violence in India*, New Delhi: Penguin.

Akhtar, Shabbir (1989) *Be Careful with Muhammad! The Salman Rushdie Affair*, London: Bellew Publishing.

—— (1990) *A Faith For All Seasons: Islam and Western Modernity*, London: Bellew Publishing.

Ali, Wijdan (ed.) (1989) *Contemporary Art from the Islamic World*, London: Scorpion Publishing Ltd.

Allaby, Michael (ed.) (1989) *Thinking Green: An Anthology of Essential Ecological Writing*, London: Barrie & Jenkins.

Amiel, Barbara (1991) 'Campus Newspeak', in *The Sunday Times News Review*, 16 June.

Amis, Martin (1989) *London Fields*, London: Jonathan Cape.

Arberry, Arthur J. (1964) *The Koran Interpreted*, London: Oxford University Press.

—— (1990) *Sufism: An Account of the Mystics of Islam*, London: Mandala Unwin Paperbacks.

Ascherson, Neal (1991) 'A forgotten people who offer the best chance for lasting peace', in the *Independent on Sunday*, 3 March.

Ashraf, Ali S. (1985) *New Horizons in Muslim Education*, Islamic Academy, Cambridge, with Hodder & Stoughton, UK.

—— and S.S. Husain (1979) *Crisis in Muslim Education*, London: Hodder & Stoughton.

Askwith, Richard (1990), 'Britain's angry Ayatollah', in *Observer Magazine*, 30 Sept.

Ateshin, H.M. (1990) *'Islamic' Architectural Education*, London: Seal Books.

Augarde, Tony (1991) *The Oxford Dictionary of Modern Quotations*, Oxford: Oxford University Press.

Augustine of Hippo (1991) *Confessions*, trans. Henry Chadwick, London: Oxford University Press.

Ba-Yunus, I. and F. Ahmad (1985) *Islamic Sociology: An Introduction*, Islamic Academy, Cambridge, with Hodder & Stoughton.

Balio, Tino (ed.) (1991) *Hollywood in the Age of Television*, London: Routledge.

Banks-Smith, Nancy (1990), 'What's eating our shan gadjy?', in *The Guardian*, 5 Sept.

Barnes, Julian (1990) *A History of the World in 10^1/2 Chapters*, London: Picador.

Barthes, Roland (1989) *Barthes: Selected Writings*, edited and introduced by Susan Sontag, London: Fontana Press.

Baudrillard, Jean (1988a) *The Evil Demon of Images*, trans. Paul Patton and Paul Foss, Australia: Power Institute Publications, No. 3.

—— (1988b) *America*, trans. Chris Turner, London: Verso.

—— (1990) *Seduction*, trans. Brian Singer, London: Macmillan.

Benton, Tim (1991) *The Villas of Le Corbusier, 1920–1930*, New Haven, CT: Yale University Press.

Bernal, Martin (1987) *Black Athena: The Afro-Asian Roots of Classical Civilization*, London: Free Association Books.

Bhutto, Benazir (1988) *Daughter of the East: An Autobiography*, London: Hamish Hamilton.

Black, Ian and Benny Morris (1991) *Israel's Secret Wars*, London: Hamish Hamilton.

Blackburn, Olly (1991) 'Oxford Blues', in *New Statesman and Society*, 21 June.

Blandford, Linda (1978) *Oil Sheikhs: In Quest of the New Arab*, London: Weidenfeld & Nicolson.

Bonner, A. (1990) *Averting the Apocalypse: Social Movements in India Today*, Durham, NC: Duke University Press.

Bose, T. *et al.* (1990) 'Report: initiative on Kashmir: on the violations of human rights by the Indian authorities in Indian-held Kashmir', New Delhi.

Boyd, William (1988) *The New Confessions*, London: Penguin Books.

Bradbury, Malcolm (1990) 'The world after the wake', in *The Guardian*, 20 Sept.

Brass, P.R. (ed.) (1984) *Ethnic Groups and the State*, London: Croom Helm.

Breakwell, Ian and Paul Hammond (1990) *Seeing in the Dark: A Compendium of Cinema-going*, London: Serpent's Tail.

Bunting, Madeleine (1990) 'Winning the race against hate', in *The Guardian*, 19 Sept.

Burckhardt, Titus (1976) *Art of Islam: Language and Meaning*, London: World of Islam Festival Publishing Co. Ltd.

Buxton, David (1990) *From The Avengers to Miami Vice: Form and Ideology in Television Series*, Manchester: Manchester University Press.

Callinicos, Alex (1989) *Against Postmodernism: A Marxist Critique*, Cambridge: Polity Press.

Campbell, Duncan (1990) 'Harassed Asians "fatalistic" over attacks', in *The Guardian*, 12 Oct.

Caroe, Olaf (1965) *The Pathans: 550 BC – 1957 AD*, London: Macmillan.

Childress, Mark (1991) *Tender: The King Lives*, New York: Viking.

Chittick, William C. (1989) *The Sufi Path of Knowledge: Ibn al-Arabi's Metaphysics of Imagination*, New York: State University of New York Press.

Ciriello, Mario (1990) 'Family ties unravel', in *The Guardian*, 12 Oct.

Clarke, Tim (1990) Book reviews of Charles Jencks 1990 and Jonathan Glancey 1990, in *Literary Review*, Dec.

Cockburn, Alexander (1991) 'Cred Menace: Political Correctness', in *New Statesman and Society*, 24 May.

Collins, Jim (1989) *Uncommon Cultures: Popular Culture and Post-Modernism*, New York and London: Routledge.

Collins, Richard (1991) *Television: Policy and Culture*, London: Routledge.

Connor, Steven (1989) *Postmodernist Culture: An Introduction to Theories of the Contemporary*, Oxford: Blackwell.

Cook, Richard (1991) 'Pop will deplete itself', in *Punch*, 30 Jan – 5 Feb.

Corner, John and Sylvia Harvey (eds) (1991) *Enterprise and Heritage: Crosscurrents of National Culture*, London: Routledge.

Cupitt, Don (1991) 'Islamic reality and tall stories', in *The Guardian*, 18 Feb.

Dafni, Reuven and Yehudit Kleiman (eds) (1991) *Final Letters, From the Yad Vashem Archives*, London: Weidenfeld & Nicolson.

Dahlgren, Peter and Colin Sparks (eds) (1991) *Communication and Citizenship: Journalism and the Public Sphere in the Media Age*, London: Routledge.

Dalrymple, William (1990) 'Thuggery rules', in *The Spectator*, 8 Dec.

Davies, Nick (1991) *White Lies*, London: Chatto & Windus.

Davis, Mike (1990) *City of Quartz: Excavating the Future in Los Angeles*, London: Verso.

Dhanjal, B. (1990) *Insight Guide to Pakistan*, Hong Kong: APA Publications (HK) Ltd.

Domb, Risa (1982) *The Arab in Hebrew Prose 1911–1948*, London: Vallentine, Mitchell & Co. Ltd.

Douzinas, Costas and Ronnie Warrington with Shaun McVeigh (1991) *Postmodern Jurisprudence: The Law of the Text in the Text of the Law*, London: Routledge.

Duncan, Emma (1989) *Breaking the Curfew: A Political Journey through Pakistan*, London: Michael Joseph.

Dunn, Ross (1989) *The Adventures of Ibn Battuta: A Muslim Traveller of the Fourteenth Century*, Berkeley: University of California Press.

Dwork, Deborah (1991) *Children With a Star: Jewish Youth in Nazi Europe*, New Haven, CT: Yale University Press.

Eagleton, Terry (1991) *Ideology: An Introduction*, London: Verso.

Eco, Umberto (1986) 'Function and the sign: an introduction to urban semiotics', in *The City and the Sign: An Introduction to Urban Semiotics* (eds) Gottdiener, M. and A. Lagopoulos, New York.

—— (1987) *Travels in Hyper-reality*, London: Picador.

Economist, The (1990) 'Goodbye to the nation-state?', 23 June.

Edwards, J. (1991) *The Jews in Christian Europe 1400–1700*, London: Routledge.

Elias, N. and E. Dunning (1986) *Quest for Excitement*, Oxford: Blackwell.

Ellis, Bret Easton (1991) *American Psycho*, London: Picador.

Elon, Amos (1985) *The Israelis: Photographs of a Day in May*, Jerusalem: Keter Publishing House, and New York: Harry Abrams, Inc. Publishers.

—— (1991) *Jerusalem*, London: Fontana.

Enzensberger, Hans Magnus (1991) 'The second coming of Adolf Hitler', in *The Guardian*, 9 Feb.

Esposito, John L. (1991) *Islam: The Straight Path*, New York: Oxford University Press (expanded edition).

Faruqi, Ismail al- (1982) *Islamization of Knowledge: General Principles and Work Plan*, Washington, DC: International Institute of Islamic Thought.

Fischer, Michael M.J. and Mehdi Abedi (1990) *Debating Muslims: Cultural Dialogues in Postmodernity and Tradition*, Madison: University of Wisconsin Press.

Fiske, John (1991) *Understanding Popular Culture*, London: Routledge.

—— and John Hartley (1988) *Reading Television*, London: Methuen.

Forster, E.M. (1967) *A Passage to India*, London: Penguin Books.

Foster, H. (ed. and introduction) (1985) *Postmodern Culture*, London: Pluto Press.

Foucault, Michel (1984) *The Foucault Reader*, ed. Paul Rabinow, London: Penguin Books.

Freund, C.P. (1990) 'Bush's golf crisis', in *The Guardian*, 29 Aug.

Fuentes, Carlos (1990) *Christopher Unborn*, London: Picador, published by Pan Books.

Gabler, Neal (1991) *An Empire of Their Own: How the Jews Invented Hollywood*, London: W.H. Allen.

Gandhi, Rajmohan (1987) *Understanding the Muslim Mind*, London: Penguin Books.

Gardner, Helen (ed.) (1972) *The New Oxford Book of English Verse: 1250–1950*, Oxford: Oxford University Press.

Garland, Robert (1991) 'Juvenile delinquency in the Graeco-Roman world', in *History Today*, London, Oct.

Geary, Conor (1990) *Terror*, London: Faber & Faber.

Geertz, Clifford (1989) *Works and Lives: The Anthropologist as Author*, Cambridge: Polity Press.

Ghazzali, Al- (1980) *The Alchemy of Happiness*, selected from *Ihya-ulum al-din*, trans. C. Field, London: Octagon Press.

Giddens, Anthony (1989) *Sociology*, Cambridge: Polity Press.

—— (1990) *The Consequences of Modernity*, Cambridge: Polity Press.

—— (1991) *Modernity and Self-Identity: Self and Society in the Late Modern Age*, Cambridge: Polity Press.

Gifford, Zerbanoo (1990) *The Golden Thread: Asian Experiences of Post-Raj Britain*, London: Grafton Books.

Glancey, Jonathan (1990) *The New Moderns*, London: Mitchell Beazley.

Gledhill, Christine (ed.) (1991) *Stardom*, London: Routledge.

Gordon, David C. (1989) *Images of the West*, Savage, MD: Rowman & Littlefield Publishers Inc.

Grant, M. (1989) *Myths of the Greeks and Romans*, London: Weidenfeld & Nicolson.

Green, J. (1990) *Them: Voices from the Immigrant Community in Contemporary Britain*, London: Secker & Warburg.

Griffin, David (1989) *God and Religion in the Postmodern World*, Albany, NY: State University of New York Press.

Grossman, David (1991a) *See Under: Love*, trans. from the Hebrew by Betsy Rosenberg, London: Pan Books. First published in 1990.

—— (1991b) *The Smile of the Lamb*, trans. from the Hebrew by Betsy Rosenberg, London: Jonathan Cape.

Haeri, Fadhlalla (1989) *Living Islam: East and West*, Longmead, Dorset: Element Books Ltd/Zahra Trust.

Hampson, Daphne (1990) 'The search for equality in the eyes of God', in *The Independent*, 14 July.

Harasym, Sarah (ed.) (1990) *The Post-colonial Critic: Interviews, Strategies, Dialogues: Gayatri Chakravorty Spivak*, London: Routledge.

Hareven, Alouph (ed.) (1983a) *Every Sixth Israeli: Relations Between the Jewish Majority and the Arab Minority in Israel*, Jerusalem: The Van Leer Jerusalem Foundation.

—— (1983b) *Can the Palestinian Problem be Solved? Israeli Positions*, Jerusalem: The Van Leer Jerusalem Foundation.

—— (1991) 'Towards a shared civility?' Lecture at Conference on Israeli Arabs at Tel Aviv University, June.

Harris, Art (1991) 'Killers on the campus', in *Weekend Guardian*, 22–23 June.

Harris, Thomas (1988) *The Silence of the Lambs*, London: Mandarin.

Harvey, David (1989a) *The Condition of Postmodernity: An Enquiry into the Origins of Cultural Change*, Oxford: Blackwell.

—— (1989b) *The Urban Experience*, Oxford: Blackwell.

Hasan, M. (1990) 'Adjustment and accommodation: Indian Muslims after Partition', Paper presented at Delhi Conference 'India: The First Decade', Delhi, Jan.

Hass, Aaron (1991) *In the Shadow of the Holocaust: The Second Generation*, London: I.B. Tauris.

Hawking, Stephen (1988) *A Brief History of Time: From the Big Bang to Black Holes*, London: Bantam Press.

Hecht, Susanna and Alexander Cockburn (1989) *The Fate of the Forest: Developers, Destroyers and Defenders of the Amazon*, London: Verso.

Heller, Zoe (1990) 'Perils abroad in the land of the veil', in *The Sunday Correspondent*, 17 June.

—— (1991) 'The Mall of God', in the *Independent on Sunday*, 2 June.

Hilton, Isabel (1991) 'The General', in *The Best of Granta Travel*, London: Granta Books.

Hitchens, C. (1990) *Blood, Class and Nostalgia*, London: Chatto & Windus.

Hodge, Robert and David Tripp (1986) *Children and Television: A Semiotic Approach*, Cambridge: Polity Press.

Hoggart, Simon (1990) *America: A User's Guide*, London: Collins.

Holt, Jim (1990) 'Washington Letter', in *Literary Review*, Aug.

—— (1991) 'New York Letter', in *Literary Review*, March.

Horrie, Chris (1991) 'Call the village women's institutes to arms', review of Eagleton (1991) in *Literary Review*, June.

Hunt, Leigh (1988) 'Another summing-up', in *In Praise of Cambridge: An Anthology for Friends*, arranged by Mervyn Horder, Bury St Edmunds, Suffolk: The Alastair Press.

Hussain, Asaf (1990) *Western Conflict with Islam: Survey of the Anti-Islamic Tradition*, Leicester: Volcano Books.

Huyssen, Andreas (1986) *After the Great Divide: Modernism, Mass Culture, Postmodernism*, Bloomington: Indiana University Press.

Independent, The (1990) 'Profile: Tariq Ali, from street fights to first nights', 29 Sept.

Iqbal, Allama M. (1986) *Allama Muhammad Iqbal: The Reconstruction of Religious Thought in Islam*, edited and annotated by M. Saeed Sheikh, Lahore: Institute of Islamic Culture.

Irving, Washington (1990) *Tales of the Alhambra* (first published 1832), Madrid, Spain: Grefol, SA.

Isaacs, H.D. (1990) 'Medieval Judaeo-Arabic medicine as described in the Cairo Geniza', in *Journal of the Royal Society of Medicine*, 83 (11), Nov.

Jameson, Frederic (1991) *Postmodernism: The Cultural Logic of Late Capitalism*, London: Verso.

Jansen, Johannes J.G. (1986) *The Neglected Duty: The Creed of Sadat's Assassins and Islamic Resurgence in the Middle East*, New York: Macmillan.

Jencks, Charles (1984) *The Language of Post-Modern Architecture*, New York: Rizzoli.

—— (1986a) *What is Post-Modernism?*, London: Academy.

—— (1986b) *Architecture and Urbanism*, extra edition, Tokyo: A & U Publishing Company, Jan.

—— (1990) *The New Moderns*, London: Academy Editions.

Jenkins, David and Rebecca Jenkins (1991) *Free to Believe*, London: BBC Books.

Johnson, Joyce (1991) *What Lisa Knew: The Truth and Lies of the Steinberg Case*, London: Bloomsbury.

Kabbani, Rana (1986) *Europe's Myths of Orient*, London: Pandora Press.

—— (1989) *Letter to Christendom*, London: Virago Press.

Kelly, J.B. (1980) *Arabia, the Gulf and the West: A Critical View of the Arabs and their Oil Policy*, London: Weidenfeld & Nicolson.

Kemp, John (1990) 'Serves him right', review of Jean Baudrillard, in *Literary Review*, Aug.

Kemp, Penny and Derek Wall (1990) *A Green Manifesto for the 1990s*, London: Penguin.

Kemp, Peter (1990) 'Pathetic phalluses of socialism: review of *Redemption* by Tariq Ali', in *The Sunday Times*, 7 Oct.

Kent, Nicholas (1991) *Naked Hollywood: Money, Power and The Movies*, London: BBC Books.

Kermode, Frank (1988) *History and Value: The Clarendon Lectures and Northcliffe Lectures (1987)*, Oxford: Clarendon Press.

Khalid, Fazlun (1991) 'When fools rushed in', in Ahsan and Kidwai (1991).

Khalil, Samir al- (1991) *The Monument: Art, Vulgarity and Responsibility in Iraq*, London: André Deutsch.

Kipling, Rudyard (1988) *Moon of Other Days: M.M. Kaye's Kipling: Favourite Verses*, London: Hodder & Stoughton.

Kmetyk, Tanis (1991) 'When killing is too ghastly for words', in *The Guardian*, 15 Jan.

Kroker, Arthur and David Cook (1988) *The Postmodern Scene: Excremental Culture and Hyper-aesthetics*, London: Macmillan Education Ltd.

Kundera, Milan (1985) *The Unbearable Lightness of Being*, trans. from the Czech by Michael Henry Heim, London: Faber & Faber. First published in 1984, New York: Harper & Row.

Kureishi, Hanif (1990) *The Buddha of Suburbia*, London: Faber & Faber.

Lamb, Alastair (1991) *Kashmir: A Disputed Legacy 1846–1990*, Wiltshire, UK: Roxford Books/Redwood Press Ltd.

Lamb, Christina (1991) *Waiting for Allah: Pakistan's Struggle for Democracy*, London: Hamish Hamilton.

Langmuir, Gavin (1991) *History, Religion and Antisemitism*, London: I.B. Tauris.

Lash, Scott (1990) *Sociology of Postmodernism*, London: Routledge.

Lee, Alison (1990) *Realism and Power: Postmodern British Fiction*, London and New York: Routledge.

Lee, Keekok (1989) *Social Philosophy and Ecological Scarcity*, London: Routledge.

Lott, Tim (1990) 'Lie of the land in the land of the lie', in *Weekend Guardian*, 14–15 July.

Louvish, Simon (1991) *The Silencer*, London: Bloomsbury.

Lyotard, Jean-François (1984) *The Post-Modern Condition: A Report on Knowledge*, trans. G. Bennington and B. Massumi, Minneapolis: University of Minnesota Press.

McKibben, B. (1990) *The End of Nature*, London: Penguin.

McLuhan, Marshall (1964) *Understanding Media: The Extensions of Man*, London and New York: Routledge (ARK edition 1987).

Mahfouz, Naguib (1990) *Palace Walk*, New York: Doubleday.

Malcolm, Derek (1991) 'In bed with the woman who dares', in *The Guardian*, 11 July.

Mandel, Gabriele (1979) *How to Recognize Islamic Art*, New York: Penguin Books.

Mansfield, Peter (1991) *A History of the Middle East*, London: Viking Penguin.

Manzoor, P. (1990) 'Politics without truth, metaphysics or epistemology: postmodernism de(con)structed for the Muslim believer', in *Muslim World Book Review*, 10 (4).

Márquez, Gabriel García (1978) *One Hundred Years of Solitude*, trans. from the Spanish by Gregory Rabassa, Pan Books. First published in Argentina in 1967 by Editorial Sudamericans, SA.

—— (1991) *The General in his Labyrinth*, London: Jonathan Cape.

Massey, Michael (1988) *Women in Ancient Greece and Rome*, London: Cambridge University Press.

Mayer, Arno J. (1990) *Why did the Heavens not Darken? The 'Final Solution' in History*, London: Verso.

Moncur, Andrew (1991) 'Diary', in *The Guardian*, 7 Feb.

Moore, Suzanne (1991) 'Stage struck', in *New Statesman and Society*, 19 April.

Mortimer, Edward (1990) 'Christianity and Islam', Paper presented at the Royal Institute of International Affairs, London, 9 Oct.

Muir, Frank (ed.) (1990) *The Oxford Book of Humorous Prose: From William Caxton to P.G. Wodehouse*, Oxford: Oxford University Press.

Mumford, Lewis (1961) *The City in History: Its Origins, its Transformations and its Prospects*, London: Martin Secker & Warburg.

Naipaul, V.S. (1981) *Among the Believers: An Islamic Journey*, New York: Alfred A. Knopf Inc.

—— (1990) *India: A Million Mutinies Now*, London: Heinemann.

Naisbitt, John and Patricia Aburdene (1990) *Megatrends 2000*, London: Sidgwick.

Nandy, Ashis (1989) *The Tao of Cricket*, New Delhi: Penguin Books.

Nasr, Seyyed Hossein (1981) *Knowledge and the Sacred*, The Gifford Lectures, Edinburgh University Press.

—— (1987) *Islamic Art and Spirituality*, Suffolk: Golgonooza Press.

—— (1990) 'On being Muslim in the West', in *Muslim Wise*, London, 7 June.

Nichols, Bill (ed.) (1976) *Movies and Methods*, vol. 1, Berkeley: University of California Press.

Njor, John (1990) 'At war with itself', in *The Guardian*, 5 Oct.

Norris, Christopher (1989) *Derrida*, London: Fontana Press.

Oppenheimer, Michael and Robert Boyle (1990) *Dead Heat: The Race Against the Green House Effect*, London: I.B. Tauris.

O'Rourke, P.J. (1991) *Parliament of Whores*, London: Picador.

Oz, Amos (1986) *A Perfect Peace*, trans. by Hillel Halkin, London: Flamingo.

Pacific Affairs (1987) 'Politics in the Punjab', 60 (1), Spring.

Paglia, Camille (1991) 'Power undressing', in the *Independent on Sunday*, 21 July.

Parekh, Bhikhu (1989) *Colonialism, Tradition and Reform: An Analysis of Gandhi's Political Discourse*, New Delhi: Sage Publications.

Park, James (ed.) (1991) *Cultural Icons: Figures Who Made the Twentieth Century What It Is*, London: Bloomsbury.

Pearce, David, Anil Markandya and Edward Barbier (1989) *Blueprint for a Green Economy*, Tonbridge Wells, Kent: Earthscan.

Pefanis, Julian (1991) *Heterology and the Postmodern: Bataille, Baudrillard, and Lyotard*, Durham, NC: Duke University Press.

Pfaff, William (1991) *Barbarian Sentiments*, London: Faber & Faber.

Pilger, John (1991a) 'Children of Gaza', in *New Statesman and Society*, 28 June.

—— (1991b) 'Terminator in bifocals', in *New Statesman and Society*, 9 Aug.

Ponting, Clive (1991) *A Green History of the World*, London: Sinclair-Stevenson.

Punch (1990) 'Going soft on Salman', by Mr Punch, 19 Oct.

Quran, The Holy (1989) Text, translation and commentary by Abdullah Yusuf Ali, Brentwood, MD: Amana Corporation.

Qureshi, Regula Burckhardt (1986) *Sufi Music of India and Pakistan: Sound, Context and Meaning in Qawwali*, Cambridge Studies in Ethnomusicology, Cambridge: Cambridge University Press.

—— (1989) 'The Urdu *ghaazal* in performance', in Shackle (1989).

Raban, Jonathan (1974) *Soft City*, London: Collins Harvill.

—— (1990) *Hunting Mister Heartbreak*, London: Collins Harvill.

Rahman, Fazlur (1984) *Islam and Modernity: Transformation of an Intellectual Tradition*, Chicago: The University of Chicago Press.

Raschid, M. Salman (1981) *Iqbal's Concept of God*, London: KPI.

Raza, Mohammad Shahid (1991) *Islam in Britain: Past, Present and the Future*, Leicester: Volcano Press Ltd.

Read, Antony and David Fisher (1989) *Kristallnacht: The Beginning of the Holocaust*, London: Michael Joseph.

Roberts, John (1990) *Postmodernism, Politics and Art*, Manchester: Manchester University Press.

Robinson, Marilynne (1989) *Mother Country*, London: Faber.

Robinson, Stephen (1991) 'Fighting for screen time', in *The Spectator*, 12 Jan.

Romer, John (1988) *Testament: The Bible and History*, London: Michael O'Mara Books Ltd.

Rose, Richard (1988) *The Postmodern President*, New York: Basic Books.

Ross, A. (ed.) (1988) *Universal Abandon? The Politics of Postmodernism*, Edinburgh: University of Edinburgh Press.

Rushdie, Salman (1981) *Midnight's Children*, New York and London: Jonathan Cape Ltd.

—— (1988) *The Satanic Verses*, London and New York: Viking Penguin Inc.

—— (1990) *Haroun and the Sea of Stories*, London: Granta Books.

—— (1991) *Imaginary Homelands*, London: Granta Books.

Ruthven, Malise (1989) *The Divine Supermarket: Travels in Search of the Soul of America*, London: Chatto & Windus.

—— (1990) *A Satanic Affair: Salman Rushdie and the Rage of Islam*, London: Chatto & Windus.

Said, Edward W. (1978) *Orientalism*, New York: Penguin Books.

—— (1981) *Covering Islam: How the Media and the Experts Determine How We See the Rest of the World*, New York: Pantheon Books.

—— (1990) 'Arabesque', in *New Statesman and Society*, 7 Sept.

Saqqaf, A. (ed.) (1987) *The Middle-Eastern City*, New York: Paragon House.

Sardar, Ziauddin (1991) 'The Rushdie malaise: a critique of some writings on the Rushdie affair', in Ahsan and Kidwai (1991).

Sardar, Ziauddin and Merryl Wyn Davies (1990) *Distorted Imagination: Lessons from the Rushdie Affair*, London: Grey Seal.

Schimmel, Anne Marie (1975) *Mystical Dimensions of Islam*, Chapel Hill, NC: University of North Carolina Press.

Schlesinger, Philip (1991) *Media, State and Nation: Political Violence and Collective Identities*, London: Sage Publications.

Seiter, Ellen, Hans Borchers, Gabriele Kreutzner and Eva-Maria Warth (eds) (1991) *Remote Control: Television Audiences and Cultural Power*, London: Routledge.

Sennett, Richard (1991) *The Conscience of the Eye: The Design and Social Life of Cities*, London: Faber & Faber.

Shackle, Christopher (ed.) (1989) *Urdu and Muslim South Asia: Studies in Honour of Ralph Russell*, London: School of Oriental and African Studies, University of London.

Sharpe, Tom (1985) *Wilt on High*, London: Pan Books.

Shavit, Ari (1991) 'Inside an Israeli prison: on Gaza beach', in *The New York Review of Books*, 18 July.

Shaw, Isobel (1989) *Pakistan Handbook*, Hong Kong: Liberty Books.

Shiblak, Abbas (1991) 'The deepening tragedy of the Palestinians', in

Victoria Brittain (ed.) *The Gulf Between Us: The Gulf War and Beyond*, London: Virago Press.

Siddiqi, M.N. (1983) *Issues in Islamic Banking: Selected Papers*, Leicester: The Islamic Foundation.

Singer, Isaac Bashevis (1986) *The Penitent*, London: Penguin Books.

Skynner, Robin (1990) 'An American family at war', in *Weekend Guardian*, 28–29 July.

Smith, Caspar Llewelyn (1990) 'Madonna: the immaculate collection', in *Varsity*, Cambridge, 23 Nov.

Smith, Huston (1989) *Beyond the Post-Modern Mind*, New York: Crossroads.

Steiner, George (1984) *George Steiner: A Reader*, London: Penguin Books.

Summerson, John (1980) *The Classical Language of Architecture*, London: Thames & Hudson.

Taplin, Oliver (1989) *Greek Fire*, London: A Channel Four Book, Jonathan Cape.

Tate, Tim (1991) *Children for the Devil: Ritual Abuse and Satanic Crime*, London: Methuen.

Taylor, John (1991) 'Are you politically correct?', in *Literary Review*, March.

Theory, Culture and Society (1988) 'Special issue on postmodernism', 5 (2–3), June, London: Sage Publications.

Theroux, Paul (1990) *Chicago Loop*, London: Hamish Hamilton.

—— (1991) 'Subterranean Gothic', in *The Best of Granta Travel*, London: Granta Books.

Thompson, John B. (1990) *Ideology and Modern Culture*, Cambridge: Polity Press.

Tibi, Bassam (1988) *The Crisis of Modern Islam: A Preindustrial Culture in the Scientific-Technological Age*, Salt Lake City: University of Utah Press.

Toffler, Alvin (1991) *Power Shift*, London: Bantam Press.

Tully, Mark (1991) *No Full Stops in India*, London: Viking Penguin.

Waddy, Charis (1990) *The Muslim Mind*, new edition with a foreword by Dr Muhammad Abdul Halim Mahmud, London: Grosvenor Books.

Walker, Martin (1991) 'Chips off that dear old tabloid block: American Diary', in *The Guardian*, 9 Feb.

Waltham Forest Council (1990) 'Beneath the surface, an inquiry into racial harassment in the London Borough of Waltham Forest', Waltham Forest Council.

Watt, William Montgomery (1988) *Islamic Fundamentalism and Modernity*, London: Routledge.

—— (1991) *Muslim-Christian Encounters: Perceptions and Misperceptions*, London: Routledge.

Wavell, Stuart (1990) 'Sabre-rattling envoy . . .', in *The Sunday Times*, 30 Sept.

Webster, Richard (1990) *A Brief History of Blasphemy: Liberalism, Censorship and 'The Satanic Verses'*, Southwold, Suffolk: The Orwell Press.

Weiner, Jonathan (1991) *The Next One Hundred Years: Shaping the Fate of our Living Earth*, London: Rider.

Wilson, Elizabeth (1991) *The Sphinx in the City: Urban Life, the Control of Disorder, and Women*, London: Virago.

Wistrich, Robert (1991) *Anti-Semitism: The Longest Hatred*, London: Thames Methuen.

Wolf, Naomi (1990) *The Beauty Myth*, London: Chatto & Windus.

Woodruff, P. (1953–54) *The Men Who Ruled India*: vol. 1, *The Founders*; vol. 2, *The Guardians*, London: Jonathan Cape.

Wright, Esmond (1991) 'The special relationship', in *History Today*, 41, April.

Zahavi, Helen (1991) *Dirty Weekend*, London: Macmillan.

Zakaria, Rafiq (1991) *Muhammad and the Quran*, London: Penguin.

Name index

Subject index